The Iran Ag~~enda~~

Based on frequent, first-hand reporting in Iran and the United States, *The Iran Agenda Today* explores the turbulent recent history between the two countries and reveals how it has led to a misguided showdown over nuclear technology. Foreign correspondent Reese Erlich notes that all the major U.S. intelligence agencies agree Iran has not had a nuclear weapons program since at least 2003. He explores why Washington nonetheless continues with saber rattling and provides a detailed critique of mainstream media coverage of Iran. The book further details the popular protests that have rocked Tehran despite repression by the country's Deep State.

In addition to covering the political story, Erlich offers insights on Iran's domestic politics, popular culture, and diverse populations over this recent era. His analysis draws on past interviews with high-ranking Iranian officials, the former shah's son, Reza Pahlavi, and Iranian exiles in Los Angeles, as well as the memory of his trip to Tehran with actor Sean Penn.

Written in skillful and riveting journalistic prose, *The Iran Agenda Today* provides inside information that academic researchers find hard to obtain.

Reese Erlich has authored five books on foreign affairs, including the national bestseller *Target Iraq: What the News Media Didn't Tell You* (co-authored with Norman Solomon). A freelance print and broadcast reporter, he has covered the Middle East since 1987 and reported from Iran since 2000.

Erlich began his journalism career in 1968 as a staff writer and research editor for *Ramparts*, an investigative reporting magazine based in San Francisco. He taught journalism for ten years at San Francisco State University and California State University, East Bay. His reporting appears in *Foreign Policy*, *Vice News*, and *The Progressive*.

He writes the syndicated column "Foreign Correspondent." His radio work airs on CBC/Radio-Canada, Reveal, and National Public Radio, among others.

Erlich earned a Peabody Award in 2007 and "best depth reporting" awards in 2002 and 2006 from the Society of Professional Journalists (Northern California). He has also received awards from Project Censored, the Chicago International Film Festival, and the Association for Women in Communication. He lives in Oakland, California.

Praise for *The Iran Agenda Today*

Reese Erlich masterfully tells the story of modern Iran through the seldom-heard voices of numerous Iranian citizens of enormous range—men and women, old and young, high government officials, university professors, shopkeepers, and semi-employed laborers. His vibrant reporting has both historical depth and contemporary immediacy, ranging from twentieth century neocolonial and revolutionary struggles, to the international controversy over Iran's nuclear program, to the social protests of 2009 and late 2017. Neither exclusively a critique of nor an apologia for Iran, the balanced, comprehensive picture Erlich paints reveals the fascinating mix of deep patriotism, social struggle, optimism, and skepticism about the future that characterizes Iranian life at present. This book is required reading for anyone who truly wishes to understand Iranian society today.

—**William O. Beeman**, *Professor of Anthropology,*
University of Minnesota and Stanford University

Ever since the 1979 Revolution, Iran has been present in practically all debates and analyses regarding the Middle East. But, due to the hostage crisis of 1979–81 and the scars that it left on the American conscience, the image of Iran that has been presented in the West, and in particular, the United States, has been greatly distorted, and is more like a cartoon of that nation, rather than anything that presents Iran with all of its strengths, shortcomings, and contradictions, as well as its historical and cultural heritage. In *The Iran Agenda Today*, Reese Erlich does a masterful job of presenting the real image of Iran: a proud and dynamic nation with a young, educated population that is connected to the rest of the world through social networks, has more bloggers per capita than any other nation, and has been struggling, not only internally between the reformists, moderates, and seculars, on the one hand, and the Islamic hardliners, on the other hand, but also externally by being in perhaps the most turbulent region. Erlich tells us about the political structure of Iran; its warring; deep wounds due to its turbulent contemporary history; and all the wrongs that have been done to it by the global powers, but also a nation that has all the prerequisites for transition to a true democracy, and wants to find its rightful place regionally and globally.

—**Muhammad Sahimi**, *N.I.O.C. Chair in Petroleum Engineering*
and Professor of Chemical Engineering and Materials Science,
University of Southern California

Reese Erlich is always in Iran at the historic moments, including nearly all elections of recent years. He has formed a network with all sides of the struggles in Iran, and his high art of storytelling captures the details I have not seen from any other Western journalist reporting on the contemporary Iran scene.

—**Goudarz Eghtedari**, *PhD, Systems Scientist and Engineer by trade,*
Social-Political and Human Rights Activist

THE
IRAN
AGENDA
TODAY

The Real Story Inside Iran and What's Wrong with U.S. Policy

REESE ERLICH

with Forewords by William O. Beeman
and Robert Scheer

Routledge
Taylor & Francis Group

NEW YORK AND LONDON

First published 2019
by Routledge
711 Third Avenue, New York, NY 10017

and by Routledge
2 Park Square, Milton Park, Abingdon, Oxon, OX14 4RN

Routledge is an imprint of the Taylor & Francis Group, an informa business

Library of Congress Cataloging-in-Publication Data
A catalog record for this title has been requested

ISBN: 978-1-138-59905-5 (hbk)
ISBN: 978-1-138-59906-2 (pbk)
ISBN: 978-0-429-48597-8 (ebk)

Typeset in Aldus LT Std
by Deanta Global Publishing Services, Chennai, India

Contents

Acknowledgments

Many people contributed directly and indirectly to the writing of this book. Omid Memarian is an incredibly talented Iranian journalist who was a chief researcher. He was studying at the Graduate School of Journalism at the University of California, Berkeley. He later went on to work with human rights groups fighting for justice in Iran. Having grown up in Iran as part of that country's younger generation, he provided important insights about current conditions in Iran, as well as contemporary history.

PoliPointPress editor Peter Richardson offered invaluable help in shaping the first edition. Editor Dean Birkenkamp at Routledge provided major contributions to the second edition. I first met University of Southern California Professor Muhammad Sahimi when I interviewed him for the book. We subsequently coauthored articles together. Special thanks to Bill Beeman at the University of Minnesota for reading the manuscript and writing the introduction to this edition.

I couldn't have written the book without the support and infinite patience of my wife Elizabeth Erlich.

Foreword

William O. Beeman

Reese Erlich, in *The Iran Agenda Today* launches readers on a deeply engaging and, for some, surprising journey into one of the most fascinating nations on Earth. This is a deeply honest book, in contrast to much that has been written about Iran in recent years. Erlich breaks through decades of misinformation and prejudicial reporting on Iran to provide factual views that have been hidden from public view for the past fifty years.

The Iran Agenda Today, thoroughly updated, is the latest accomplishment in Erlich's award-winning journalistic career, having pursued investigative reporting for years, working in Syria, Iraq, and Cuba amid conflict and serious personal danger. He proves his superb skill as a reporter and analyst in *The Iran Agenda Today*. This achievement is not the result of some quicky "parachute" reporting venture. Rather, it is the result of ten extensive journeys to Iran over sixteen years. During this extensive contact, Erlich conducted hundreds of interviews with Iranians of all economic, political, and social classes and traveled extensively throughout the country, observing and noting changes through four successive Iranian presidential administrations. His vivid descriptions and clear style will draw readers into the streets, offices, and public spaces of the modern Iranian state.

Erlich demonstrates how in today's world Iran may be one of the least understood nations in the world. To those who know Iran well, it is a land of enormous beauty and infinite fascination. One of the most ancient continuous civilizations in the world, its soaring literary, artistic, political, and economic heritage has shaped the history and culture of the world. It's intelligent, handsome people are cultivated, educated, and sophisticated, with notably extravagant warmth shown toward guests and visitors. Its stunningly gorgeous landscape and historical monuments are awe inspiring.

But Iran is also a nation of intriguing, often contradictory complexity, as Erlich demonstrates admirably. On the positive side, everyday life can be delightful with sumptuous cuisine, rich family life, and exuberant celebrations. The nation is thoroughly modern with an extensive transportation and industrial infrastructure, well-stocked retail stores with every conceivable consumer good, and abundant food supplies. Public safety is strong with little personal danger for Iranian citizens and visitors. Women have a vibrant role in Iran's political and economic life and young people are highly educated and politically savvy.

However, Erlich understands well that concerns over human rights for ordinary Iranian citizens constitute a serious social problem. Restrictions on public morality, especially for women, as well as dissident political activity have resulted in high rates of incarceration and capital punishment. Economic pressures, including unemployment for young people, create distress for Iranian families. Government expenditures on defense agreements with Iran's regional allies are concerning both to Iranians and non-Iranians alike. The tension between individuals and government authorities occasionally break out in demonstrations and public resistance to heavy-handed conservative regulation and economic conditions—events that Erlich covers admirably.

For non-Iranians—especially international relations professionals—the ability to understand this rich and complicated Iranian social and political fabric requires sophisticated knowledge. Unfortunately, that knowledge is utterly lacking in the United States today. The reasons for this lack of knowledge lie in the history of U.S.–Iranian relations over the past half-century.

In recent decades, Iran's image has suffered in the eyes of Euro-American states. The Islamic Revolution of 1978–9 altered Iran's relationship with the United States and Europe. Whereas Iran's leaders had been compliant and cooperative with Western powers following the Industrial Revolution, suddenly with the revolution, they were perceived to be radically opposed to the West. In particular, Americans saw the Anti-American protest resulting in the sequestering of U.S. Embassy personnel in Tehran for 444 days in 1979 as a monumental insult that has yet to be ameliorated. The United States broke off diplomatic relations with Iran because of this action, and has yet to restore them after forty years of estrangement.

A coterie of Iranian experts, fluent in Persian and adept at deciphering Iran developed after World War II. I am one of these, having worked steadily in Iran as a linguist and anthropologist since 1968. However, after the revolution, this pool of expertise began to dwindle. Now the pre-revolutionary experts are near or past retirement age, and few younger experts are replacing them. This has created a dearth of accurate knowledge about Iran in U.S. government circles, resulting in uninformed and inaccurate assessments of Iranian political and social life, which has led to poor decision-making. American administrations have thus operated more from prejudice than from accurate information. They have been ruthlessly negative toward Iran during the post-Revolutionary period, to the point that U.S. officials were for many years even prohibited from so much as greeting Iranian officials in public.

As Erlich points out, American print and broadcast media have tended to follow the lead of government leaders in their reporting. He devotes an instructive chapter of his book (Chapter 11— "What the U.S. Media Didn't Tell You") to the distorted, inaccurate reporting and commentary directed toward Iran since 1978.

Ordinary Americans, too, have been deprived of face-to-face contact with Iranian citizens. They have little exposure to, or experience with modern Iranian life, and they are burdened with outdated, occasionally bizarre views of the Iranian people and their way of life. Although Americans can travel to Iran with relative ease, many believe they are not able to do this. Those who do make the journey nearly always experience an epiphany. They return home to report their surprise and delight at the modern travel amenities, the warmth, and the hospitality of Iranians and the wonders of the sights they encounter. They also discover that Iran is full of international visitors from every other nation on earth, many of whom return repeatedly with pleasure.

Because our American experience with Iran has grown so remote, *The Iran Agenda Today* fills a great need for Americans starved for accurate knowledge. Erlich provides a trenchant, fine-grained portrait of Iran from the ground level to the highest echelons of power. The personalities of Erlich's interviewees leap off the page. It is as if the reader is right there with him, experiencing Iran on a highly personal basis. They speak with an immediate honesty that brings a three-dimensional quality to his reportage.

Although the heart of Erlich's book is focused on Iran and Iranian citizens, he also provides interviews with an extensive range of commentators on Iran in the United States and Europe, including many detractors and skeptics, particularly regarding Iran's nuclear energy development. Since Iran's nuclear program has been such an area of controversy in Iran's relations with the United States and the rest of the world, this view is particularly instructive for readers wishing to obtain a balanced perspective regarding the 2015 Joint Comprehensive Plan of Action (JCPOA), the "Iran Nuclear Deal," which continues to be a major factor in international foreign policy.

Erlich tries to correct the imbalance in Western views of Iran, but he also provides a balanced perspective of Iranians' attitudes toward their own country and government. Economic concerns, questions about Iran's foreign military activities, and attitudes toward Iran's current political leadership are all pursued with vigor in the pages of this book. The result is a picture of Iran that truly favors neither Iran's supporters nor its detractors.

It is my hope that readers of *The Iran Agenda Today* will be fascinated with the vivid, varied picture of Iran that Erlich creates. I hope that they will be inspired to examine media and government pronouncements about Iran—both from the Western media and from Iran's own media—with discrimination and care. A nation and a civilization of such richness and complexity deserve careful attention. The effort, I guarantee, will be highly rewarding.

William O. Beeman is Professor of Anthropology at the University of Minnesota. He has conducted research in the Middle East for more than forty years with special expertise in Iran and the Persian Gulf region. His expertise has been widely sought as an advisor to the U.S. State Department, the Department of Defense, the United Nations, and the European Union. He is author or editor of more than 100 scholarly articles, 500 opinion pieces and 14 books, including *Language, Status and Power in Iran*, and *The "Great Satan" vs. The "Mad Mullahs": How the United States and Iran Demonize Each Other*. In addition, he has written extensively on music and performance traditions both in Western and non-Western traditions. His latest book on this topic is *Iranian Performance Traditions*. He is currently Visiting Scholar at Stanford University where he is completing two books: *Understanding Iran* and *Music, Emotion and Evolution*.

Foreword to *The Iran Agenda: The Real Story of U.S. Policy and the Middle East Crisis*

Robert Scheer

Historical mischief has stark consequences, not at all mitigated when world leaders, including Americans, claim the best of intentions. Steeped in the mythology of innocence since our own revolt against British imperial rule, the United States has consistently presented its own imperial drive as an effort to extend rather than suppress the freedoms of the peoples conquered.

The pattern has repeated itself many times since World War II, but it has never been clearer than in the persistent but disastrous effort of the United States to direct the politics of oil-rich Iran. Never admitting to an overriding interest in controlling that nation's and the region's precious resource, U.S. leaders have always insisted that they care only to expand the universe of peace and freedom. That charade now stands exposed since the U.S. invasion of Iraq. Despite that debacle, the longer-standing goal of dominating Iran remains all the more compelling to the United States.

In this perceptive analysis, Reese Erlich writes in the spirit of Graham Greene, whose classic *The Quiet American* captured the naive but nonetheless murderous impact of U.S. intervention in the "third world" of the Cold War era. Like Greene, Erlich blends an on-the-scene familiarity with everyday life in the target country with a piercing critique of the purportedly high motives of the foreign invader.

The United States has interfered with Iran for more than fifty years, and the consequences of that sorry history will continue to haunt us well into the future. Our capricious disregard for the nationalist and religious complexity of Iran began with the 1953 overthrow of its last democratically selected leader, the secular populist Mohammad Mossadegh. His crime was to begin the nationalization of foreign oil companies. He assaulted our sacred faith in the divine right of corporate plunder that trumped all other concerns, including the will of the Iranian people to control their own resources, and hence their own destiny.

After a well-documented coup paid for and engineered by the CIA, the United States replaced Mossadegh with the self-proclaimed Shah of Shahs, Mohammad Reza Pahlavi, who based his legitimacy on a highly questionable royal lineage. Despite U.S. and Israeli support, the shah's regime eventually collapsed under the weight of its own corruption and selfish opulence, which wasted oil revenues on an array of unnecessary purchases, including U.S. military hardware. The shah was replaced by religious fanatics who claimed the mantle of incorruptibility. Because the shah had governed in the name of modernization, it is no wonder that the ayatollahs' appeal to the glories of a fundamentalist world found a following among those whom the shah had ignored.

It is also no wonder that the theocrats who ascended to power should prove hostile to Israel and the United States. But of course, given the general acceptance of American virtue in foreign policy, the 1979 taking of hostages by the Iranian revolutionaries was interpreted as a totally unprovoked attack. American politicians and media figures have accepted this interpretation uncritically. Although the Iranian leadership has undergone many changes since then—from militant to somewhat reasonable and back again—most Americans have never wavered from the view that Iranian leaders are nothing but treacherous.

Call it the cartooning of Iran, in which the motives and actions of Iran's various (and sometimes competing) leaders are never plumbed for profound explanations but rather dismissed as the pure caprice of the malevolent. Hence, we see the all-too-easy classification of Iran as part of the "axis of evil" by the Bush Administration. That designation is now an embarrassment, given that Bush's invasion of Iraq has left the Iraqi disciples of the Iranian ayatollahs very much in power in Baghdad.

Erlich provides an invaluable insight into the contradictions that drive U.S. policy toward Iran and threaten to take us into yet another disastrous war in a region that has ample reason to question U.S. motives. He questions the demonization of Iran's leadership without underestimating the theocracy's record of suppressing the people it rules. Having witnessed modern ideological wars, he brings a nuanced and—dare one say it—objective view of the contending forces attempting to define modern Iran. The book is particularly useful in dissecting the trite, politically motivated threat assessments of Iran's nuclear program and its alleged support of international terrorism. In both instances, there are painful reminders of the phony case made to justify the invasion of Iraq.

Erlich's analysis opens up possibilities for change other than those that rely on the military option, which has proved so disastrous in neighboring Iraq. Indeed, Erlich questions the value of a belligerent U.S. stance when its primary impact is to enhance the popularity of hardliners and undermine those working for genuine reform in Iran. For that reason, this is a hopeful book, as well as a well-written work on a difficult subject, for it suggests the truly revolutionary prospect that the Iranian people might be trusted with the difficult task of engineering their future. After a half-century of heavy-handed U.S. interference, they can hardly do a worse job on their own.

But Iran is not some banana republic to be toyed with as a matter of whim; it is rather the historic seat of a major civilization whose legacy, both politically and religiously expansionist, cannot be ignored. A U.S. foreign policy based on ignorance of Iran's rich history and preoccupied only with U.S. interests has wrought horrible consequences. Those consequences—unintended as they sometimes were, and authored by politicians oblivious to the complexity of the world upon which they intruded—now dominate the key drama of international politics. The value of this excellent treatise is that it exhibits rare humility in attempting to grasp why modern-day Iranians have proved so difficult for the U.S. government to deal with. While critical of the clerical tyranny that has controlled Iranian politics since the anti-shah revolution, Erlich avoids the path of crude demonization that has characterized most popular writing on this subject. Instead, he skillfully melds personal observations with a scholar's insight into the historical record that informs today's passions—passions that we ignore at our peril.

Robert Scheer is Editor-in-Chief of the Webby Award-winning online magazine *TruthDig*, Professor of Communication at the University of Southern California's Annenberg School for Communication and Journalism, and co-host of *Left, Right & Center*, a weekly syndicated radio show broadcast from NPR's west coast affiliate, KCRW. He is the author of ten books, including his most recent, *They Know Everything About You: How Data-Collection Corporations and Snooping Government Agencies are Destroying Democracy.*

ONE

In Tehran with Sean Penn

All our senses were assaulted simultaneously as we walked slowly down the inclined road into the Tehran bazaar. We smelled the fragrance of fresh spices, heard the cacophony of merchants hawking their wares, and saw the yellow saffron rice and deep purple eggplant. It was June 2005.

The crowds jostled Sean Penn, Norman Solomon, and me as we worked our way deep into the narrow byways of the bazaar. Sean was there on assignment for the *San Francisco Chronicle*; Norman was writing for his media analysis column; and I was reporting as a freelancer for the *Dallas Morning News* and Canadian Broadcasting Corporation Radio. I had visited the bazaar during my previous trip in 2000 and figured this was a good way for Sean and Norman to get acquainted with ordinary people.

Middle East bazaars were the first shopping malls. Tehran's main bazaar consists of a vast underground network of stalls, shops, and stores. You can buy anything from ridiculously expensive hand-knotted Persian silk carpets to ladies' underwear. Both are clearly displayed for passersby. There are no fixed prices. Bargaining is a proud tradition in Iran. If you pay the first price asked, you are clearly not from around these parts.

As we walked past the many shoppers, our translator and guide, Maryam Majd, suddenly became aware that this would be no ordinary visit to the bazaar. "Everyone is whispering Sean's name," she said a bit apprehensively. Although I don't speak Farsi, I could hear the mumbled recitation "Sean Penn" and see the startled looks on people's faces. We had arrived in Tehran two days before, without any prior announcement. So most people were very surprised to see the world-famous actor, with his wavy hair and piercing eyes, just ambling by.

In meetings at Sean's house north of San Francisco before our departure, we all agreed that the purpose of the trip was to learn the views of Iranians toward the United States and their own government. Sean was visiting as a writer, not an actor or celebrity. He did not want to become the focus of the story and refused to give any media interviews.

"Do you think they know me over there?" he asked me during one preparation session. "Oh yes," I responded. But none of us had any idea *how* well known Sean was in Tehran—nor the buzz his trip would have, even years later.

We were walking in the bazaar, looking at the incredible array of clothing, household goods, food, and antiques. We stopped at a stall where Moshtabor was selling small home appliances such as irons and blenders. He asked that we use only his first name.*

We asked him about the U.S. assertion that Iran's quest for nuclear power disguises a plan to build nuclear weapons. Moshtabor said Iran is not building nuclear weapons. He defended Iran's desire to have nuclear power. "Every country needs to have access, and it's our right," he told us.

Moshtabor told us that compared to the 1980s, cultural restrictions are much more relaxed in Iran. The government usually looks the other way if people choose to drink alcohol in their own homes or

---

* My experience is that Iranians approached randomly on the street are about as willing to talk as Americans. I asked interviewees if they wanted to use their full names. Often if sensitive political questions were asked, they preferred to use first names only. Our interview with Moshtabor took place June 11, 2005, in Tehran.

see their girlfriends without male relatives present. The government won't allow most Western films to be shown in theaters or on television, but the films are readily available on pirated DVDs. In fact, major Hollywood films often reach Tehran before being released in the United States. Moshtabor told us that many Iranian young people are obsessed with Hollywood movie stars.

At that point Sean, who had been interviewing someone else, walked over to join us. "That guy looks just like Sean Penn," Moshtabor told us with a big grin. Suddenly he realized that he was talking to the real Sean Penn. "I'm going to see *The Interpreter*," he blurted out. "I know you were married to Madonna."

Great. We've come halfway round the globe to meet ordinary Iranians and discuss matters of grave international concern. And Iranians want to talk to us about Madonna.

That encapsulates the contradictions in today's Iran. Ten thousand people chant "Death to America" at Friday prayers. But afterward, those same people invite us home for lunch. In part, that reflects traditional Iranian hospitality toward strangers. But it's also a genuine friendliness and fascination with things American. Many Iranians studied in the United States in the 1960s and 1970s. I've met Iranians who speak with a Bostonian or even a valley girl accent.

But most Iranians strongly criticized U.S. government policy. Yes, they are bombarded with clerical propaganda denouncing the United States and Israel. But they also haven't forgotten the U.S. support for the shah's dictatorship* or the American navy ship that shot down an Iranian civilian airliner, killing all 290 people on board.† They may love Sean Penn, but they would take up arms against Donald Trump.

---

* While those of us born before 1965 vividly remember the reign of Shah Mohammad Reza Pahlavi, I realize than many younger readers do not. The shah (king) was crowned with British backing in 1941. A democratic movement in parliament restricted his powers in the early 1950s, but he was restored to full power in a CIA-led coup in 1953. The shah ran a brutal dictatorship until 1979, when he was overthrown by a popular revolution.

† I describe the 1988 USS *Vincennes* incident in greater detail in Chapter 5.

Since the 1979 revolution overthrew the U.S.-backed shah, successive Democratic and Republican administrations have vilified Iran. They have argued that Iran poses a threat to U.S. national security, with the reason varying by the year: It spreads Islamic revolution; it supports terrorists; it plans to develop a nuclear bomb; it kills American soldiers in Iraq. That hostility has remained, even when some of the U.S. justifications have disappeared. For example, the United States rarely mentions Iran's trying to spread its Islamic revolution anymore, because Iran largely stopped doing so in the 1980s. The United States just shifts the goalposts and comes up with new ways to score the game.

U.S. policy is controlled by a relatively small ruling elite of corporate executives, military leaders, government bureaucrats, and politicians. That elite is supposed to be subject to democratic control. In practice, however, the American people have little influence over its decisions.

The U.S. ruling elite always want to confuse national security with corporate/military interests. The people of the United States face no immediate threat from Iran. Iran cannot and would not launch a military attack on U.S. territory. While it supports groups that have used terrorist tactics in Israel and other parts of the Middle East, it is no supporter of Al Qaeda, the Islamic State, or other terrorist organizations that pose a real threat to the United States.* If the current government of Iran disappeared tomorrow, Americans would be no more or less secure. But Iran does threaten the interests of the political, military, and corporate elite who run the United States.

The Great Game in the Internet Era

In the early part of the twentieth century, Britain competed with Russia, the Ottoman Turks, and other imperialist powers to control

---

* I go into much greater detail about the antagonism between Iran and Al Qaeda and the Taliban in Chapter 4.

the oil wealth of the Middle East. Oil was vital to power navy ships and home-front industry. The British had no oil of their own, so they had to control colonies and neocolonies that did. The imperialist powers called this scramble for natural resources the Great Game. For them it was a game; for the people of the region, it was deadly.

Today the players have changed, but the Great Game continues. Charles Freeman, Jr., was U.S. ambassador to Saudi Arabia (1989–92) and Under Secretary of Defense for International Security Affairs (1993–4). He welcomed me into his office at the Middle East Policy Council in Washington DC, and was jovial and outspoken as he explained U.S. national interests in Iran. "There is a hierarchy of American interests at stake, which begins with secure access to energy supplies," he told me.[1]

U.S. oil companies never come pounding on his door demanding that the United States overthrow the Iranian regime or invade Iraq, he explained. They don't have to. U.S. politicians and military men understand that the country must have secure sources of oil. And the oil companies automatically benefit because they are trusted to develop and market the oil.

Freeman said the United States wants Middle Eastern governments "that are not hostile, countries that are willing to work with American companies to provide energy. It means governments that are sufficiently competent to maintain stability rather than engage in acts that disrupt the flow of energy."

Iran sits on approximately 10 percent of the world's proven oil supplies and has the second-largest amount of natural gas.* Iran also sits between the Persian Gulf and the Caspian Sea, two critical oil regions. The world's oil tankers slip down Iran's coast at the Strait of

---

* Estimates vary about which countries are number one or two in oil and gas reserves, depending on how the figures are computed. Iran clearly has some of the largest oil and natural gas reserves in the world. Iran has oil reserves of 133 billion barrels and natural gas reserves of 26.6 trillion cubic meters, according to the CIA's *World Factbook—Iran*, which is available online.

Hormuz, which narrows to thirty-one miles at one point. Control of that strait means control of the whole region. No wonder the British, Russians, Germans, and Americans have all sought to dominate Iran.

Freeman also noted that because the United States buys so much oil from the region, it needs to sell products to keep a favorable balance of trade. "This is a significant market for our products and services. We have to sell things to the people who sell oil in order to buy oil. Dollars that we give them have to be recycled."

Freeman said U.S. generals and admirals worry about the Strait of Hormuz as well. "The United States is a global power. We have forces both in Europe and Asia. From a military point of view, this is a vital choke point. It's vital that it stays open."

Paul Pillar was the CIA's national intelligence officer for the Near East and South Asia (2000–5). He is retired from teaching at Georgetown University's Security Studies Program. He told me, "Everyone is quite conscious, not least of all U.S. military planners, about the capability of the Iranians to cause—if they had the motive to do so—a lot of mischief in regard to closing the strait or necessitating considerable military measures on the opposite side to keep it open, that is to say, on the part of the United States."[2]

The U.S. ruling elite not only wants to dominate the region but works to prevent any other country from doing so. Since its inception in 1979, the clerical government in Iran has thumbed its nose at U.S. oil companies and military brass. Robert Hunter, U.S. ambassador to NATO from 1993 to 1998, said the U.S. "goal with Iran is not even regime change, but regime change as a means to eliminating Iran as a competitor for power and influence."[3]

Please note, dear reader, that none of these "national interests" have much to do with you and me. Sure, we need gasoline to drive cars and natural gas to power electricity plants, although less as renewable energy becomes more widely used, but the United States can buy those energy resources on international markets, as do other countries. In order to maintain a steady supply of oil, Sweden doesn't unilaterally impose sanctions, prop up dictatorships, or overthrow governments. Apparently, God has given that mandate to the United States of America. In reality, U.S. strategic interests benefit corporations whose profits depend on domination of the region.

"Aha!" some neoconservatives are mumbling to themselves right now. If you oppose U.S. policy, you must be a supporter of the Iranian mullahs. Actually, no. Iran is ruled by a reactionary, dictatorial clique that oppresses its own people. However, that doesn't make Iran a threat to Americans. As we will see in later chapters, those Iranians fighting hardest to get rid of Iran's government are also strong opponents of U.S. policy.

The U.S. ruling elite can't very well tell the American people that we may go to war with Iran to improve the long-term profits for Exxon Mobil and Halliburton. So the United States creates threats, or exaggerates those that do exist.[4] And that's one of the reasons we visited Iran.

Sean, Norman, and I visited one of the most highly guarded locations in Tehran, a place where ordinary Iranians never go. It's the compound where Ayatollah Ruhollah Khomeini once ruled, and today it is home to some of the country's top officials.

In the early years of the revolution, Ayatollah Khomeini spoke to throngs of followers while seated on the second-story balcony of his home. That's where we visited. They've preserved Khomeini's living quarters since his death, as a kind of museum that Iranians can't visit.

"This is the famous balcony," said Mohammed Hashemi, a grizzled old man and former Khomeini bodyguard. "This is where he first called the USA the Great Satan. This is where everything started. This is the place," he said with a hearty chuckle.[5]

We were there to interview Hassan Khomeini, grandson of the late ayatollah, who then headed the influential Khomeini Foundation. Hassan Khomeini welcomed us into a meeting room in his grandfather's house. He sported a ginger-colored beard, wore long white clerical robes, and wrapped his head in the black turban indicating he was a descendant of the prophet Mohammed. Some of us sat on chairs. Others rested, Iranian style, on thick carpets and cushions.

We asked for his response to U.S. charges that Iran is a major sponsor of terrorism. "What is the yardstick that defines Iran as a terrorist-supporting nation yet dismisses such a claim against Israel?" he said.[6] Bush uses the issue as an excuse, he said. If Iran met all U.S. demands, Bush would come up with new ones. "I don't know about his intentions" about a military attack, he told us. "I don't believe the USA has enough power to attack Iran. American public opinion, as well as what America is facing in Iraq, as well as world situation, won't allow the Americans to do that."

Khomeini conceded that U.S.–Iran relations have been bad for a long time, but he blamed President George W. Bush for making things worse. After all, it was Bush who referred to Iran as part of the "axis of evil ... The first thing is to recognize the Iranian government as an independent government," Khomeini told us. "The U.S. public should force its government to change its opinion in this regard."

A Wrestler, the Foreign Ministry, and a Cup of Coffee

Two days later we covered a women's rights demonstration in front of the University of Tehran. Plainclothes police and paramilitaries known as Basijis blocked hundreds of people from attending the demonstration and strong-armed the press. Sean got shoved around by a cop. Dozens of Iranians were clubbed by the police. The government even turned off cell phone service in that part of Tehran to block communication among demonstrators.

We got back to the hotel that night tired and angry. By this time, Sean's visit was making headlines all over Iran. So the hotel assigned a 300-pound former wrestler to escort Sean while inside the hotel and shoo people away while we were in the lobby. The wrestler had secured a table for Hamid-Reza Asefi, then Iran's deputy foreign minister, who had decided to stop by for an unannounced chat with us. Boy, did he pick the wrong night.

I pulled out my microphone, hooked up the cables to the recorder, and let fly. Why did the police attack peaceful demonstrators demanding equal rights for women? I asked. "If [the demonstrators] had permission, they should be protected," he answered rather lamely.[7] He knew that it's impossible to get official permission for demonstrations critical of the government. So demonstrators are always subject to attack and arrest.

Sean followed up by asking Asefi if it's government policy for police to beat up reporters. Asefi claimed that the government works transparently with journalists. "I don't know why they [beat people]. They were wrong." In fairness to Asefi, he was part of reformist President Mohammad Khatami's government. A parallel intelligence service within the judiciary, Revolutionary Guard, and Basijis operated independently of any governmental control and sometimes even jailed Khatami supporters.

But neither was Asefi willing to criticize those forces within the government who trampled on people's basic rights. He reminded us that Iran was far more democratic than Saudi Arabia or other Middle East dictatorships supported by the United States. True, but also irrelevant. Iran says it is an Islamic democracy but hardly lives up to the claim. Asefi's responses encapsulated the problem with Iran's political reformists. They wanted to liberalize Iran, allow greater individual freedoms within the context of an Islamic republic, but they wouldn't take effective action against those who broke the law and undercut the positive reforms.

But the people of Iran aren't relying on politicians to make change. Slowly, and sometimes in small ways, Iranians are rebelling against the tight strictures that once bound them to a reactionary version of Islam.

From the time of the revolution until the early 1990s, the government required women to wear a manteau or the all-encompassing chador. The chador is a full-length cloth cut into a semicircle and wrapped around the body and head. It is the traditional Iranian hijab, or "cover" for women. Translated literally, *chador* means "tent." A manteau is a cloth raincoat that comes in various lengths.

According to Islamic teachings, women should be modest and cover themselves while in public. But the type of covering varies widely depending on the country and culture. Saudi Arabian and Afghan women cover themselves head to toe, without even their eyes visible. Some Muslim women in Lebanon wear stylish suits and matching head scarves with the scarves pushed well back, revealing a lot of hair.

Iranian clerics, all men, mandated a very conservative interpretation of the dress code in the early years of the revolution. Unmarried couples couldn't even attend a party together. Film director Jafar Panahi skewered this government repression in his excellent 2003 film *Crimson Gold*. In one scene a delivery man on a motorbike brings a pizza to an upscale apartment building in Tehran. He discovers men arresting unmarried couples leaving a party.

> *Male Policeman:* Come out here.
> *Man with Woman:* What's going on? But we're married. Let me explain.
> *Policeman:* Yeah, right. Who goes out with his wife?

But rebellion from below gradually forced the government to loosen its policies. By the time of President Khatami's election in 1997, authorities had all but given up trying to enforce those moral codes inside people's homes.

One day I visited an upscale shopping mall in north Tehran. Wealthy Iranians wandered through stores stocked with imported cosmetics, Italian designer clothes, and hi-tech sound systems. In a cell phone store, I met fifteen-year-old Michelle and her mom shopping for a new cell phone. Michelle had the unfortunate habit of losing her cell phone, and they were bargaining for an inexpensive replacement.

Michelle's mom was wearing a head scarf and manteau. Michelle was wearing a head scarf, sandals, jeans, and a green manteau about the length of a long shirt. "When we bought the manteau, it was up to here," said mom, pointing to her daughter's mid-calf. "But we shortened it." In the United States, teens like to wear short skirts, and the shortening urge is apparently international. "It's more stylish," said Michelle with a big grin.

Then I asked about a more controversial topic. Does Michelle ever go to parties? The resulting dialogue was revealing.

Michelle: Yes, of course.
Mom: But only girls.
Michelle: No! Not these days.
Mom: Maybe brothers of a couple of girls.
Michelle: No, Mom! We go to parties. There are boys. We hang out.
    [giggling] Mommy![8]

When the boys and girls get a little older, the parties get a lot wilder. At several north Tehran parties I attended, people not only drank alcohol but smoked hashish and even snorted coke. I was more worried about a police raid than they were. (I could see the next day's headline: "American spy found consorting with drug-crazed teens and unaccompanied women.")

By far the most popular illegal activity behind closed doors is watching satellite TV. The government has tried to stop news and entertainment from the outside world. And it has failed.

Satellite TV—Now You See It, Now You Don't

The satellite TV revolution hit the Middle East in the 1990s. For the first time, people of the region could see timely news and entertainment shows banned on state-run TV. People were fascinated with everything from English-language news on BBC or CNN to videos of scantily clad belly dancers undulating on screen.

The Iranian government first tried to prohibit satellite dishes in 1995, and it has waged a largely unsuccessful effort to enforce the ban ever since. Satellite dish prices have dropped. Friends in Iran told me you could buy a satellite dish and descrambler for $100. Most stations are pirated, so viewers don't pay monthly fees. The dishes are affordable to middle-income and even working-class Iranians.

I sat down one evening and counted over 500 channels available on the Hotbird satellite, including foreign news broadcasts, American film channels, and even pornography. The vast majority of sites seemed to be Arabic music video stations, judging from the women dancing and lip synching on screen. But over a dozen channels broadcast in Farsi, including the Voice of America and some Los Angeles-based Iranian exile stations.

After Mahmoud Ahmadinejad was elected president in 2005, he tried yet another crackdown. Police using helicopters and airplanes located satellite dishes on rooftops. Then the police went to each building, demanding that the dishes come down and forcing residents to pay a fine.

But residents didn't miss their favorite programs for very long. The system is so corrupt that sometimes a simple bribe allowed the dishes to remain pointing skyward. In other cases, residents were more creative. One journalist friend told me how the police came to his building and took away the forest of dishes. But since he was a foreign reporter, he was legally entitled to keep his. So all the neighbors hooked up their cables to his dish, and he is now the most popular guy in the building. Another friend took his satellite dish off the roof and placed it on his balcony.

The dishes and descramblers are imported from abroad, often with the assistance of corrupt officials. Some Revolutionary Guard leaders get a cut from the illicit smuggling of satellite dishes, liquor, and drugs.

The underground economy functions rather efficiently. Friends wanting liquor one night simply called a local bootlegger, who delivered a variety of name-brand bottles that evening. When I visited a private apartment in Tehran, the satellite system suddenly stopped working.

The owner went up on the roof but couldn't figure out the problem. He called the satellite man, who came out within two hours and replaced the receiver immediately. I can't get that kind of service at home in Oakland.

A Memorable Trip

Sean, Norman, and I visited Iran in June 2005 during the country's tumultuous presidential election. In August Sean published a five-part series in the *San Francisco Chronicle* that amassed one of the highest numbers of online readers in the paper's history.[9] The articles were translated, e-mailed, and posted on blogs all over Iran.

On our first day in Tehran, we interviewed some people at a coffeehouse. Afterward, all the customers cleared out and went out front to take cell phone pictures with Sean. One of those images got e-mailed to friends, who forwarded it to friends until it became like a Hollywood chain letter. One of my friends got twenty copies of the e-mail from different people. Sean's trip became headline news every day, and dozens of fans camped out in the hotel lobby, hoping to get an autograph.

When I returned to Iran in November 2006, I assumed our trip had been quickly forgotten, one of those blips on the celebrity radar. In numerous spontaneous discussions, however, people asked proudly if I knew that Sean Penn had visited Iran. They would then launch into a detailed description of his trip, which I didn't have the heart to correct in any way. Even in 2017, people remembered Sean's trip, although the details have been forgotten.

Sean's articles, an excellent introduction to Iran for Americans, showed the nature of the ruling dictatorship. They showed how every day, sometimes in little ways, Iranians express their discontent with the system. At the same time, Iranians reject U.S. plans to "help build democracy in Iran" and certainly oppose any U.S. military action against their country.

Former ambassador Freeman likened U.S. policy to someone with mental illness. "A psychotic thinks that $2 + 2 = 5$," he told me.

"But a neurotic knows that 2 + 2 = 4, but he's very unhappy about it. Washington falls in the neurotic category, unwilling to accept reality happily."

These days the neuroses begin when U.S. officials look at Iran's nuclear program.

Notes

1. Charles W. Freeman, Jr., interview with author, Jan. 19, 2007, Washington DC.

2. Paul Pillar, interview with author, Jan. 18, 2007, Washington DC.

3. Robert Hunter, comments posted on Gulf 2000 list serve, Mar. 2, 2007, quoted with permission.

4. Norman Solomon provides numerous examples of the lies used to justify previous U.S. wars. Norman Solomon, *War Made Easy*, chapter 3 (New York: John Wiley and Sons, 2005).

5. Mohammed Hashemi, interview with author, June 11, 2005, Tehran.

6. Hassan Khomeini, interview with author, June 11, 2005, Tehran.

7. Hamid-Reza Asefi, interview with author, June 12, 2005, Tehran.

8. Interview with author, June 14, 2005, Tehran. This dialogue appeared in my radio documentary "On the Ground in Iran," *Making Contact Radio*, Aug. 24, 2005 (www.radioproject.org/archive/2005/3405.html).

9. Sean Penn's series in the *San Francisco Chronicle* began Aug. 22, 2005 (www.sfgate.com/entertainment/article/SEAN-PENN-IN-IRAN-2615110.php).

TWO

United States Tells Iran: Become a Nuclear Power

Top Democratic and Republican leaders absolutely believe that Iran would like to develop nuclear weapons. And one of their seemingly strongest arguments involves a process of deduction. Since Iran has so much oil, they argue, why develop nuclear power?

James Woolsey typifies the view. The director of the CIA under both George Bush (the elder) and Bill Clinton said, "There is no underlying reason for one of the greatest oil producers in the world to need to get into the nuclear [energy] business ... unless what they want to do is train and produce people and an infrastructure that can have highly enriched uranium or plutonium, fissionable material for nuclear weapons."[1]

In an op-ed commentary, former secretary of state Henry Kissinger wrote, "For a major oil producer such as Iran, nuclear energy is a wasteful use of resources," a position later cited approvingly by the Bush administration.[2]

But U.S. leaders are engaging in a massive case of collective amnesia, or perhaps more accurately, intentional misdirection. In the 1970s the United States encouraged Iran to develop nuclear power precisely because Iran will eventually run out of oil.

A declassified document from President Gerald Ford's administration, during which Kissinger was secretary of state, supported Iran's push for nuclear power. The document noted that Tehran should "prepare against the time—about fifteen years in the future—when Iranian oil production is expected to decline sharply."[3]

The United States ultimately planned to sell billions of dollars' worth of nuclear reactors, spare parts, and nuclear fuel to Iran. Muhammad Sahimi, a professor and former department chair of the Chemical and Petroleum Engineering Department at the University of Southern California, told me that Kissinger thought "it was in the U.S. national interest, both economic and security interest, to have such close relations in terms of nuclear power."[4]

The shah even periodically hinted that he wanted Iran to build nuclear weapons. In June 1974, the shah proclaimed that Iran would have nuclear weapons "without a doubt and sooner than one would think."[5] Iranian embassy officials in France later denied the shah made those remarks, and the shah disowned them. But a few months later, the shah noted that Iran "has no intention of acquiring nuclear weapons but if small states began building them, then Iran might have to reconsider its policy."[6]

If an Iranian leader made such statements today, the United States and Israel would denounce them as proof of nefarious intent. They might well threaten military action if Iran didn't immediately halt its nuclear buildup. At the time, however, the comments caused no ripples in Washington or Tel Aviv because the shah was a staunch ally of both. Asked to comment on his contradictory views then and now, Kissinger said, "They were an allied country, and this was a commercial transaction. We didn't address the question of them one day moving toward nuclear weapons."[7]

Kissinger should have added that consistency has never been a strong point of U.S. foreign policy.

Nukes and Party-Mad Dictators

To fully understand the hypocrisy of U.S. foreign policy, we must travel back to the era of bell-bottoms, funny-looking polyester shirts, and party-mad dictators. In the early 1970s, Iran's repressive dictator was perhaps most famous in the West for his prodigious partying. In October 1971, Shah Mohammed Reza Pahlavi celebrated the 2,500th anniversary of the Persian Empire with a lavish, three-day party on the site of the ancient city of Persepolis. Luminaries such as Vice President Spiro Agnew, Britain's Prince Philip, and Ethiopian dictator Haile Selassie consumed 2,500 bottles of French wine, 5,000 bottles of champagne, and massive quantities of caviar flown in by Maxim's of Paris. Iran's per capita income was only $350 per year; the party cost an estimated $100 million.[8] The excesses of the party helped fuel anger against the shah at home and abroad.

But in those days, successive U.S. presidential administrations were tickled pink with the shah's regime. As far as the United States was concerned, the shah had a stable government that was modernizing an economically and religiously backward society. True, he ran a brutal dictatorship unconstrained by elections or an independent judiciary. The National Security and Intelligence Organization (SAVAK), his secret police, was infamous for torturing and murdering political dissidents. But the shah made sure that Iran provided a steady supply of petroleum to U.S. and other Western oil companies. He had his own regional ambitions and also acted as a gendarme for the United States.

Need an ally for Israel in the surrounding Arab world? The shah entered into military and intelligence agreements with the Israelis starting in 1958. Got a rebellion in the Gulf state of Oman? In the early 1970s, the shah sent 3,000 troops to put down the leftist rebels[9] and to ensure the region's oil fields remained safe for him and the United States. Iran became America's single biggest arms buyer. It bought $18.1 billion worth of U.S. arms from 1950 to 1977.[10]

U.S. anti-communist diplomacy, military expansion, and business profit all melded together nicely. And that's where nuclear power comes in.

Beginning in the late 1960s, the shah began to worry about Iran's long-term electric energy supplies. Iran had fewer than 500,000 electricity consumers in 1963, but those numbers swelled to over 2 million in 1976. The shah worried that Iran's oil deposits would eventually run out and that burning petroleum for electricity would waste an important resource. He could earn far more exporting oil than using it for power generation.

Hermidas Bavand, second in command of Iran's Mission to the United Nations under the shah and now a professor of international law at Allameh Tabatabaee University in Tehran, told me that the position of the shah on nuclear power was almost identical to that of the current Iranian government. Back then, proponents of nuclear power said Iran had to prepare for the day when the oil runs out. Second, said Bavand, "Iran had to keep up with scientific and technological" progress in the world. And Iran craved international prestige. Bavand said, "Many countries—Brazil, Argentina, Israel—were developing nuclear energy. So they thought that Iran should have nuclear power" as well.[11]

Successive Republican and Democratic administrations in the United States backed the shah's elaborate plans to make nuclear power an integral part of Iran's electrical grid, in no small part because he would buy a lot of his nuclear equipment from the United States. The United States established Iran's first research reactor in 1967 at the University of Tehran. In November of that year, the U.S. corporation United Nuclear provided Iran with 5.85 kilograms of 93 percent enriched uranium.[12]

By the 1970s, nuclear power was becoming increasingly unpopular in the United States and around the world, as hundreds of thousands of people marched and blockaded nuclear facilities. Even before the Three Mile Island, Chernobyl, and Fukushima disasters, the antinuclear movement pointed out that many reactors were unsafe. In addition, the industry had no long-term, secure method for transporting and storing nuclear waste produced at the reactors. Massive demonstrations and rising costs meant U.S. nuclear power companies were having a hard time getting permits to build reactors. In later years the nuclear industry tried numerous times to build new reactors, claiming nuclear power was environmentally preferable because it didn't use fossil fuels. The high cost of nuclear still required massive government subsidies, however, and new permits were hard to get.

Permits never seemed to be a problem in Iran, however. In 1974, Richard Helms, then U.S. ambassador to Iran and later head of the CIA, wrote to Shah Mohammad Reza Pahlavi, "We have noted the priority that His Imperial Majesty gives to developing alternative means of energy production through nuclear power. This is clearly an area in which we might most usefully begin on a specific program of cooperation and collaboration." Helms went on to write, "The Secretary [of State Henry Kissinger] has asked me to underline emphatically the seriousness of our purpose and our desire to move forward vigorously in appropriate ways."[13]

General Electric and Westinghouse ultimately won contracts to build eight reactors in Iran. By the time of the Iranian revolution in 1979, the shah had plans to buy a total of eighteen nuclear power reactors from the United States, France, and Germany.[14]

Evidence has emerged since the 1979 Iranian revolution that the shah did more than make embarrassing public references to building nuclear weapons. Documents show that Israel and Iran had discussed modification of Israel's Jericho missiles, which could have been fitted with nuclear warheads.[15] A research report from the Nuclear Threat Initiative, an organization founded by conservative Democrat and former senator Sam Nunn, explained that the shah was suspected of experimenting with nuclear weapons design, plutonium extraction, and laser-enrichment research.[16]

Nuclear expert Sahimi argued that presidents Nixon and Ford "would not have minded if the shah developed the bomb because the shah was a close ally of the United States. Remember, Iran had a long border with the Soviet Union. If the shah did make a nuclear bomb, that would have been a big deterrent against the USSR."[17] Neither Sahimi nor other experts say the shah had actually developed a nuclear bomb, but the United States denounces the current Iranian government for activity at least as suspicious as that carried out by the shah.

Since the United States wasn't terribly concerned about an Iranian bomb in the 1970s, it also wasn't worried about Iran's enriching its own uranium. The United States gave approval when the shah bought a 25 percent stake in a French company making enriched uranium. But the shah wanted to build enrichment facilities inside Iran, as well. No country wants to be reliant on others for fuel whose absence could shut down a portion of its electricity grid. The United States actually encouraged Iran to enrich its own uranium.[18]

Starting in the 1990s when Iran demanded that it be able to enrich uranium for nuclear power under strict international supervision. The United States said that was proof Iran wanted to develop nuclear weapons.

Weapons Inspections

Mohamed ElBaradei looks every inch the international diplomat. The Egyptian keeps his shoes shined and suits sharply pressed. Glasses and a balding pate give him the look of authority. Indeed, he steered the International Atomic Energy Agency (IAEA) through very troubled waters from 1997–2009. Prior to the U.S. invasion of Iraq in 2003, ElBaradei correctly said Saddam Hussein did not have a nuclear weapons program. In retaliation, the Bush administration tried to block his reelection to head the IAEA. ElBaradei gathered widespread international support, however, and beat back administration efforts. He won reelection to his post at the end of 2005.

Oh, and did I mention that he and the IAEA won the Nobel Peace Prize in 2005?

I was on the phone from Oakland when ElBaradei entered the radio studio at the UN headquarters in New York to be interviewed by Walter Cronkite for a radio documentary I was producing about nuclear weapons. I was surprised that ElBaradei expressed an almost teenage giddiness about being in the presence of Cronkite.

"It is an honor to be here with you, Mr. Cronkite. I watched your news broadcasts for many years as a young man."[19] There was something special about listening to these two eminent authorities in their fields. Cronkite had long reported on nuclear issues and was very concerned about nuclear weapons proliferation. When Cronkite asked ElBaradei about Iran, the answer was succinct. "Some people suspect [the Iranians] have the intention to develop a nuclear weapon," said ElBaradei. "This is a matter of concern to us. But this is not [an] imminent threat."

ElBaradei, unlike successive U.S. administrations, based his conclusions on facts unearthed through analysis of data and on-the-ground inspections. As a signer of the Non-Proliferation Treaty (NPT), Iran followed the treaty requirements to allow IAEA inspectors into its nuclear facilities. ElBaradei has criticized the Iranian government for lack of transparency and restricting some access in recent years, but has never accused Iran of planning to make a nuclear weapon.

Yukiya Amano took over the top job at IAEA in 2009. He was far more sympathetic to the U.S. position and raised many more questions about Iran's nuclear power program. But even he never claimed that Iran had a current nuclear weapons program.[20]

So if the guys in charge of inspecting nuclear sites say there is no proof Iran is developing the bomb, why are so many people in the United States convinced that it is? For that understanding, we'll have to go back to the years just after the Iranian revolution of 1979.

Is Nuclear Power Islamic?

Shortly after coming to power, Iran's Supreme Leader Ayatollah Ruhollah Khomeini scrapped the shah's nuclear power programs as un-Islamic. In fact, he called nuclear power "the work of the devil."[21] Not coincidentally, the United States and Europeans had completely halted their devil's work in Iran. Germany had stopped construction on the Bushehr nuclear reactor. The United States, Germany, and France had cut off supplies of equipment and nuclear material. All three governments had refused to refund any money already paid, despite the cancellation of the nuclear contracts. So while Koranic scholars might disagree on whether nuclear power was consistent with Islam, as a practical matter, Iran wasn't getting any.

Starting in 1980, Iran fought a bloody war with Iraq. Each side feared the other might develop nuclear weapons. Iraq repeatedly bombed Iran's unfinished nuclear facilities, further setting back any possibility of completing them. By the end of the war in 1988, Iran was in the midst of a population explosion. Iran's population grew from 39.2 million in 1980 to 68.7 million in 2006. Iran's energy planners could see that demand would far outstrip supply. Continuing to extract oil and natural gas at the projected levels wouldn't be enough to guarantee a steady supply of electricity.[22]

So nuclear power was back on the table. In 1989 Iranian President Akbar Hashemi Rafsanjani signed a ten-point agreement with the USSR to provide nuclear materials and related equipment. The Soviets were going to finish the Bushehr reactor started by the Germans in the 1970s. In 1990 Iran signed a ten-year nuclear cooperation agreement with China.

Although it was kept secret at the time, Iran also bought parts and technology from A. Q. Khan, Pakistan's so-called father of the atomic bomb, who also had nuclear dealings with Libya and North Korea. Iran built a secret nuclear facility in the central Iranian city of Natanz. Later, after three years of inspections, the IAEA also determined that Iran had used lasers to purify uranium starting in 1991 and had researched a rare element called polonium-210, which could be used in a nuclear bomb trigger.[23]

The Iranians argued that they had engaged in the secret activity to prevent the United States from stopping their plans for nuclear power development and that they had no intention of developing nuclear weapons. Discussing the issue of secrecy, Sahimi told me, "Let's say Iran had announced back in 1985 that 'Hey guys, we want to make a uranium enrichment facility.' What do you think would have happened? Would the U.S. and [European Union] have rushed to help Iran? No, they would have done everything in their power to deny Iran's rights."[24]

In 2003 Supreme Leader Ayatollah Ali Khamenei issued a fatwa, an official religious ruling, that declared Islam forbids the building or stockpiling of nuclear weapons.[25] Before dismissing such a ruling as propaganda, it's worth noting that similar religious reasoning stopped Iran from using chemical weapons during the Iran–Iraq War, despite Saddam Hussein's numerous chemical assaults against Iranian troops and civilians.

The United States asserts that Iran's desire to enrich uranium demonstrates its desire to develop nuclear weapons. So what is enrichment anyway? Raw uranium must go through a process to raise the concentration of the isotope U-235 in order to either produce fuel for a nuclear reactor or make a nuclear bomb. Iran has a small number of domestic uranium mines. The ore must be milled and subjected to an acid bath to leach out the uranium. The resulting yellowish ore is called yellow cake. Then it's combined with fluorine to produce uranium hexafluoride, or UF6.

Then the process gets really hairy. The uranium hexafluoride must pass through a series of thousands of spinning centrifuges. Imagine a bunch of pipes and whirling motors passing the liquid through cascading cylinders like a water filtration system.[26] The cascades can produce 5 percent enriched U-235 for use in nuclear power plants. Iran would have to make 93 percent enriched uranium to make a nuclear bomb but can do so using the same technical process. Getting those centrifuge cascades to work properly is a big technical challenge, according to experts. The centrifuges "spin 60,000 rounds per minute," said Sahimi. "They generate a lot of vibrations, which must be controlled. The centrifuges can't be contaminated because they are easily corroded. Once the centrifuges start working, it's not wise to shut them down and start them again. This damages them. There are all sorts of technical problems."

As of the signing of the nuclear accord between the United States, Iran, and other powers in 2015, Iran had not produced enough enriched uranium to make even a single nuclear weapon. Strict IAEA inspections since then have guaranteed none has been produced subsequently.

Iran Is Just Five to Ten Years from Making a Bomb, Really

Every few years U.S. intelligence officials estimated Iran was just years from making a bomb. In 1995, a "senior U.S. official" estimated Iran was five years from making the bomb.[27] A 2005 National Intelligence Estimate, representing a consensus among U.S. intelligence agencies, predicted Iran could have the bomb somewhere around 2015.[28] In early 2006 Israeli intelligence, on the other hand, argued that Iran is much closer to having a bomb, perhaps one to three years away. In citing such estimates, the U.S. media don't provide any corroboration nor explain why the Israeli assessment differs so widely from the CIA's and IAEA's. Indeed, Israel keeps postponing its estimates of when Iran will have the bomb. At the end of 2006, Meir Dagan, head of the Mossad intelligence agency, claimed Iran could have a bomb by 2009 or 2010.[29]

Israel's estimates are clearly influenced by its political and military goals. Using President Mahmoud Ahmadinejad's statements attacking Israel and questioning the existence of the Holocaust, Israel proclaims Iran an immediate military threat. In reality, Ahmadinejad poses no offensive nuclear threat to Israel.[30] Iran would be insane to launch a first strike against the militarily far superior Israel, let alone a nuclear strike with an arsenal of one or two bombs. Such an action would give the United States and Israel a political excuse to wreak havoc on Iran and gain lots of international support.

But Israel does have a vested interest in creating anxiety around a possible Iranian bomb. While Iran has no ability to wipe Israel off the map, it does support the Palestinian groups Hamas and Islamic Jihad, and the Lebanese political party/militia Hizbollah. Iran gives them political, financial, and military backing. Israel doesn't want to suffer another defeat like its 2006 war against Hizbollah. Rather than give up occupied territory and agree to establishing a Palestinian state, Israeli leaders blame outsiders. Israel seeks to weaken or, preferably, overthrow Iran's government.

Israeli officials, along with U.S. hawks, argue that Iran will soon reach "a point of no return," in which it will have both the theoretical knowledge and the practical ability to create weapons-grade plutonium. After that point, the hawks argue, Iran must be confronted militarily. The advantage of this argument, of course, is that it's all hypothetical. The Iranians cross this point of no return at whatever time the hawks allege. Who can prove otherwise?

In the spring of 2006, Bush seemed to echo those sentiments, justifying a military attack by setting the bar impossibly high for Iran. "The world is united and concerned about [Iranians'] desire to have not only a nuclear weapon, but the capacity to make a nuclear weapon or *the knowledge as to how to make a nuclear weapon*" (emphasis added), Bush said in an April 2006 press conference.[31] No one can possibly prove what knowledge scientists might have in their brains. But according to Bush's logic, Iran is a dangerous enemy so long as its scientists might, at some time in the future, think about building a bomb.

On July 31, 2006, the United States rounded up European powers, and got China and Russia to acquiesce, to pass UN Security Council Resolution 1696. The resolution demanded that Iran stop "all enrichment-related and reprocessing activities."[32] (Reprocessing involves removing highly radioactive plutonium from nuclear waste products, a procedure that can lead to the production of bomb-grade fuel.) A month later, in a report not released to the public, IAEA Director ElBaradei indicated that Iran was *not* reprocessing uranium.

ElBaradei criticized Iran, however, for continued attempts at uranium enrichment. "Iran has not addressed the long outstanding verification issues or provided the necessary transparency to remove uncertainties associated with some of its activities," wrote ElBaradei.[33]

An IAEA official told the *New York Times*, "the qualitative and quantitative development of Iran's enrichment program continues to be fairly limited."[34]

The IAEA report was hardly a smoking gun. But the Bush administration huffed and puffed that Iran's failure to uphold the Security Council resolution meant the world should impose more sanctions. On March 24, 2007, the UN Security Council voted to impose another round of sanctions, prohibiting the sale of Iranian weapons to other countries and freezing the overseas assets of more Iranian individuals and organizations.

The United States failed to get any backing for military attacks on Iran to enforce the sanctions. The March resolution even restated the UN position that the Middle East region should be nuclear free, a criticism of Israel's large nuclear arsenal.

U.S. officials told the *New York Times* that the new sanctions went beyond the nuclear issue. "The new language was written to rein in what [U.S. officials] see as Tehran's ambitions to become the dominant military power in the Persian Gulf and across the Middle East."[35]

President Obama initially continued the tough line against Iran. He declared that the United States was keeping "all options on the table," including military attacks. But he softened the approach and eventually signed the nuclear accord (see Chapter 3). President Trump has resumed the hostile rhetoric and unilaterally tore up the agreement in 2018.

So What Would You Do?

When I speak at college campuses and before community groups, someone inevitably asks me a legitimate question: "OK, U.S. policy

toward Iran is wrong. If you were president, what would you do?"
Glad you asked.

First, no more demonizing Iran. I would apologize for years of U.S.
aggression against Iran. I would lift all existing sanctions against Iran
and offer to restore full diplomatic relations.[36] That would get Iran's
attention. More important, it would set the basis for easing tensions
on other issues.

I would announce plans to reduce the unconscionable number
of nuclear weapons maintained by the United States in violation of
the Non-Proliferation Treaty. Most Americans have no idea that the
Non-Proliferation Treaty not only limits other states from obtain-
ing nuclear weapons but also requires disarmament by the existing
nuclear states, including the United States.[37]

Then I would do something neither side expects. I would tell them
we will phase out our nuclear power reactors for safety reasons and
because we can't safely store nuclear waste. I would then suggest that
Iran not develop nuclear power. Nuclear reactors and their tons of
radioactive waste are disasters waiting to happen. They are prohibi-
tively expensive. Iran has the potential to develop a lot more wind
and geothermal power as well.[38] In the meantime Iran could harness
its tremendous natural gas resources as a relatively efficient source of
electricity generation.

I don't know how Iranian leaders would react. These suggestions
would certainly spark a lot of discussion among Iranians, who are
much more willing to debate the issue today than in years past.
Journalist and opposition leader Akbar Ganji told me, "I am very
worried that something like Chernobyl will happen to Iran. If that
happens, the Iranian people will pay the heaviest price."[39] I would like
to see Ganji's views prevail. But if, after a genuine debate, Iranians
decided they wanted nuclear power, so be it.

Should the world simply trust that Iran's leaders will stick to the
peaceful use of nuclear power? No. We don't have to assume good
faith. The IAEA is quite capable of detecting NPT violations because

radioactive particles inevitably show up in water and soil. Over a period of time, and allowed full access, the IAEA can detect illegal nuclear activity. Since even U.S. intelligence agencies agree Iran is many years from building a bomb, why not allow the IAEA to do its job?

In the long run, the people of Iran must change their government and revisit the nuclear power issue. I hope they choose to develop safer forms of energy. But that's a decision to be made by the people of Iran, not rulers in Washington.

Notes

1. James Woolsey, quoted in Thomas Stauffer, "Unlike Dimona, Iran's Bushehr Reactor Not Useful for Weapons-Grade Plutonium," *Washington Report on Middle East Affairs*, Sept. 2003, pp. 28–9.

2. Henry Kissinger, *Washington Post*, Mar. 29, 2005, op-ed article.

3. Dafna Linzer, "Past Arguments Don't Square with Current Iran Policy," *Washington Post*, Mar. 27, 2005.

4. Muhammad Sahimi, interview with author, Oct. 17, 2006, Los Angeles.

5. John K. Cooley, "More Fingers on Nuclear Trigger?" *Christian Science Monitor*, June 25, 1974. See also Elaine Sciolino, "Nuclear Ambitions Aren't New for Iran," *New York Times*, June 22, 2003.

6. *Der Spiegel*, Feb. 8, 1975, as cited in Muhammad Sahimi, "Iran's Nuclear Program, Part V," *Pavand Iran News*, Dec. 22, 2004 (www.pavand.com).

7. Linzer, *Washington Post*.

8. David Wallechinsky and Irving Wallace, *The People's Almanac*, 1981 (www.trivia-library.com/c/excesses-of-the-rich-and-wealthy-shah-of-iran-party.htm).

9. Federal Research Service, "The Dhofar Rebellion," *Persian Gulf States: Oman* (Library of Congress, 1993).

10. "Background Information on the Crisis in Iran," Institute for Policy Studies, Washington DC, 1979 (www.irvl.net/USMI.htm).

11. Hermidas Bavand, interview with author, June 15, 2005, Tehran.

12. Nuclear Threat Initiative (NTI), "Nuclear Chronology 1957–1985," *Iran Country Profile* (www.nti.org/e_research/profiles/1825_1826.html).

13. Richard Helms, "Issues and Talking Points: Intensified Bilateral Cooperation," *Department of State Brief*, Digital National Security Archive (http://nsarchive.chadwyck.com/marketing/index.jsp).

14. Alexander Montgomery, *Social Action: Rogue Reaction*, PhD thesis, Stanford University, Sept. 2005, p. 163.

15. Elaine Sciolino, "The World: Nuclear Ambitions Aren't New for Iran," *New York Times*, June 22, 2003 (www.nytimes.com/2003/06/22/weekinreview/the-world-nuclear-ambitions-aren-t-new-for-iran.html).

16. Nuclear Threat Initiative (NTI), "Nuclear Overview," *Iran Country Profile*, May 1, 2006 (www.nti.org/e_research/profiles/Iran/index_1822.html).

17. Sahimi interview.

18. Linzer, *Washington Post*. Also, Alfred L. Atherton, "Strategy for Your Visit to Iran," confidential Department of State Briefing Memorandum, Oct. 20, 1974, in Digital National Security Archive (http://nsarchive.chadwyck.com/marketing/index.jsp).

19. Mohamed ElBaradei, interview for radio documentary *Lessons from Hiroshima 60 Years Later*, Reese Erlich producer, May 2, 2005 (excerpts from the interview available online at www.peacetalksonline.org/NoMoreHiroshima/HiroshimaSummary.htm).

20. Yukiya Amano, "Director General's Remarks on Iran, the JCPOA and the IAEA," Nov. 14, 2017, www.iaea.org/newscenter/statements/director-generals-remarks-on-iran-the-jcpoa-and-the-iaea.

21. Montgomery, PhD thesis, p. 159.

22. Muhammad Sahimi, "Iran's Nuclear Energy Program: Part IV," Dec. 7, 2004 (www.pavand.com). Sahimi points out that Iran's oil production had declined from 5.8 million barrels per day in 1974 to 3.9 million in 2004, and that the oil fields are far more depleted today than during the shah's time.

23. William Broad and Elaine Sciolino, "Iran's Secrecy Widens Gap in Nuclear Intelligence," *New York Times*, May 19, 2006.

24. Sahimi interview.

25. Robert Collier, "Nuclear Weapons Unholy, Iran Says Islam Forbids Use, Clerics Proclaim," *San Francisco Chronicle*, Oct. 31, 2003.

26. Steve Coll, "The Atomic Emporium," *The New Yorker*, Aug. 7 and 14, 2006.

27. Mark D. Skootsky, "US Nuclear Policy Toward Iran," June 1, 1995, p. 3 (http://people.csail.mit.edu/boris/iran-nuke.text).

28. Dafna Linzer, "Iran Is Judged 10 Years from Nuclear Bomb," *Washington Post*, Aug. 2, 2005.

29. Greg Myre, "Abbas Repeats Call for Vote as Truce Erodes," *New York Times*, Dec. 19, 2006.

30. I explain the military issues between Iran and Israel in Chapter 4.

31. George W. Bush, Rose Garden Press Conference, Apr. 28, 2006 (www.whitehouse.gov/news/releases/2006/04/print/20060428–2.html).

32. IAEA Director General's Report.

33. IAEA Director General's Report.

34. Elaine Sciolino, "Highly Enriched Uranium Is Found at an Iranian Plant," *New York Times*, Sept. 1, 2006.

35. Thom Shanker, "Security Council Votes to Tighten Iran Sanctions," *New York Times*, Mar. 25, 2007.

36. Some mainstream analysts advocate a similar negotiating position. Ray Takeyh, senior fellow at the Council on Foreign Relations, wrote "Time for Détente with Iran," *Foreign Affairs*, Mar.–Apr. 2007, p. 29.

37. Nuclear Age Peace Foundation (www.nuclearfiles.org).

38. Muhammad Sahimi, "Iran's Nuclear Energy Program: Part IV." Sahimi estimates total nonnuclear alternative energy sources could meet 25 percent of Iran's needs under current conditions.

39. Akbar Ganji, interview with author, July 30, 2006, Berkeley CA.

THREE

The United States, Iran, and the Nuclear Accord

Avasta Yazdi was stacking weights in a fitness gym when I met him. The stocky and muscular twenty-five-year-old lives in a working-class neighborhood in south Tehran. Yazdi told me that politics in Iran's working-class neighborhoods are volatile. Many people vote for religious and populist conservatives such as former President Mahmoud Ahmadinejad. And many opposed the nuclear agreement.

But Yazdi and his friends, like most Iranians, supported the deal. They voted twice for centrist President Hassan Rouhani, whose administration negotiated the agreement. When Rouhani got elected the first time in 2013, Yazdi said, "We were all happy and went out onto the streets and celebrated. The fact that he helped lift sanctions was a very good thing to do. Although we haven't yet seen the concrete economic improvement in our daily lives, the overall spirits and morale of people is much better."[1]

After years of conflict, in 2015 Iran agreed to a nuclear deal with the United States, China, Russia, France, Germany, and the UK. The Joint Comprehensive Plan of Action (JCPOA) imposed stringent restrictions on Iran's nuclear power program in return for lifting international sanctions.[2] The JCPOA generated immediate controversy. Conservative Republicans and Democrat Party hawks argued that the

United States had made too many concessions and that Iran would be in a better position to develop a nuclear bomb after fifteen years when some restrictions would be lifted. In addition, they argued, the JCPOA didn't stop Iran from testing ballistic missiles and supporting Hizbollah, Hamas, and what they termed terrorist groups.

The JCPOA was controversial in Iran as well. Some hardline political, intelligence, and military leaders strongly opposed it. They argued that the JCPOA gave away too much. The United States would never lift sanctions enough to improve the economy. And, most significantly, critics worried that a post-Obama administration might go back on the agreement. Ruhollah Hosseinian, a conservative member of Iran's parliament, told me the accord could allow the United States to spy on Iran's military bases under the guise of inspections. "What has this deal brought to the Iranian nation?" he asked. "We have seen that the United States has always reneged."[3]

Is Iran Planning to Build a Bomb?

The United States and Israel have asserted since 1995 that Iran was on the cusp of building a nuclear weapon. In the mid-aughts the International Atomic Energy Agency raised questions about Iran's nuclear power program. "Our reports often stated that Iran was not very forthcoming in clarifying unresolved issues," said IAEA Chair Yukiya Amano. But the IAEA never asserted that Iran had a nuclear weapons program after 2003.[4]

Iran argues, while it enriched uranium for medical research and to produce electric power, it never had a nuclear weapons program. A 2007 National Intelligence Estimate (NIE), reflecting the views of the top U.S. intelligence agencies, indicated Iran had no nuclear weapons program since 2003.[5] That conclusion was reaffirmed in a 2011 NIE report.[6] If Iran had no bomb and didn't even have a program to develop one, why did the United States get its jockey shorts in such a twist?

The Washington elite argued that, even without an active program, Iran was only months away from enriching enough uranium to make one bomb, what they call a "nuclear breakout." Washington, Tel Aviv, and European capitals fiercely debated whether Iran could break out in just a few months (Israel) or in a year (Obama administration). So, it's worth meeting someone who advocates the conservative viewpoint.

Patrick Clawson welcomed me into his Washington DC office with a smile. The office was empty during our early morning meeting. His shelves were lined with books, including *The Iran Agenda*. So he knew we don't agree on Iran. But he's an articulate spokesperson for a view on Iran that was considered fringe under Obama and is now mainstream under Trump. Clawson was a former leftist who marched in demonstrations against the shah of Iran in the 1970s. He became a conservative, he said, after working for the International Monetary Fund and witnessing what he called the hypocrisy of third-world, leftist governments.

Clawson has been suspicious about Iran's nuclear power program from the beginning. Referring to uranium enrichment facilities, he said, "Iran has put a lot of effort, a lot of money and a lot of prestige into building facilities which don't have any obvious civilian use but do have a very clear potential military use."[7] I asked if he believed, even when the nuclear accord was in place, that Iran is developing atomic weapons? "I think the program is aimed at having that option and that's disturbing," he replied.

But those assertions only misdirect the public. Given enough time, Iran could enrich bomb-grade fuel. But it would be detected by inspectors. The IAEA closely monitored all uranium in Iran, from the mining, to refining, to enrichment.[8] And that's only step one in having a functioning nuclear weapon. As described in Chapter 2, Iran would have to miniaturize the uranium to fit into a bomb or missile warhead, develop a way to detonate the bomb, and then test the system. This process would take years to produce a handful of nukes.

In a worst-case scenario, Iran would have a handful of nuclear bombs compared to an estimated 200 in Israel and 6,800 in the United States. Iran could not launch offensive nuclear attacks on the United States or Israel without assuring its own destruction. Above all, Iran's leaders want to survive; they aren't crazy. So the concept that Iran would launch an offensive nuclear attack is a myth.

Iran certainly engages in reprehensible activity, including brutally repressing its own people. Iranian leaders seek to expand their regional power in pursuit of a conservative, religious agenda. Iran expanded its conventional weapons, including short-range ballistic missiles and drones, and developed a sophisticated cyber warfare program. It has armed and trained militias in Iraq, Syria, and Lebanon.

But Iran's policies are quite different than those of the hegemonic United States, as admitted by the Pentagon in a 2014 report: "Iran's military doctrine is defensive. It is designed to deter an attack, survive an initial strike, retaliate against an aggressor, and force a diplomatic solution to hostilities while avoiding any concessions that challenge its core interests."[9]

On several occasions before signing the JCPOA, Iran offered to negotiate the nuclear issue. In 2003, reformist President Mohammad Khatami sent a message to the Bush administration offering political negotiations without prior conditions on a range of issues, including nuclear enrichment and a two-state solution for Israel and Palestine. The Bush administration, still flush from early successes in the Iraq War, ignored the message and even denied receiving it.[10]

The next president, populist Mahmoud Ahmadinejad, took a much harder line. He installed new and more sophisticated centrifuges. Iran enriched uranium to 20 percent, much higher than what is needed for nuclear power, but still legal under the Non-Proliferation Treaty (NPT). Uranium enriched to that level can be used for medical research. Ahmadinejad, a right-wing populist like Trump, turned the nuclear power program into an issue of national pride. He defiantly challenged the U.S. superpower while creating bargaining chips for future negotiations. However, even under Ahmadinejad, Iran had no nuclear weapons program.

In 2010 Obama encouraged Brazil and Turkey to act as intermediaries with Iran to develop a nuclear agreement. But when the presidents of those countries announced a solid proposal that would have shipped much of Iran's enriched uranium out of the country, Secretary of State Hilary Clinton immediately rejected it.[11] At that time the United States insisted that Iran could never enrich its own uranium, a demand flatly rejected by Iran.

Rather than explore a peaceful settlement at that time, the Obama administration intensified sanctions against Iran. It pressured some European countries and the UN Security Council to pass sanction resolutions. The United States claimed that the sanctions excluded food and medicine, and were only aimed at the Iranian leadership. In fact, the sanctions squeezed ordinary Iranians.

Impact of U.S. Sanctions

It was July of 2013 when I saw many dozens of people lined up at the 13th of Aban government-run pharmacy in Tehran. This was their last stop to find drugs in short supply. One man unable to fill his prescription shouted angrily as he stomped out. "A lot of people are angry when they can't get their medicine," Yusuf Abadi told me. He was waiting to get a chemotherapy drug and asked that his real name not be used. Tahereh Karimi, a woman standing in the same line, knew that, officially, pharmaceuticals are excluded from the sanctions. But, she said, the U.S. government put the squeeze on ordinary people in hopes they would pressure the government. "The United States knows what it is doing," Karimi told me. "Tell Obama not to hurt ordinary people."[12]

Ever since the United States imposed stringent sanctions in 2011, the Iranian economy had been in freefall. Oil revenues dropped by 50 percent, the local currency was devalued by 300 percent, and inflation hit 40 percent. The drop in the rial's purchasing power made importing foreign drugs and medical devices particularly expensive.

In addition, the United States threatened international banks with severe penalties if they violated the sanctions. So while banks were supposed to allow fund transfers for medicine and medical devices, many found it easier to ban Iranian transactions altogether. "We can't get certain vitamin tablets because we can't send money abroad through the banks," Khodadad Asna'ashari told me. He's the administrative director at the Sapir hospital in Tehran.

An authoritative study of sanctions issued by the Woodrow Wilson Center noted, "Bank hesitation is understandable given that a mistake could earn a bank the wrath of the U.S. Treasury Department and fines that exceed $1 billion."[13]

Ghader Daemi Aghdam, owner of a private pharmacy, told me even affluent Iranians in north Tehran were struggling to pay the high cost of medicine. "I estimate 30 percent of my customers walk out when they see the cost of filling their prescriptions," he said.

So many Iranians took a walk down Nasser Khosro Street where they hoped to find scarce drugs. The massive thoroughfare, not far from the city's famous Bazaar, was crowded with midday shoppers. The street was clogged with cars, motorcycles, and pedestrians all trying hard not to collide with one other. Within a few minutes of walking down the street, a young man whispered "medicine?" He and dozens of others operated like drug dealers, which they were. They just sold drugs for chemotherapy, diabetes, and other hard to find pharmaceuticals. The dealers weren't educated men and may or may not have been familiar with the requested drug. The patient usually provided a prescription. Street dealers then made a quick mobile phone call to check availability and price. This day a common chemo drug was available, but at three times the cost at a government pharmacy.

"Our drugs are of the finest quality," claimed the dealer with the polished confidence of a used car salesman. "All the drugs are from Europe." He said the pharmaceuticals were smuggled from Iraq and

Iraqi Kurdistan, usually in people's luggage. It was impossible to determine the age or quality of drugs, and patients took real risks when making purchases.

Drug smugglers weren't the only people making money from sanctions. One businessman, who asked to use only the first name Abbas, explained how corrupt officials profited as well. Abbas needed to buy raw materials for his business. He deposited rials in an account with a money changing store in Tehran. The store worked with a partner business in Dubai, which converted rials to dollars and then wired the money to foreign suppliers. The process was reversed when the Abbas sold his products abroad.

The currency shop made money converting currency and charging for the wire transfers. In turn, shop owners paid off Iranian officials in order to stay in business. "Some people are getting very rich off the sanctions," said Abbas, "while most people are suffering."

Cyberwar and Assassinations

But these tough sanctions weren't enough in Washington's view. The Obama administration imposed even harsher measures, sometimes using illegal means. The United States worked with the Israeli government to develop a computer virus, later known as the Stuxnet worm, to disable Iranian nuclear facilities. The worm was first introduced at Iranian nuclear facilities in 2006 although it was not discovered until 2010.[14]

Stuxnet resulted in widespread damage to enrichment centrifuges and other sensitive equipment. It also caused major computer crashes in India and Indonesia, whose industrial computers were apparently inadvertently infected. The Stuxnet incident was the first weaponization of a computer virus by one country against another, a tactic now widely denounced when used against the United States.

From 2010–12 Israeli agents assassinated six Iranians they accused of being nuclear scientists.[15] The Iranians arrested one of the assassins who confessed to have been trained by Israeli Mossad.[16] In that case one scientist's personal details were passed by the International Atomic Energy Agency (IAEA) "to Western intelligence agencies, and then at least one of them gave it to the Israelis," Seyed Mohammad Marandi told me.[17] He is an assistant professor at the University of Tehran and was part of the Iranian delegation to the Vienna nuclear talks.

Then in March of 2012, without UN Security Council authorization, the United States and some EU countries disconnected Iran from the SWIFT banking system, which coordinates international wire transfers. Iran could no longer transfer U.S. dollars internationally, a huge economic blow. Even when selling products to India, for example, banks change rials to dollars and then to rupees. So even many non-dollar denominated transfers were blocked.

Nevertheless, Iran survived. It created a "resistance economy" in which domestic production replaced some imports, and Iranians cut back on domestic consumption. Businesses transferred funds through third countries such as Dubai by carrying suitcases full of currency. Russia and China ignored unilateral U.S. sanctions and continued trade in consumer goods not prohibited by the UN.

"Sanctions never stopped their [nuclear] program," admitted Wendy Sherman, an important U.S. nuclear negotiator. "Every year that went by, they had more centrifuges, more capacity, and more capability."[18]

In July 2012 the Obama administration opened secret, direct talks with Iran in the Gulf country of Oman. Over the next three years both countries engaged in fierce and contentious negotiations. Both sides agreed to limit the talks to the nuclear issue. U.S. negotiators didn't insist that the agreement cover Iran's human rights violations and troops stationed in Syria and Iraq. Iran didn't insist that U.S. police stop murdering African Americans or that the United States pull its troops out of Iraq and Syria. Both sides realized that introducing non-nuclear issues would doom the talks.

Iran and the United States both made significant concessions. Previously, the United States had demanded that Iran not enrich uranium, relying instead on nuclear fuel imported from countries such as Russia. For Iranians, that was a non-starter. It couldn't risk a shutdown of the country's electrical grid because of a dispute with Russia. During secret negotiations in the Spring of 2013, Obama formally accepted Iran's right to enrich uranium.

The United States dropped demands that Iran explain documents that allegedly showed Iran had done nuclear bomb and related research in years past.[19] The Obama administration agreed to lift all sanctions related to the nuclear issue.

Iran also made major concessions. It agreed to IAEA inspections at all stages of the nuclear cycle: mining, processing, enrichment, use, and waste disposal. Iran cut its stockpile of enriched uranium by 97 percent and shipped large amounts of heavy water, potentially useful in making bombs, out of the country. Iran agreed not to enrich uranium to more than 3.87 percent for fifteen years and agreed to enrich uranium at only one facility with old centrifuges for ten years. After fifteen years, Iran can expand its nuclear power program, but the JCPOA prohibits making nuclear weapons in perpetuity.[20]

Iran accepted the "additional protocol" of the Non-Proliferation Treaty, which they had previously rejected. It allows intrusive inspections of existing nuclear sites and of suspected secret sites for valid reasons. Yukiya Amano, head of the IAEA noted that "Iran is subject to the world's most robust nuclear verification regime."[21] In 2015 the UN Security Council approved the JCPOA and lifted nuclear-related sanctions. The deal was done! Or so it seemed.

There were a few loose ends. The United States had not refunded Iran's money for the undelivered 1979 fighter jets, which had been paid for by the shah. The Obama administration knew it would lose a pending case before arbitrators in the International Court of Justice in the Hague. So the United States negotiated the return of $1.7 billion, which included interest since 1979. The deal made international headlines because $400 million of it was shipped on a cargo plane with cash stacked on pallets. The United States paid cash because

U.S. banking sanctions, in effect at the time, made wire transfers impossible.[22] Iran also released *Washington Post* correspondent Jason Rezaian and his wife Yeganeh Salehi, both of whom had faced phony espionage charges.

And then there was a huge drama over releasing Iranian funds that had been embargoed because of sanctions. During the 2016 presidential campaign, Donald Trump and other conservatives argued that the JCPOA would give Iran $150 billion even if the United States didn't sign the agreement.[23] Conservatives claimed Iran would use the windfall to sponsor terrorism and other nefarious activities.

First of all, the United States wasn't giving any money to Iran. Iran would receive its own money that was being held abroad because of sanctions. Second, the total amount embargoed was about $100 billion, not $150 billion. About half of that remained in banks abroad to pay off existing debts.[24] The Rouhani government used most of the remaining money on domestic spending to spur economic growth. And, of course, Iran continued to fund its nuclear power plant.

Is Nuclear Power a Good Idea?

Nuclear power generation is extremely expensive, one of the main reasons why U.S. electricity companies have been forced to shut down nuclear plants in recent years. Nuclear reactors are also very dangerous, as seen in the disaster at Fukushima, Japan. Iran has one functioning nuclear reactor, Bushehr, located along the Persian Gulf coast. It was originally built by German companies in the 1970s, and more recently has been refurbished by Russia. It provides about 2 percent of Iran's current electricity. Western experts have warned that aging equipment and lack of safety precautions at Bushehr could cause another Chernobyl disaster.[25]

University of Tehran Professor Marandi told me that the Soviet nuclear plant in Chernobyl, which suffered a catastrophic explosion in 1986, was an old model. "The technology now used by the Russians and Chinese is very different today than it was in the past."[26] He conceded, however, that the cost of building nuclear power plants is very high indeed. The government has not revealed the overall costs, but a RAND Corp study estimated the nuclear program cost Iran $100 billion.[27] The cost of the program is "a big discussion right now," Mehrdad Khadir admitted to me. He is chief editor of the weekly magazine, *Omid Javan* (*Hope of the Youth*). "How much money did we lose over the past ten years?"[28]

A startling admission came from Abbas Araghchi, Iran's chief nuclear negotiator in the nuclear talks at Vienna. He spoke off the record to Islamic Republic of Iran Broadcasting, but his remarks were posted online before being hastily removed. "I have always said that if we judge our nuclear program on purely economic criteria, it is a big loss—meaning that if we calculate the cost of the products, it makes no sense at all," said Araghchi. "But we paid these costs for our honor, our independence and our progress ... Our program ... will become cost-effective in time."[29]

The high cost of nuclear power has provoked some controversy in Iran. I stopped young people at random in various parts of Tehran. Farzad Yazdoneh, a twenty-five-year-old student, said he would like to see an end to nuclear power. "Iran is only pursuing nuclear energy because of regional rivalry," he told me. Iran should develop more wind, solar, and hydro power. "Iran does not need nuclear energy, because other sources are cheaper."

Pulling Out of the Nuclear Accord

President Trump made the JCPOA a key campaign issue in 2016. He viscerally hated all of Barack Obama's policies and claimed that the nuclear accord was "catastrophic for America, for Israel and for the whole of the Middle East."[30] Republicans swept the presidency and elected majorities in both the House and Senate in 2016. The Republicans set to work figuring how to cancel an agreement that had been accepted by five other major powers and the UN Security Council. They floated various arguments during the first months of 2017.

Four conservative Republican senators sent Trump a letter calling for an end to the JCPOA. "Iran continues to wage a campaign of regional aggression, sponsor international terrorism, develop ballistic missile technology, and oppress the Iranian people," they wrote. "A continuation of current policy would be tantamount to rewarding Iran's belligerence."[31]

Throughout 2017 Trump took a series of actions that fell just short of withdrawing from the JCPOA. In February, after Iran had tested a new medium-range ballistic missile, the White House imposed sanctions on individuals and companies involved in producing those weapons. In July the United States sanctioned six additional Iranian companies. In August Trump signed a law imposing sanctions on Iran, Russia, and North Korea. And in October he imposed new sanctions on Iran's Revolutionary Guard.

Technically these new sanctions didn't violate the JCPOA because they weren't aimed at Iran's nuclear program. The Obama administration had always reserved the right to sanction Iran on other issues. But Trump's sanctions were unilateral and were criticized by close allies such as Britain and France.[32]

In October of 2017 Trump decertified Iran's compliance with the JCPOA under the Iran Nuclear Agreement Review Act, a U.S. law which is not part of the JCPOA. When the Obama administration sought legislative approval of the JCPOA in 2015, it agreed to the review act in which the president must certify Iranian compliance with the JCPOA every ninety days or else Congress can take action against Iran. It was not sanctioned by the UN or any of the other JCPOA signatories. Congress took no action in response to the decertification because of deep divisions over support for the JCPOA among Republicans and Democrats.

Nevertheless, the hostile rhetoric coming out of Washington and behind the scenes maneuvering raised doubts about whether foreign companies should invest in Iran. The Trump administration was violating terms of the JCPOA by pressuring companies not to do business with Tehran. "It was death by a thousand cuts," according to Trita Parsi, president of the National Iranian American Council.[33]

Trump also pressured the CIA and other intelligence agencies to create some Iranian violations of the JCPOA.[34] He sent UN Ambassador Nikki Haley to Vienna to tell the IAEA it must inspect Iranian military bases for the presence of nuclear materials. The only problem: the United States couldn't offer any proof that illegal activity was taking place there. So the IAEA refused.[35]

The one Trump argument that caused the most confusion, however, was Iran's newly tested ballistic missiles. After all, didn't these missiles demonstrate Iran's aggressive behavior?

Prior to the JCPOA, the UN Security Council prohibited Iran from having ballistic missiles that could carry nuclear weapons. Here's the relevant section of resolution 1920 passed in 2010. "Iran *shall not* undertake any activity related to ballistic missiles capable of delivering nuclear weapons, including launches using ballistic missile technology" (emphasis added).[36]

The Iranians had long objected to that resolution, arguing that they had the right to develop conventional weapons for self-defense. All parties to the JCPOA negotiated new terms, which were subsequently incorporated into UN Security Council Resolution 2231 in 2015. It only *"calls upon* Iran not to undertake any activity related to ballistic missiles designed to be capable of delivering nuclear weapons" (emphasis added).[37]

The Iranian government argues that since it has no nuclear weapons, it's missiles can't deliver nuclear bombs. Regardless of whether that argument is valid, the change in wording means the resolution is not binding regarding ballistic missiles. So while conservatives and the Trump administration may not like the Iranian missiles, they are legal under UN Security Council resolutions.

Through the first months of 2018 the United States demanded that Iran renegotiate the JCPOA. Iran refused as did the UK, Germany, France, China, and Russia. The Trump administration position on JCPOA became more isolated. Even many Israeli intelligence officials, who had been among the strongest critics when the JCPOA was proposed, had come around to supporting it. The JCPOA "has been a clear success," wrote Carmi Gillon, former Shin Bet director, Israel's internal security agency. Many colleagues "now acknowledge that it has had a positive impact on Israel's security and must be fully maintained by the United States and the other signatory nations."[38]

But Prime Minister Benjamin Netanyahu barreled ahead despite the objections of some Israeli intelligence officials. At a major press conference in May, he claimed Israel had seized Iran's nuclear archives, and they proved Iran had violated the JCPOA by conducting prohibited nuclear research. Critics quickly pointed out, however, that none of the supposedly top-secret documents indicated Iran had a nuclear weapons program prior to 2003 and that information revealed by Netanyahu had been known for years.[39]

However, the press conference did set the stage a few days later for the Trump administration to renounce the JCPOA and impose nuclear-related sanctions on Iran, allowing 90–180 days for the sanctions to take effect. The United States planned to reimpose the harsh sanctions used in 2010 and force European countries to comply by threatening to cut them off from the U.S. banking system.

Meanwhile, the IAEA had certified that Iran was living up to the terms of the JCPOA. All the other signatories of the JCPOA agreed and strongly criticized the Trump pullout. Even Trump admitted that Iran has no nuclear weapons or even a nuclear weapons program. So why does Washington continue its hostility?

Real Reasons for U.S. Hostility

Washington's beef with Iran's leaders was never really about them attacking the United States or Israel with nuclear weapons. It's about finding an issue that will get you—the American public—very, very worried. For decades after World War II, the Soviet Union was the scary enemy trying to spread communism in the Middle East. Later, the danger came from Saddam Hussein and his weapons of mass destruction. Now it's Iran and the terrorist threat. To assert U.S. hegemony in the Middle East, Washington must have a truly evil enemy to combat. Mad mullahs with nukes fit the bill.[40]

So What Are the Real Reasons for U.S. Hostility?

Geopolitics. Iran occupies a strategic location in the greater Middle East. It's a Shia power in a predominantly Sunni neighborhood. Prior to 1979 the United States and Israel used Iran as an economic and military force to combat Arab nationalism. After the 1979 revolution, Iran left the U.S. sphere of influence and eventually created new alliances with governments in Iraq, Lebanon, and Syria. Iran directly challenges U.S. hegemony.

Iranian leaders would like to see conservative, pro-Iranian, Islamic governments throughout the region. That would be disastrous for the people of the Middle East, but they are capable of dealing with that issue themselves. U.S. political, economic, and military intervention only makes the situation worse.

Oil. Iran has the some of the largest oil reserves in the world.[41] Prior to 1979, U.S., British, and French oil corporations had contracts to develop, pump, and distribute Iranian oil. After 1979 Iran's nationalized oil company was willing to continue business with U.S. firms, but on terms more favorable to Iran. For both political and economic reasons, U.S. oil companies pulled out of Iran. They much prefer that Iran return to the U.S. camp where far more profitable agreements can be made.

Military presence. Under the rule of Shah Mohammad Reza Pahlavi, the United States embedded over 50,000 troops within the Iranian military, supposedly to protect the region from communist aggression. In reality those troops protected U.S. oil and geopolitical interests, and tried to assure the shah's despotic rule. The U.S. military demanded extraterritoriality, which meant that the American personnel couldn't be tried in Iranian courts. That issue created tremendous resentment and was a significant factor in the overthrow of the shah. The 1979 revolution and its aftermath led to the withdrawal of U.S. troops.

For years U.S. administrations have sought to either pressure Iranian leaders to accept U.S. hegemony or to overthrow them altogether, what is euphemistically called "regime change." During the Trump years, the cries for regime change intensified.

Senator Tom Cotton (Republican—Arkansas) is a close Trump ally. He called for political and covert action against Iran, hoping to incite the country's ethnic minorities to rebel against the central government. "The policy of the United States should be regime change in Iran," he said. "I don't see how anyone can say America can be safe as long as you have in power a theocratic despotism."[42]

But as we'll see in Chapters 7 and 8, while the Iranian people strongly oppose their government's policies, that doesn't mean they want to replace the current autocrats with a pro-U.S. regime. Gym worker Yazdi, who we met at the beginning of the chapter, offered his own solution for how ordinary Americans can lessen tensions between the United States and Iran.

"I hear that they call Iranians terrorists or they are bad people," he told me. "My suggestion is not to judge. Come to Iran if they can for a few days and see for themselves. Don't make judgments from media or people lying. There are good and bad people everywhere."

I must add a quick footnote. Over the years the United States issued blustery condemnations of Iran's alleged violatations of the Non-Proliferation Treaty, which prohibits the developments of nuclear weapons. But neither Washington officials nor mainstream media mention the long-standing U.S. violations of the NPT. The United States and other nuclear powers are supposed to negotiate an end to their nuclear arsenals.

Title VI of the NPT states: "Each of the Parties to the Treaty undertakes to pursue negotiations in good faith on effective measures relating to cessation of the nuclear arms race at an early date and to nuclear disarmament, and on a treaty on general and complete disarmament under strict and effective international control."[43]

The United States doesn't even make a pretense of making "good faith" efforts toward negotiations. It has ignored this provision and, in fact, plans to spend $1.3 trillion to modernize its nuclear weapons.[44]

Notes

1. Avasta Yazdi, interview with author, Feb. 25, 2016, Tehran.

2. Joint Comprehensive Plan of Action, Vienna, July 14, 2015 (www.state. gov/documents/organization/245317.pdf).

3. Ruhollah Hosseinian, interview with author, Aug. 2, 2015, Tehran.

4. Yukiya Amano, "Director General's Remarks on Iran, the JCPOA and the IAEA," Nov. 14, 2017 (www.iaea.org/newscenter/statements/director-generals-remarks-on-iran-the-jcpoa-and-the-iaea).

5. CIA, "The 2007 NIE Report on Iran's Nuclear Intentions and Capabilities," May 2007 (www.cia.gov/library/center-for-the-study-of-intelligence/csi-publications/books-and-monographs/csi-intelligence-and-policy-monographs/pdfs/support-to-policymakers-2007-nie.pdf).

6. Seymour Hersh, "Iran and the Bomb," *The New Yorker*, June 6, 2011 (www.newyorker.com/magazine/2011/06/06/iran-and-the-bomb-seymour-m-hersh).

7. Patrick Clawson, interview with author, Jan. 9, 2018, Washington DC.

8. IAEA, "Report by the Director General: Verification and Monitoring in the Islamic Republic of Iran in light of United Nations Security Council Resolution 2231 (2015)," Nov. 13, 2017 (www.iaea.org/sites/default/files/17/11/gov2017-48.pdf).

9. U.S. Department of Defense, "Annual Report on Military Power of Iran," Jan. 2014 (http://freebeacon.com/wp-content/uploads/2014/07/Iranmilitary. pdf).

10. Glenn Kessler, "In 2003, U.S. Spurned Iran's Offer of Dialogue," *Washington Post*, June 18, 2006 (www.washingtonpost.com/wp-dyn/content/article/2006/06/17/AR2006061700727.html).

11. Trita Parsi, "The Turkey-Brazil-Iran deal: Can Washington Take 'Yes' for an Answer?" *Foreign Policy*, May 5, 2010 (http://foreignpolicy.com/2010/05/18/the-turkey-brazil-iran-deal-can-washington-take-yes-for-an-answer/).

12. This and other interviews in this section originally appeared in Reese Erlich, "Iranians Say US Sanctions Hit Wrong Target," *GlobalPost*, July 26, 2013 (www.pri.org/stories/2013-07-26/iranians-say-us-sanctions-hit-wrong-target).

13. Siamak Namazi, "Sanctions and Medical Supply Shortages in Iran," Woodrow Wilson Center, Feb. 8, 2013 (www.wilsoncenter.org/publication/sanctions-and-medical-supply-shortages-iran). Ironically, the author of this report, which is highly critical of U.S. policy, was arrested by Iranian authorities in 2015 and sentenced to ten years in prison on false allegations of spying.

14. David E. Sanger, "Obama Order Sped Up Wave of Cyber Attacks Against Iran," (www.nytimes.com/2012/06/01/world/middleeast/obama-ordered-wave-of-cyberattacks-against-iran.html?_r=1). See also, Kim Zetter, "An Unprecedented Look at Stuxnet, the World's First Digital Weapon," *Wired*, Nov. 3, 2014 (www.wired.com/2014/11/countdown-to-zero-day-stuxnet/).

15. Ronen Bergman, "When Israel Hatched a Secret Plan to Assassinate Iranian Scientists," *Politico*, March 5, 2018 (www.politico.com/magazine/story/2018/03/05/israel-assassination-iranian-scientists-217223).

16. Reese Erlich, "Who's the Bad Guy?" *Vice News*, Aug. 28, 2015 (https://news.vice.com/article/whos-the-bad-guy-the-view-on-foreign-policy-from-tehran).

17. Seyed Mohammad Marandi, interview with author, July 29, 2015, Tehran.

18. Trita Parsi, *Losing an Enemy: Obama, Iran and the Triumph of Diplomacy*, p. 180, (New Haven: Yale University Press, 2017).

19. Many of those documents were of suspicious origin. For example, the U.S. claimed to be in possession of an Iranian laptop that contained proof that Iran had drawn up plans to make a nuclear weapon that could be mounted on a missile. The documents were phony. See Gareth Porter, *Manufactured Crisis: the Untold Story of the Iran Nuclear Scare*, pp. 191–216, (Charlottesville, VA: Just World Books, 2014).

20. Arms Control Association, "Section 3: Understanding the JCPOA," (www.armscontrol.org/reports/Solving-the-Iranian-Nuclear-Puzzle-The-Joint-Comprehensive-Plan-of-Action/2015/08/Section-3-Understanding-the-JCPOA).

21. Yukiya Amano, "Director General's Remarks on Iran, the JCPOA and the IAEA," Nov. 14, 2017 (www.iaea.org/newscenter/statements/director-generals-remarks-on-iran-the-jcpoa-and-the-iaea).

22. Karl Vick, "Why the U.S. Owed Iran That $400 Million," *Time* magazine, Aug. 5, 2016 (http://time.com/4441046/400-million-iran-hostage-history).

23. Lauren Carroll, "Donald Trump: Iran Gets to Keep $150 billion even if U.S. Rejects Nuclear Deal," *Politifact*, Aug. 16, 2015 (www.politifact.com/truth-o-meter/statements/2015/aug/16/donald-trump/donald-trump-iran-gets-keep-150-billion-even-if-us/).

24. Reese Erlich, "Iran's President Is Betting Billions on Economic Reform," *VICE News*, April 19, 2016 (https://news.vice.com/article/irans-president-is-betting-billions-on-economic-reform). See also Carol E. Lee and Jay Solomon, "A Tally of Iran Sanctions Relief Includes More Than $10 Billion in Cash, Gold," *Wall Street Journal*, Dec. 30, 2016 (www.wsj.com/articles/a-tally-of-iran-sanctions-relief-includes-more-than-10-billion-in-cash-gold-1483112751?mod=trending_now_5).

25. Tom Hamburger, "Iran Reports Safety Concerns at Nuclear Plant," *Los Angeles Times*, Feb. 27, 2011 (http://articles.latimes.com/2011/feb/27/world/la-fg-iran-nukes-20110227).

26. Interview with author, Tehran, July 29, 2015.

27. Scott Peterson, "How Much Is a Nuclear Program Worth? For Iran, well over $100 billion," *Christian Science Monitor*, Apr. 3, 2013 (www.csmonitor.com/World/Middle-East/2013/0403/How-much-is-a-nuclear-program-worth-For-Iran-well-over-100-billion).

28. Mehrdad Khadir, interview with author, July 27, 2015, Tehran.

29. Reese Erlich, "Who's the Bad Guy?" *Vice News*, Aug. 28, 2015, op. cit.

30. PBS News Hour, "Trump May Scrap the Iran Nuclear Agreement. Here's What You Need to Know," Oct. 10, 2017 (www.pbs.org/newshour/show/trump-may-scrap-iran-nuclear-agreement-heres-need-know).

31. Josh Rogin "GOP Senators Want Tillerson to Get Tougher on Iran," *Washington Post*, July 11, 2017 (www.washingtonpost.com/news/josh-rogin/wp/2017/07/11/gop-senators-want-tillerson-to-get-tougher-on-iran/?utm_term=.600bf10c35a6).

32. Julian Borger, "Europe's Governments Look to Bypass Trump to save Iranian Nuclear Deal," *The Guardian*, Oct. 4, 2017 (www.theguardian.com/world/2017/oct/04/iran-nuclear-deal-europe-trump-congress).

33. Trita Parsi and Ryan Costello, "Trump Vindicates Iranian Hardliners and Victimizes Ordinary Citizens," *Huffington Post*, May 8, 2018 (www.huffingtonpost.com/entry/opinion-parsi-iran-deal_us_5af239fce4b0a0d601e78d40?lbs).

34. Julian Borger, "White House 'Pressuring' Intelligence Officials to Find Iran in Violation of Nuclear Deal," *The Guardian*, Aug. 28, 2017

(www.theguardian.com/world/2017/aug/28/iran-nuclear-deal-violations-white-house-search-intelligence).

35. Reuters Staff, "Nuclear Inspectors Should Have Access to Iran Military Bases: Haley," *Reuters*, Aug. 25, 2017 (www.reuters.com/article/us-iran-nuclear-usa-haley/nuclear-inspectors-should-have-access-to-iran-military-bases-haley-idUSKCN1B524I).

36. UN Security Council Resolution 1929, June 9, 2010 (www.un.org/sc/suborg/en/s/res/1929-%282010%29).

37. UN Security Council Resolution 2231, July 20, 2015 (https://web.archive.org/web/20150819092747/http://www.un.org/en/sc/inc/pages/pdf/pow/RES2231E.pdf).

38. Carmi Gillon, "The Iran Nuclear Deal Has Been a Blessing for Israel," *Foreign Policy*, July 13, 2017 (http://foreignpolicy.com/2017/07/13/the-iran-nuclear-deal-has-been-a-blessing-for-israel-jcpoa/).

39. Gareth Porter, "The Latest Act in Israel's Iran Nuclear Disinformation Campaign People," *Consortium News*, May 3, 2018 (https://consortiumnews.com/2018/05/03/the-latest-act-in-the-israels-iran-nuclear-disinformation-campaign/).

40. For excellent background on this and related topics, see William Beeman, *The Great Satan vs. the Mad Mullahs: How the United States and Iran Demonize Each Other* (Chicago: University of Chicago Press, 2008).

41. World Atlas, "The World's Largest Oil Reserves By Country," (www.worldatlas.com/articles/the-world-s-largest-oil-reserves-by-country.html).

42. Bryan Bender, "Trump Allies Push White House to Consider Regime Change in Tehran," *Politico*, June 25, 2017 (www.politico.com/story/2017/06/25/trump-iran-foreign-policy-regime-change-239930).

43. "The Treaty on the Non-proliferation of Nuclear Weapons," United Nations, May 2005 (www.un.org/en/conf/npt/2005/npttreaty.html).

44. William J. Broad and David E. Sanger, "Trump Plans for Nuclear Arsenal Require $1.2 Trillion, Congressional Review States," *New York Times*, Oct. 31, 2017 (www.nytimes.com/2017/10/31/us/politics/trump-nuclear-weapons-arsenal-congressional-budget.html).

FOUR

Iran, Hizbollah, and Israel: The Real Story

What I remember most clearly about Eliyahu Ben-Elissar was his goatee. It wasn't just any goatee. It resembled an elegant, carefully trimmed shaving brush. The goatee descended directly from the great European facial hair of the early 1900s.

When I met Ben-Elissar in Jerusalem back in 1987, he was a ranking member of the Knesset (parliament) foreign affairs committee and a former ambassador to Egypt. Ben-Elissar later became the Israeli ambassador to the United States and died in 2000. But in 1987 he welcomed me into his house on a quiet Jerusalem street and offered coffee. The hospitality matched the goatee.

Ben-Elissar assumed that, as an American Jew, I would be sympathetic to Israel's current policies. Once the pleasantries were over, however, our differences became quite clear. Ben-Elissar strongly advocated hard-right views as a leader of the then-ruling Likud party. Ultra-right-winger Yitzhak Shamir was prime minister, and Ben-Elissar reflected Shamir's views. Israel opposed establishing a Palestinian state, claiming that Palestinians already had their own state, Jordan. Ben-Elissar favored annexing the West Bank. He justified torture by Shin Bet, the Israeli intelligence agency.

But Ben-Elissar took what seemed to be an incongruous position on Iran. He defended Israeli government support of Iran in the Iran–Iraq War. Top Iranian leaders opposed the existence of the Jewish state and regularly spewed anti-Jewish rhetoric. Yet Israel sold spare parts and other arms to Iran. Israel was an integral part of the Iran-Contra scandal, providing arms to both Iran and the Contras in Nicaragua.* Ben-Elissar admitted to me that "the decision to sell arms to Iran was made in secret by [Israel's] prime minister, minister of defense, and foreign minister."[1]

Ben-Elissar explained that Israel considered Iraq the more-dangerous enemy. He said Ayatollah Ruhollah "Khomeini is full of anti-Israeli rhetoric, but that's all." Israel "would not like to see Iran completely defeated because this would make ... Iraq a big winner."[2]

U.S. congressional investigations confirmed what Ben-Elissar told me that day. The United States had been the main arms supplier to Iran before 1979, and the new clerical government desperately needed to restock its arsenal. Israel had many of the same U.S. weapons, such as TOW and HAWK missiles, as well as spare parts for jet fighters. In its chronology of the Iran-Contra scandal, the National Security Archive wrote, "Iran badly wanted what Israel could provide. ... Since Israel had those weapons in its inventory, ... Israel was more than happy to provide those weapons to Iran."[3]

Why would Israel support the rabidly anti-Zionist government in Iran? Israel had been a close ally of Shah Mohammad Reza Pahlavi almost to the moment of his overthrow and had a policy of supporting non-Arab governments in the region as a wedge against Arabs. Israel had supported Iran, Turkey, and Ethiopia. So Israel saw no

---

*   In what became known as the Iran-Contra scandal, the administration of President Ronald Reagan sent missiles and other armaments to Iran in return for Iran using its influence to release U.S. hostages held in war-torn Lebanon. Administration officials then used the profits from these sales to illegally fund the right-wing Contra guerrillas, who carried out terrorist bombings and assassinations against the elected leftist government of Nicaragua.

contradiction in supporting the clerical government of Iran despite its frequent and public calls for "Death to Israel." Yitzhak Rabin, Israeli prime minister from 1974 to 1977 and then again from 1992 to 1995, told a 1987 press conference, "Iran is Israel's best friend, and we do not intend to change our position in relation to Tehran, because Khomeini's regime will not last forever."[4]

But times have changed, and Israel now seeks to demonize Iran rather than Iraq.

Does Iran Want to Kill the Jews?

Shimon Peres said in a speech that President Mahmoud Ahmadinejad "is the only person in the world calling for the annihilation of another people." Peres was a former Labor Party prime minister and later became president. "We need to expose his real face, which is just like Hitler, to the world. ... Here we have a man with a dangerous personality, just like Hitler, who wants to build dangerous weapons. These kinds of threats we hear from Ahmadinejad have not been heard since Hitler."[5]

Well, actually, Israel's supporters make that claim all the time. The Hitler analogy has been made against Saddam Hussein, Palestine Liberation Organization (PLO) Chairman Yasser Arafat, Egypt's President Anwar Sadat (before he signed a peace treaty with Israel), and many other leaders opposed to Israeli policies.[6] In reality, Ahmadinejad was no Hitler, if for no other reason than Iran is no Germany. Both the United States and Israel intentionally distort his words for maximum negative impact. On the other hand, some people in the Muslim world idealize Ahmadinejad as a hero, a reputation he clearly doesn't deserve.

At various times Ahmadinejad has been quoted as saying "Israel must be wiped off the map." In reality, according to several Farsi speakers I consulted, Ahmadinejad is quoting an old slogan from Ayatollah Ruhollah Khomeini that means "this regime occupying

Jerusalem must vanish from the page of time." That phrase does not imply Iranian military action against Israel.

But Ahmadinejad really angered world opinion by holding a conference in December 2006 to question the existence of the Holocaust. The conference was a political disaster for Ahmadinejad and led some members of the Majlis to criticize him. A group of a hundred leading Iranian intellectuals, inside and outside Iran, denounced the conference as a "distortion of historical facts."

Ahmadinejad's statements and actions indicate he is profoundly wrong about Jewish history and current Middle East politics. His rhetoric harms the Palestinian people, providing the United States and Israel easy propaganda points. But neither Ahmadinejad nor other major political leaders call for annihilating the Jews.[7]

President Hassan Rouhani, a centrist elected in 2013, did not offer the same easy target. He backed the nuclear accord, which prohibits Iran from developing nuclear weapons, and took steps to lower tensions with the West. But that didn't stop ultra-right-wing Prime Minister Benjamin Netanyahu from vilifying Iran. He continued to compare Iran to Nazi Germany, claiming it had a "ruthless commitment to kill Jews."[8]

What are Iranian leaders' real views toward Israel and Jews? "Iran officially supports the one-state" in Palestine, explains Tehran University Professor Foad Izadi in an interview.[9] That means all the estimated 5 million Palestinians now living in exile should return home. Then Israeli Jews and Palestinians would hold a referendum on what kind of government they want. Such a position would eliminate Israel as a Jewish state and would not be accepted by Israelis.

Iran has a fall-back position that leaves open the option for a two-state solution, in which Israeli and Palestinian states live peacefully side by side. Izadi explains, "Iran will not be more Palestinian than the Palestinians, that is, Iran will not do anything to harm any decision the majority of Palestinians make in resolving the problem of occupation." So, if the Israelis and Palestinians agree on a two-state solution, Iran will agree as well. The Iranian government offered to support a two-state solution in a 2003 proposal sent to the George W. Bush Administration through the Swiss ambassador to Iran.[10]

The Palestine Liberation Organization rejected the one-state solution in the 1990s and later in a formal Arab League peace plan adopted in 2002 at its summit in Beirut.[11] Most Palestinians and Arabs continue to believe in a two-state solution. Israel would have to return occupied Arab land and agree to recognize a viable Palestinian nation with Jerusalem as its capital. In return, Palestinians and Arab states would recognize and live in peace with Israel.

The United States and Israel maintain that Hamas, the conservative political Islamist party that won the 2006 parliamentary elections in the Palestinian Authority, does not accept a two-state solution. In fact, Hamas has modified its views over time and today would accept two states. It signed an accord with the Palestinian Authority, the body that governs occupied Palestinian territory, which agrees to accept a Palestinian state in Gaza and the West Bank with Jerusalem as its capital. Hamas leader Khalid Meshal confirmed Hamas acceptance of a two-state solution in an interview with me.[12]

But Israeli leaders have blocked the possibility of a two-state solution by continuing to expand and build new settlements on occupied Palestinian land. Netanyahu stopped all negotiations with the Palestinians. In early 2018 the Trump administration moved the U.S. embassy to Jerusalem, a decision that angered Palestinians because it implies no part of Jerusalem would ever become part of Palestine. The hard line pursued by Netanyahu and Trump has led some Palestinians to re-open the question of demanding one state. But the consensus remains that two states are the only practical solution for both sides.

The rhetoric from some Iranian leaders remains fiercely anti-Zionist, but Israeli leaders know Iran doesn't have a nuclear bomb. If Iran ever launched an offensive attack on Israel, let alone a nuclear attack, the Iranian government would be isolated at home and internationally. The United States and Israel would destroy Iran in counterattacks.

Mark Heller, principal research associate at the Institute for National Security Studies in Tel Aviv, told me succinctly, "An unprovoked, direct military attack [by Iran] on Israel is on the bottom of the list of probabilities."[13] Iran's rulers are angry, not insane.

Israel doesn't have to worry about an offensive first strike, but if Iran ever did develop nuclear weapons, the United States and Israel would have a much harder time attacking Iran. They would have to calculate whether Iran would use its nuclear arsenal in self-defense. Israeli leaders' scaremongering about Iran's nuclear threat hides their real agenda. Iran supports Lebanon's Hizbollah and the Palestinian group Hamas. Israel seeks to weaken or eliminate those groups. It argues that without the outside support of Iran and Syria, those two groups would no longer pose a threat to Israel.

That argument has a familiar ring. Israel has always blamed the indigenous resistance on outsiders. In the early 1970s, the Israeli government argued that the PLO survived only because of support in Jordan. After it was driven from Jordan in 1971, the PLO survived only because of its bases in Lebanon. When Israel invaded and occupied southern Lebanon and expelled the PLO in 1982, the outside threat became Syria and Iraq. But somehow opposition to Israeli occupation continued to grow. Now the outside agitator is Iran.

Outsiders are not the cause of Palestinian or Lebanese resistance. Military might cannot guarantee Israel's security. Israel must resolve the Palestinian issue and return occupied Arab land. If the Palestinians agree to a two-state settlement, the views of Iran, Syria, or any other country become irrelevant.

Is Hizbollah a Terrorist Organization?

But what about Lebanon? Western analysts argue that Iran created Hizbollah. Should the world be worried about Iran's influence there?

Back in 2003 I wanted to visit the headquarters of Hizbollah in Beirut, but it wasn't easy. The problem was not security. Rather, I was stumped by Beirut's confusing system of addresses. For many Shiite neighborhoods, you drive to the general location and then ask a passerby for the specific destination. This works great for locals but can be a problem for someone who doesn't speak Arabic.

"Don't worry," Haidar Dikmak, Hizbollah chief press officer, told me over the phone, "any taxi driver will know how to get you here." He was right. I told the grizzled old man driving my taxi to take me to the Hizbollah offices. We arrived about thirty minutes later, after stopping to ask a passerby, of course.

Many Americans have an image of Hizbollah as a group of wild-eyed terrorists with their turbans in a twist. In reality, Hizbollah has become the most popular Shia Muslim political party in Lebanon. In 2018 Hizbollah candidates won thirteen seats in the parliamentary elections and have been a leading political force in the cabinet for many years. Hizbollah has garnered support by operating hospitals, schools, and social service agencies. On the other hand, it's strict interpretation of Islam teaches that Muslim clerics should play a leading role in government, Hizbollah takes a hard line against Israel and maintains its own armed militia. In 2012 Hizbollah sent its troops into Syria to put down a rebellion against Bashar al Assad, a controversial action that angered many Lebanese.

But engaging in armed struggle doesn't mean a group is terrorist as admitted to me by an American diplomat in Beirut. Speaking off the record, the diplomat downplayed the official terrorism designation. While the United States still considers Hizbollah an enemy, the diplomat said the group had changed significantly. "No one in Lebanon thinks Hizbollah is a terrorist organization. We recognize they do social work. They've become more sophisticated in military terms as well as fund-raising and providing services."

Hizbollah is also quite open about its political ties to Iran. Walk down the street in the Shiite districts of Lebanon, and you'll see posters of Hizbollah leader Sheik Hassan Nasrallah, Ayatollah Khomeini, and Iran's current Supreme Leader Sayyed Ali Khamenei. Of course, those bearded visages also decorated the walls of Hizbollah's modest office when I visited.

Visiting Hizbollah

It was an oppressively hot summer day in Beirut, and the sweat poured down my back as I hiked up the stairs to Hizbollah Press Officer Dikmak's office. I had traveled to Lebanon as a freelancer on assignment for the *San Francisco Chronicle*. Dikmak's place was the first stop in getting permission to visit Hizbollah-controlled areas of southern Lebanon. In theory, anyone could travel anywhere in Lebanon. But in reality, Hizbollah controlled a sizable swath of Lebanese territory.

I watched with fascination as Dikmak typed the *Chronicle's* name into his computer database. He scanned several articles that staffers and freelancers had written about Hizbollah. Luckily, the most recent visitor had been Robert Collier, a fine *Chronicle* reporter without the usual Middle East ax to grind. Dikmak had even mastered the mainstream media terminology. "Ah, yes," he said with a slight smile, "Mr. Collier's articles were quite objective." An assistant brought in strong Arabic coffee, and we had an informal chat.

At one point, almost in passing, he mentioned the "Four Mothers." I had no idea who they were. I found out later that the Four Mothers were a group of Israeli women who became famous for organizing against the Israeli occupation of Lebanon, which ended in 2000. Any Israeli would have recognized the reference. Luckily, I did not.

Israel periodically sends spies into Lebanon disguised as journalists. Had I been more familiar with recent Israeli history, I might have been mistaken for an agent, the 007 of Oakland. But seeing as how I was a writer for an objective newspaper and not a spy, I was given permission to visit and interview people in southern Lebanon.

The drive south of Beirut in those days was quite beautiful. The modern highway gave way to winding roads. Spectacular views of the

Mediterranean slowly disappeared only to be exchanged for scenic, rolling hills. Much of this land was destroyed in the 2006 Israel–Lebanon War.

On a 2003 trip, I eventually drove all the way down to the Lebanese–Israeli border. We stopped at the Fatima Gate, a long-closed border crossing point. Standing on a hill, I could see the developed towns and agricultural fields of Israel. I could also shop at outdoor stands selling tsotchkes to tourists: Hizbollah lapel pins, CDs, flags, and T-shirts. After a bit of haggling, I finally bought a genuine Hizbollah coffee mug.

We drove back up the coast and then inland for a meeting with Mohammed Raad, the head of Hizbollah's parliamentary group. Raad explained that Iran provides political and moral support for Hizbollah. But despite these close ties, he said, Hizbollah makes its own decisions.[14] Hizbollah emerged in the early 1980s when it split from Amal, the Lebanese Shiite political party and militia. Hizbollah rejected Amal's vaguely leftist political stands and its corruption. Iran played an important role from the beginning, offering political, military, and financial support to Hizbollah. Iranian Revolutionary Guards helped train Hizbollah in the Bekaa Valley of Lebanon and provided financial aid, although neither side has ever revealed the amount. Some years ago, Farid El Khazen, a political science professor at the American University of Beirut, told me he estimated Iran provided $100 million in military and civilian assistance annually.[15] Iran publicly pledged $500 million to Hizbollah during the 2006 war.[16] The subsidies have increased substantially since Hizbollah's militia entered Lebanon.

Iranian and Hizbollah leaders share a common ideology. Both take a hard line on the Israeli–Palestinian conflict. Both see a central role for Shia Islam in government. Hizbollah initially favored forming an Islamic state in Lebanon, similar to what exists in Iran. Since the 1990s, however, Hizbollah has recognized that a majority of Lebanese would not support the establishment of a Shia Islamic state.

So Hizbollah pushes for Islamic rule in areas it controls, without trying to impose that on the entire country.

El Khazen told me, "Ultimately, Hizbollah knows that a country like Lebanon, with so many different communities and sects—Sunni, Shia, Christians—they know it's not easy to establish an Islamic state."

While relations between Iran and Hizbollah are close, Hizbollah remains a nationalist party with its focus on Lebanon. In the long run—after Israel eventually returns occupied land to Lebanon, resolves the Palestinian issue, and the Syrian civil war is settled—Hizbollah must still function as a political party in Lebanon. That means Hizbollah has no future as a proxy for Iran.

I had the pleasure of working with Iranian journalist and documentary filmmaker Maziar Bahari during my 2000 trip to Iran. He has studied Iran's and Hizbollah's leaders and remains a sharp critic of both. He notes, however, that Hizbollah is no puppet. "Hizbollah, to a great extent, makes decisions independently of Iran," he wrote. "Hizbollah is an indigenous Lebanese armed resistance group that owes its popularity to Israeli atrocities, biased American policies, and corrupt Lebanese politicians. When the United States and Israel try to portray Hizbollah as an Iranian proxy, they are pointing the finger in the wrong direction."[17]

Who Won the 2006 Israel–Lebanon War?

In June 2006, Israel sent troops back into Gaza, after having unilaterally withdrawn in September 2005.* Fierce fighting broke

---

* Israel withdrew unilaterally from Gaza in September 2005 but continued to economically strangle the territory by prohibiting sea, air, and land access. Palestinians were rarely allowed outside Gaza to work in Israel. On June 25, 2006, Palestinian militants attacked an Israeli post just outside Gaza and captured a soldier. That led directly to Israel's re-occupation of parts of Gaza a few days later. While Israeli troops eventually pulled out, they returned in subsequent clashes.

out between Palestinians and the Israeli army. In a particularly horrendous incident, Israeli warships shelled a beach in Gaza on June 9, killing seven civilians and wounding fifteen. The chilling images were captured by TV cameras and broadcast around the world. The Israeli government claimed that the people had been killed by Palestinian land mines, but Human Rights Watch investigators held the Israeli navy responsible.[18]

In this context, Hizbollah launched a well-planned raid from Lebanon into northern Israel on July 12. It ambushed Israeli soldiers, killing eight and capturing two. It hoped to exchange the Israeli soldiers for Lebanese prisoners held in Israel. In previous years, Israel had retaliated for border incidents with artillery and air strikes inside Lebanon. Hizbollah leader Nasrallah later said he expected such retaliation once again. But this time the recently elected government of Prime Minister Ehud Olmert decided to pummel Hizbollah into submission with a full-scale air bombardment, followed by a ground invasion. Why adopt such a hard-line policy?

Clearly, Israel wanted to punish Hizbollah, both for its support of the Palestinians and for holding Israeli soldiers captive. But the United States played a strong role as well. In the spring of 2006, the Bush Administration had been ramping up its rhetoric and threatening military strikes against Iran. The United States feared, however, that if it attacked Iran, the clerical government would encourage Hizbollah and Hamas to retaliate. So the United States urged Israel to severely weaken and, if possible, wipe out Hizbollah.

Seymour Hersh wrote in the *New Yorker*:

> The Bush Administration ... was closely involved in the planning of Israel's retaliatory attacks. President Bush and Vice President Dick Cheney were convinced, current and former intelligence and diplomatic officials told me, that a successful Israeli Air Force bombing campaign against Hizbollah's heavily fortified underground-missile and command-and-control complexes in Lebanon could ease Israel's security concerns and also serve as a

prelude to a potential American preemptive attack to destroy Iran's nuclear installations.[19]

Hersh quotes a former senior intelligence officer who characterized Cheney's views. "What if the Israelis … [are] really successful? It'd be great. We can learn what to do in Iran by watching what the Israelis do in Lebanon."

Or what not to do.

Hizbollah was a lot better armed and organized than either the United States or Israel imagined. In the first days after Israel's attack, Hizbollah sank an Israeli warship with an Iranian-made C-802 missile, the first such sinking since Israel's founding in 1948. Despite a month of aerial bombardment throughout Lebanon, Hizbollah kept up a daily barrage of Iranian-supplied missiles fired into Israel. Israeli ground troops in Lebanon faced fierce house-to-house combat, including weaponry that destroyed some of their heavily armored tanks.

Israeli aerial bombardments damaged many of Lebanon's bridges, roads, and other infrastructure, including some Lebanese army bases and towns inhabited by Lebanese Christians. Many Christians had sided with Israel in the 1980s, but that apparently didn't matter this time. Israel hoped that the bombardments would force non-Shiite Lebanese to blame Hizbollah for starting the war and ultimately isolate the guerrillas politically. The strategy backfired, as Lebanese from all backgrounds cheered Hizbollah for beating back Israeli attacks.

Richard Armitage, a Republican and former deputy secretary of state, said, "The only thing that the bombing has achieved so far is to unite the population against the Israelis."[20] Israel admitted using phosphorous artillery shells, a weapon many experts consider illegal under international law.[21] The UN reported that in the final days of the war, the Israel Defense Forces fired as many as four million cluster bomblets into civilian areas of southern Lebanon, of which an estimated one million failed to explode.[22]

The Israelis used American-made cluster bombs, which are less likely to detonate and therefore pose a greater threat to civilians. From the end of the war until the end of January 2007, thirty Lebanese civilians had died from these cluster bombs and another 180 had been injured.[23] U.S. law prohibits other countries from using American cluster bombs in civilian areas, but it appeared unlikely the Bush Administration would sanction Israel for its violations. For years to come, children and other civilians who stumble on the bomblets face maiming or death.

Jan Egeland, the UN's under-secretary for humanitarian affairs, noted, "What's shocking—and I would say to me completely immoral—is that 90 percent of the cluster bomb strikes occurred in the last 72 hours of the conflict, when we knew there would be a resolution. Every day people are maimed, wounded and are killed by these ordnance."[24] Why would Israel fire cluster bombs when it had already agreed to a cease-fire? Israel wanted to make parts of Lebanon uninhabitable in order to weaken Hizbollah's political support.

Hizbollah also engaged in illegal activities by intentionally targeting civilians. Human Rights Watch reported that Hizbollah fired 113 rockets with about 4,400 cluster bomblets into northern Israel.[25] Human Rights Watch accused Hizbollah of war crimes for firing rockets indiscriminately into Israel, which killed both Israeli and Arab residents. In its report, Human Rights Watch wrote, "International humanitarian law (the laws of war) obliges warring parties to distinguish between combatants and civilians and, when attacking legitimate military targets, to ensure that the military advantage gained in the attack outweighs any possible harm caused to civilians."[26]

But the atrocities committed by both sides were hardly equal. According to official Israeli figures, 120 IDF soldiers and thirty-nine Israeli civilians died because of the fighting.[27] Experts have a harder time compiling accurate figures for Lebanon. The Higher Relief Commission, a Lebanese government agency, estimates the overall death toll at 1,181, including thirty-four Lebanese soldiers.[28]

Hizbollah says sixty-eight of its guerrillas died. Using those figures, Hizbollah killed roughly three Israeli soldiers for every civilian. The IDF killed roughly seventeen Lebanese civilians for every combatant.

Israel claims that it killed about 500 Hizbollah fighters, a figure that hasn't been corroborated elsewhere. But even assuming that figure is accurate, Israel still killed more than two civilians for every combatant.

Hizbollah clearly won the war politically. Opinion polls conducted immediately after the war showed 80 percent popular support for Hizbollah inside Lebanon, including backing from Sunni Muslims and Christians. In contrast, Israeli politicians and generals immediately began squabbling, blaming each other for the failure to decisively defeat Hizbollah. Prime Minister Olmert's popularity ratings sank below 40 percent among Israelis. Even some staunch defenders of Tel Aviv admitted Israel lost. Former CIA analyst Kenneth Pollack noted, "Hizbollah did what no Arab government ever has: They fought Israel and didn't lose."[29]

So the war that was to strengthen the United States and Israel in the entire region resulted in a huge setback for both. Combined with the defeat of the United States in Iraq, the impact of the Israel–Lebanon War on Middle East relations reverberated for years.

But to fully understand U.S. policy in the region, we must understand more about its recent history. For many Americans, U.S.–Iranian relations begin with the seizure of the hostages at the U.S. Embassy in 1979. But for Iranians, the history goes back twenty-six years earlier.

Notes

1. Eliahu Ben-Elissar, interview with author, June 23, 1987, Jerusalem.

2. Ben-Elissar. See also Reese Erlich, "Behind Israel's Role in the Iran-Contra Arms Scandal," *San Francisco Chronicle*, Aug. 26, 1987.

3. National Security Archive, *The Chronology, the Documented Day-by-Day Account of the Secret Military Assistance to Iran and the Contras*, p. 116 (Warner Books, 1987).

4. Trita Parsi, "Teheran and Jerusalem Are Not Natural Enemies," *South Asia Analysis Group* (www.saag.org/Bb/view.asp?msgID=27964).

5. "Peres: Treat Ahmadinejad like Hitler," *Israel Today*, Oct. 22, 2006 (www.israeltoday.co.il/default.aspx?tabid=178&nid=9919).

6. Jewish Task Force, "Fighting to save America and Israel from Islamic terrorism," (www.jtf.org/israel/israel.arab.moderates.part.one.htm). The web page accuses Egypt's presidents Gamal Abdel Nasser and Anwar Sadat and other Arab leaders of being pro-Nazi.

7. On April 2, 2006, on CNN's *Late Edition with Wolf Blitzer*, Iran's ambassador to the International Atomic Energy Agency Ali Asghar Soltanieh was asked about Iran's position on Israel and Jews. Blitzer: "But should there be a state of Israel?" Soltanieh: "I think I've already answered to you. If Israel is a synonym and will give the indication of Zionism mentality, no. But if you are going to conclude that we have said the people there have to be removed or we they have to be massacred or so, this is fabricated, unfortunate selective approach to what the mentality and policy of Islamic Republic of Iran is. I have to correct, and I did so." (http://transcripts.cnn.com/TRANSCRIPTS/0604/02/le.01.html).

8. Amir Tibon, "Netanyahu at Saban Forum: Iran, Like Nazi Germany, Has 'Ruthless Commitment to Murdering Jews,'" *Haaretz*, Dec. 3, 2017 (www.haaretz.com/us-news/netanyahu-iran-like-nazi-germany-has-commitment-to-kill-jews-1.5627565).

9. Foad Izadi, email interview with author, Mar. 22, 2018.

10. Gareth Porter, "Iran Proposal to U.S. Offered Peace with Israel," *Inter Press Service*, May 24, 2006 (www.ipsnews.net/2006/05/politics-iran-proposal-to-us-offered-peace-with-israel/).

11. www.al-bab.com/arab/docs/league/peace02.htm.

12. Khalid Meshal, interview with author, Dec. 18, 2008, Damascus. See also Reese Erlich, *Conversations with Terrorists: Middle East Leaders on Politics, Violence and Empire*, pp. 20–1, (Sausalito: Politpoint Press, 2010).

13. Mark Heller, interview with author, Oct. 23, 2013, Tel Aviv.

14. Mohammed Raad, interview with author, June 27, 2003, southern Lebanon.

15. Farid El Khazen, interview with author, July 30, 1998, Beirut.

16. Ali Nouri Zadeh, "Iranians Upset at Government's Financial Aid to Hizbollah in Lebanon," *Asharq Alawsat* (Arabic newspaper in London), Aug. 21, 2006 (http://aawsat.com/english/news.asp?section=1&id=6077).

17. Maziar Bahari, "Sweating Out the Truth in Iran," *International Herald Tribune*, op-ed page, Aug. 25, 2006.

18. Human Rights Watch, "Israel: More Evidence on Beach Killings Implicates IDF," *Human Rights News*, June 15, 2006 (http://hrw.org/english/docs/2006/06/15/isrlpa13570.htm).

19. Seymour Hersh, "Watching Lebanon, Washington's interests in Israel's war," *The New Yorker*, Aug. 21, 2006.

20. Hersh, Aug. 21, 2006.

21. Meron Rappaport, "IDF Commander: We Fired More Than a Million Cluster Bombs in Lebanon," *Haaretz* (Israeli daily newspaper), Sept. 12, 2006. See also "Official: Israel Used Phosphorous Bombs," AP wire story, *USA Today*, Oct. 23, 2006.

22. Human Rights Watch, "Lebanon/Israel: Hizbollah Hit Israel with Cluster Munitions During Conflict," *Human Rights News*, Oct. 19, 2006 (http://hrw.org/english/docs/2006/10/18/lebano14412.htm).

23. David S. Cloud and Greg Myre, "Israel May Have Violated Arms Pact, U.S. Officials Say," *New York Times*, Jan. 28, 2007.

24. Rory McCarthy, "Cluster Bombing of Lebanon 'Immoral' UN Official Tells Israel," *The Guardian* (London), Aug. 31, 2006.

25. Human Rights Watch, Oct. 19, 2006.

26. Human Rights Watch, Oct. 19, 2006.

27. Steven Erlanger, "Israeli Admits Big Errors in Lebanon War, but Won't Resign," *New York Times*, Jan. 3, 2007.

28. "Mideast War, by the Numbers," AP wire story, Aug. 18, 2006.

29. Neil King, Jr., "War Emboldens Iran Ahead of Nuclear Talks," *Wall Street Journal*, Aug. 16, 2006.

FIVE

A Brief History of U.S.–Iranian Relations

November 4, 1979, has gone down in history. That day, a group of militant, Islamic students took over the U.S. Embassy in Tehran. Although they didn't know it at the time, they altered U.S.–Iranian relations for decades. The United States had backed the dictatorial shah for twenty-six years, and then after his overthrow, President Jimmy Carter allowed the shah to enter the United States for medical treatment. Iranians feared the United States was planning to return the shah to power as it had done in 1953.

At the time, I guessed the embassy takeover might last a few days or even a few weeks. I thought the hostages would be released, and Iranians could get on with sorting out their revolution. That was not to be. The crisis lasted 444 days. Ayatollah Ruhollah Khomeini used the mass anti-imperialist sentiment stirred up by the takeover to consolidate his power and wipe out opposition groups. That part is well known. What's not known, or often forgotten, is that inside the United States, we saw a huge rise in racism and xenophobia against Middle Easterners.

Some of my Iranian friends were attacked on the streets of San Francisco for simply being Iranian. Similar incidents took place around the country. Some Americans saw images of American diplomats blindfolded and paraded on TV and retaliated against any dark-skinned foreigner they could find. The embassy takeover became a metaphor for U.S.–Iranian relations. For people in the United States, it demonstrated international humiliation and the pure evil of an extremist regime intent on harming Americans. For Iranians, it showed that the United States was trying to abort a popular revolution. Those two sharply different perceptions of reality continue today.

Iran has never been a formal colony, but the British exercised virtual colonial control over Iran starting in the early 1900s. A British financier found oil in Iran in 1908. By 1919, the British imposed the Anglo-Persian agreement on Iran. British troops made sure that a British oil company controlled the country's oil production and export. The British imposed martial law and ran the country's army, treasury, and transport system.

British Foreign Secretary Lord George Curzon explained why Iran was so important to the British Empire. He asked rhetorically why Persia, as the country was then called, shouldn't rule itself. "The answer is that her geographical position ... renders it impossible. ... Further if Persia were to be alone, there is every reason to fear that she would be overrun by Bolshevik influence from the north. Lastly, we possess ... great assets in the shape of oil fields, which are worked for the British navy and which give us a commanding interest in that part of the world."[1]

That argument, with a few variations, has been used by British and American governments ever since. Iran is blessed and cursed with a critical geographic location along shipping lanes of the Persian Gulf. Apparently, Iranians are not capable of handling those blessings without outside assistance.

The British remained the dominant power in Iran between the world wars. But the country emerged in turmoil at the end of World War II. As part of the wartime alliance, Soviet troops occupied northern Iran and British troops controlled the south. The British had forced Shah Reza Pahlavi to abdicate in 1941 and crowned his son Mohammad Reza Pahlavi as king. But the young shah was inexperienced and weak. Both Kurds and Azerbaijanis briefly established leftist, independent states, and the Tudeh (communist) Party was growing in strength.

Iran was supposed to be a constitutional monarchy with both a king and a parliament. But for most of the 1900s, the British and the shah made sure the parliament played a subservient role or no role at all. But Iranians, like many people in the developing world, were no longer willing to settle for the old power structure and traditional subservience to colonial powers. Starting in 1944, Shah Mohammad Reza Pahlavi lost power to the elected parliament.

The recently invigorated parliamentary opposition was led by Mohammad Mossadegh, a wealthy and aristocratic nationalist who had been active in Iranian politics for thirty years. He strongly believed in western-style democracy, a free press, multi-party politics, and an independent judiciary—what today we would call civil society. He also strongly opposed British domination of Iran.

Mossadegh led the National Front, which was allied with a variety of religious, nationalist, socialist, and communist groups. Mossadegh supported what leftists called a united front. Each party figured it would benefit from the alliance and opening up of democracy while maintaining its own views on the best long-term solutions for Iran. The United States vilified such coalitions because, supposedly, Moscow-controlled communists used them to sneak into power. In reality, the U.S. leaders wanted everyone to oppose the USSR and allow Western companies to pump Iran's oil.

Mansour Farhang, a former Iranian ambassador to the United States who later taught at Bennington College, said U.S. officials "didn't believe in neutrality, they didn't believe in authentic democratic development within a country that was not an ally of the West or the East."[2]

The Oily British

The stakes were high in Iran. A corrupt shah in 1901 had sold a British financier exclusive rights to develop oil and gas in Iran for sixty years. The British government later bought part of the financier's stake and became 50 percent owner of Anglo-Iranian Oil. Under tremendous Iranian pressure in 1933, Britain modified the agreement to give more money to Iran but also expanded the exclusive contract until 1993. While Iran was supposed to share in the profits, in practice Anglo-Iranian made out like the robber barons of old. In 1947, Anglo-Iranian reported profits of $112 million, but only $19.6 million went to the Iranian government.[3]

The Majlis (parliament) demanded that the British share 50 percent of their profits and open their books to Iranian auditors. American oil companies had set up a 50 percent ownership deal with Saudi Arabia's government in 1950, so Iran's proposal was quite reasonable. But Anglo-Iranian Oil and the British government refused and insisted on the terms of the old contract. The crisis led directly to the Majlis' electing Mossadegh prime minister by an overwhelming 79 to 12 vote in April 1950. The Majlis then voted, in principle, to nationalize British oil interests altogether.

Remember, this was still the colonial era, in which the British Empire stretched across the globe. The British officials took the Majlis vote as a challenge to their colonial hegemony and immediately conspired to get rid of the democratic government.

In May 1951 the Majlis formally established a state-run oil company. The British refused to cooperate with the new company and later withdrew managers and skilled personnel. The huge Abadan oil refinery in southern Iran eventually ground to a halt. British tankers refused to export Iran's crude oil. The British navy established an illegal sea blockade of Iran's ports and stopped any other country from transporting the oil. Britain acted unilaterally, without a UN vote. The International Court of Justice at The Hague eventually ruled against Britain and Anglo-Iranian Oil, but that didn't stop Britain from continued illegal military activity.

While Iran began to suffer economically from the oil embargo, Mossadegh remained tremendously popular. So Britain tried to convince President Harry Truman to support a coup. Truman refused and suggested that Britain reach a compromise with Iran. Mossadegh became a hero worldwide. Iran's defiance of British imperialism became a popular cause in Asia, Africa, and Latin America. Many in the United States sympathized with Iran as well. Mossadegh came to New York to speak before the UN and received a warm welcome. *Time* magazine named him Man of the Year in 1951, calling him the "Iranian George Washington."

Then Dwight Eisenhower got elected. Even before the new president took office in January 1953, his top advisors were planning to support a coup in Iran. The British, who were fighting to maintain their oil monopoly, argued that the Soviet Union might take over Iran because of Mossadegh's weak control of the government. That was the argument that won over the Eisenhower Administration.[4]

The CIA dispatched Kermit Roosevelt, Jr., grandson of President Teddy Roosevelt, to Tehran, where he set about conniving, lying, and bribing anyone available. British spies turned over their agents to the CIA, who promptly put them and various members of the Majlis on the CIA payroll. The CIA secretly shipped Roosevelt over $1 million in cash, a considerable sum in those days. The United States sought to erode Mossadegh's majority in the Majlis, as well as win over police and military officials. But underhanded political deals and bribery proved insufficient. So the CIA turned to violence.

Terrorism, the Clergy, and the Coup

On April 19, 1953, Iranians on the CIA payroll kidnapped the pro-Mossadegh Tehran police chief, General Mahmoud Afshartus. They held him in a cave outside of Tehran. As police came to his rescue, a captor shot him. Of course, the United States kept its role in the kidnapping secret. Stephen Kinzer wrote in his excellent book

All the Shah's Men, "The murder had the desired effect. It shocked the country and also eliminated a popular officer who might have been a formidable obstacle to the success of the forthcoming coup."[5]

Some major Muslim clergy had initially supported Mossadegh and opposed the British. The CIA worked hard to break that alliance. As explained in a declassified CIA report on the coup, CIA agents issued "black propaganda in the name of the Tudeh Party, threatening these [religious] leaders with savage punishment if they opposed Mossadeq. Threatening phone calls were also made to them, in the name of Tudeh, and one of several planned sham bombings of the houses of these leaders was carried out."[6] Similarly, the CIA had agent provocateurs organize phony Tudeh demonstrations that ransacked the offices of another political party, thus driving a wedge between the two.[7]

Ayatollah Abulqasim Kashani was an ultra-conservative Shiite mullah very much admired by today's clerical leaders. He had fought in the desert against the British, been imprisoned, and then exiled by the shah. He was elected to the Majlis while exiled in Beirut. Popular support forced the shah to allow his return. Kashani initially supported Mossadegh and his decision to nationalize the country's oil. But CIA-allied politicians managed to alienate Kashani from Mossadegh and eventually involve him in the coup plot. Roosevelt sent Kashani $10,000 the day before the coup, and Kashani helped mobilize pro-shah demonstrators at a crucial moment.[8] Kashani showed up at the airport to welcome the shah's return to Tehran and was personally greeted by him.[9]

Most mainstream American newspapers, magazines, and radio broadcasts of the time reflected the official U.S. propaganda line that Iran had gone through a popular uprising against an unstable and communist-leaning Mossadegh. Universal Newsreel releases distributed to movie theaters nationwide every week were typical: "In the quick shift of power, Mossadegh was finally apprehended and held for treason. The shah, who had fled to Rome, comes home, backed by General Zahedi, military strongman who engineered his return to power. ... Iranian oil may again flow—westward!" The Newsreel segment ends with a mighty musical flourish.[10]

In fact, American historians now admit to what Iranians have known since 1953: the CIA and British engineered a coup against a parliamentary government in order to install a pro-Western, anticommunist dictatorship. Mark Gasiorowski, a political science professor at Louisiana State University and expert on the coup, wrote,

> The CIA extensively stage-managed the entire coup, not only carrying it out but also preparing the groundwork for it by subordinating various important Iranian political actors and using propaganda and other instruments to influence public opinion against Mossadeq. ... In my view, this thoroughly refutes the argument that is commonly made in Iranian monarchist exile circles that the coup was a legitimate 'popular uprising' on behalf of the shah.[11]

After the coup, the shah turned over most of the country's oil production to foreign firms. U.S. oil companies ended up taking a 50 percent share of Iranian oil production while Anglo-Iranian Oil got only 40 percent.[12] Ironically, Britain would have come out ahead if it had accepted Iran's earlier offer of half ownership. But the American victory in the 1953 coup was just one indication that the British Empire was in decline.

When the coup initially met setbacks, Shah Mohammad Reza Pahlavi fled to Baghdad and then Rome. When the coup proved successful, he returned to Tehran to serve as figurehead for the United States. His military and police cracked down hard on the democratic forces, jailing opponents, closing newspapers, and banning political parties. The U.S. government, the great promoter of democracy, had crushed it in Iran. But, of course, that's not what U.S. officials said publicly.

The U.S. government, echoed by the media, praised the shah as a modernizer who saved his country from chaos and doom. Soon after the coup, the shah visited New York and met with Mayor Robert

Wagner, Jr. In a broadcast of that visit on WNYC public radio, the announcer intoned, "The shah has always had one thing uppermost in mind to improve the lot of his people. ... The shah's well-rounded personality is felt throughout Iran and has resulted in the balanced manner in which he has handled crises in Iran."

The United States established close military ties with the shah, and that led to a major dispute regarding the legal status of U.S. military personnel. The United States had stationed soldiers in Iran since 1947 to train local armed forces and police. By the end of the shah's rule, the United States had 185 military trainers in Iran, the largest U.S. mission in any third world country at the time.[13]

Then, as now, the United States insisted that its military personnel not be subject to other countries' civil or criminal courts. The United States argues that local judicial systems cannot fairly judge U.S. military personnel, or even their family members. So the United States coerces other countries to sign treaties that stipulate Americans can be tried only by American courts. Few Americans give this system of extraterritoriality a second thought. But in many parts of the world, it's a major flash point. The shah's signing of such a treaty in 1964 is known to Iranians as "the capitulation."

Ayatollah Khomeini rose to national prominence because of his outspoken opposition to the capitulation. In October 1964 he criticized the United States and the shah. Stanford University Iran expert Professor Abbas Milani said Khomeini used a famous example. "If an American sergeant kills the shah of Iran, we can't take him to court. But if the shah of Iran does the slightest thing to an American, they will take him out." Milani said, "Before that [speech] Khomeini was a secondhand cleric," but after his criticism, he became known throughout Iran.[14]

In direct response to that criticism of the capitulation, the shah exiled Khomeini in November 1964. Khomeini went first to Turkey then later to Najaf, Iraq. Khomeini continued to agitate against the shah and gained considerable popularity. By the late 1970s, Iran was ready to explode.

The 1979 Revolution and Embassy Takeover

By 1978 the shah's power had begun to fade. Students, workers, women, and the religious community were fed up. But the United States always focused on the supposed communist threat, was largely unaware of the ferment among Iranian Muslims. In January 1978, religion students in the holy city of Qom demonstrated, demanding that Ayatollah Khomeini be allowed to return from exile. Police opened fire and killed seventy students.

Shiites traditionally commemorate martyrs forty days after their deaths. So forty days later, Iranians demonstrated in Tabriz, and police killed over a hundred. The demonstrations and repression escalated until the infamous "Black Friday," September 8, when the foreign media reported that forces loyal to the shah murdered several hundred in Tehran, although some historians put the number at less than a hundred.[15]

By October, workers had gone on strike, including oil workers. The shah declared martial law, but strikes and massive demonstrations continued. On January 16, 1979, the shah fled for his life. By mid-February Ayatollah Khomeini had returned to declare the Islamic Republic. Khomeini initially enjoyed support from all the non-monarchist groupings in Iran. He appointed Mehdi Bazargan, a cabinet minister under Mossadegh, as prime minister. Bazargan appointed a cabinet made up mostly of nationalists, with clerics assigned to sub-cabinet-level posts. Political parties operated freely; newspapers of various stripes published and circulated widely. But all that changed very rapidly.

In October 1979 the shah entered the United States for cancer treatment. We now know that the shah was indeed seriously ill with cancer, but at the time, many Iranians suspected a trick. Militant students knew that Iranian government officials had met with President Jimmy Carter's representatives and feared Iran would normalize relations with the United States.

On November 4, militant students marched up to the U.S. Embassy in Tehran, a block-long fortress with concrete walls. They pushed past the Marine guards and occupied the building. They tied up the embassy staff and demanded that the United States return the shah to Iran for trial and punishment. The students captured a total of sixty-six hostages that day, but released some women and African Americans over the next few weeks. Ultimately, fifty-two diplomatic personnel were held at the embassy.

Massoumeh Ebtekar, press spokesperson for the students, then known as Tehran Mary, explained the widely different perceptions of Americans and Iranians at the time. She had become vice president in charge of the environment ministry when I interviewed her in 2000. "America had lost a lot," she told me. "They had lost an ally. They had lost what they called the gendarme of the region. So something serious was going on." Ebtekar said the students knew the history of the CIA coup against Mossadegh. "Many people felt that history was being repeated."[16] She said the students originally planned to stay a few hours at the embassy to make their point. But the situation shifted rapidly.

The student takeover crystallized anti-imperialist sentiment among Iranians and became incredibly popular. After years of coups, repression by the shah, extraterritoriality, and other indignities, Iranians saw someone standing up to the United States. The U.S. government spread a lot of disinformation in those days, claiming the occupiers weren't really students acting independently.

The people inside the embassy were indeed students drawn from several Tehran universities. They had acted without the advance knowledge of Khomeini or the Iranian government. Prime Minister Bazargan and his cabinet, however, realized the seriousness of the crisis. The students had seized a diplomatic compound, which is legally U.S. territory, and the resulting publicity had blackened the eye of the Iranian government. Bazargan and his cabinet, realizing that their power was on the wane, resigned en masse one day after the student takeover.

Khomeini backed the students and their demands. As a result the standoff went from a few hours to weeks, and ultimately to 444 days.

Barry Rosen, press spokesman for the embassy in 1979, told me in a 2000 interview that the first few weeks of captivity were horrendous.

> We were tied hand and foot. They would take some of the cord from the drapes and tie you up. I was forced to sleep bound hand and foot for several days. They were so frightened of us. They thought we were all members of the CIA. They had seen many motion pictures of James Bond over the years. They were frightened and thought that we were supermen. There were moments when the Iranians interrogated us. There were times when they put guns to our heads and counted from ten to one and said answer or we'll shoot you.[17]

Rosen said that physical conditions got better after a few weeks. But the hostages still had to endure mental anguish, sometimes held in dank cellars and prisons. Even twenty years later, however, Ebtekar doesn't apologize for that treatment. "It's a matter of collective rights [versus] individual rights," she said. "It is very difficult to compare the sufferings that the Iranian nation felt during fifty years of foreign domination and comparing that to the sufferings or the pain they may have faced during these 444 days."[18]

While many of the former leaders of the embassy takeover won't apologize for their actions, they do admit that reactionary forces within the clerical elite used the event to consolidate power. A number of former captors, including Ebtekar and Abbas Abdi, became leading advocates of political reform. Many of the former student leaders want a democratic, Islamic government. Ebtekar told me the former students have become part of "a reform movement that genuinely believes that Islam and democracy can go along with each other, believes in the freedom of expression, believes in the fact that an Islamic society can tolerate ... a wide spectrum of different viewpoints and different interpretations."*

---

* Ebtekar left national office during the administration of President Ahmadinejad, but President Rouhani appointed her vice president for women and family affairs in 2017.

Abdi told me his ideas about the revolution have matured. "At the time of the shah, our picture of a democratic system was not a very realistic one. Obviously people who live under a despotic regime may aspire and wish for a democratic regime, but the image that they have may be a variation of that same despotic regime."[19]

In 1997 Abdi flew to Paris to meet with Barry Rosen. In a sense, Rosen had exchanged roles with his former captors. He no longer felt the pressure of being an embassy spokesperson. But Abdi faced tremendous responsibilities as a prominent political reformer who had been jailed several times for his outspoken views. Rosen told me about his thoughts before the meeting.

"I didn't know if I could forgive," he said. "I don't forget what went on. I will never forget that. As soon as we met, we started to talk. It's as if everything melted away. We still had different points of view. Abbas Abdi is now a man who is fighting for some law and order in Iran, to build a democratic system within the country."

Rosen and Abdi reconciled themselves on a personal level, but the rendezvous did nothing to warm up relations between the U.S. and Iranian governments. Abdi later published the results of a survey indicating 70 percent of Iranians wanted a political reconciliation with the United States, for which he was arrested and served three years in jail. Ironically, the people that Americans most hated are now the ones who want to reach out to the United States.

Back in 1979, President Carter knew his presidency was on the line when the hostage crisis continued to drag on, month after month. The ABC news program *Nightline* began as a series of specials covering the hostage crisis. Each night, host Ted Koppel prominently displayed the number of days the hostages had been held. Carter adopted increasingly belligerent and aggressive policies.

Carter initially cut off diplomatic relations and seized $8 billion in Iranian assets, including airplanes and other equipment already paid for. The United States imposed a trade embargo and cut off all Iranian oil imports. In April 1980, the United States attempted a clandestine military mission to rescue the hostages, called Operation Eagle Claw. It was a disaster. A sandstorm caused so much confusion at a rendez-vous point fifty miles outside Tehran that the mission was aborted. Then a U.S. helicopter collided with a C130 cargo plane, killing eight soldiers. That sealed the fate of the hostages and Carter himself, who lost to Ronald Reagan in the 1980 election.

The public didn't know at the time, but Reagan emissaries met secretly with Iranian officials to arrange the release of embassy hostages after the election.[20] Under terms of the hostage release formally negotiated by the Carter Administration after the 1980 election, the United States signed the Algiers Agreement,[21] under which the United States returned some of Iran's impounded money, gave Iran immunity from lawsuits, and pledged not to intervene politically or militarily in Iran's internal affairs.* The hostages were put on airplanes and left Iranian airspace just minutes after Reagan formally took office on January 20, 1981. And this came courtesy of politicians who said "never negotiate with terrorists."

The Iran-Contra Affair

In August 1985, Israeli intelligence officials approached the Reagan Administration with an unlikely proposal: Israel wanted to help arm Iran.[22] At first such a proposal would seem strange. After all, Iran stood as a sworn enemy of the "Zionist entity." But Israel at the time saw Iraq as a greater danger, and it therefore tilted toward Iran in its war with Iraq. The Reagan Administration also liked the plan because in return for arms, the Iranians promised to free American hostages held in Lebanon. The deal was done.

In August 1985, Israel provided one hundred anti-aircraft missiles to Iran as a first installment. Both the United States and Israel would

---

* The Algiers Agreement legally prohibits the United States from attacking Iran, some-thing conveniently forgotten by both leading Democrats and Republicans ever since it was signed in 1980.

supply tens of millions of dollars in aircraft spare parts, ammunition, and armaments to Iran. Iran paid the United States for the arms, and then the Reagan Administration secretly used the money to arm the Contras fighting the leftist government of Nicaragua.

The Reagan Administration violated all kinds of laws with this scheme, from failing to notify Congress of covert operations, to arming the Contras in direct violation of the Boland Amendment passed by Congress. A few Reagan officials were prosecuted for minor aspects of the scandal. The main perpetrators, including Lieutenant Colonel Oliver North, got off. Reagan himself never faced impeachment. While Iran-Contra has gone down in American history as a horrible scandal, it's rarely mentioned in Iran. The Iranian government was pleased to receive much-needed arms. Iranian officials I interviewed admitted that Iran accepted help from Israel, but they dismissed cooperation as a wartime necessity.

Shooting Down of Iranian Airliner

I still remember the day that the USS *Vincennes* shot down Iranian Air flight 655 on July 3, 1988. I was teaching journalism at California State University, Hayward (now East Bay), when initial news reports indicated the USS *Vincennes* had fired in self-defense to stop an attack by an Iranian aircraft.[23] I told my students that something was very wrong with this story and to watch it closely in the days ahead.

It made no sense for an Iranian plane to attack the far-superior U.S. Navy, then stationed in the Persian Gulf. If something makes no sense politically, then it probably makes no sense militarily. I told my students about the 1964 Gulf of Tonkin incident, in which North Vietnamese naval vessels allegedly attacked U.S. ships on the high seas. The Lyndon Johnson Administration used the attack-that-never-happened to justify the Vietnam War.[24]

I didn't think the *Vincennes* incident was a prelude to war, but I suspected the United States was engaging in the same kind of confabulation. The United States quickly admitted that it had shot down a civilian airliner but tried to blame the Iranians for the incident. Ronald Reagan issued a statement on July 3 that read, in part, "The course of the Iranian civilian airliner was such that it was headed directly for the USS *Vincennes* ... When the aircraft failed to heed repeated warnings, the *Vincennes* followed standing orders and widely publicized procedures, firing to protect itself against possible attack."[25]

The administration later claimed that Iran Air flight 655 failed to turn on its transponder identifying itself as a civilian plane, was flying outside the proper civilian air corridor, and was rapidly descending toward the USS *Vincennes*, then sailing in international waters. The Reagan Administration said that while the United States regretted the tragic loss of life, the U.S. Navy did nothing wrong.

None of the administration's key assertions turned out to be true. The USS *Vincennes* was illegally inside Iranian waters. It wasn't under attack. Iran Air flight 655 was within the corridor for civilian flights and was ascending, not descending. In short, the United States had shot down a civilian airliner doing nothing out of the ordinary.[26]

The Iranian government argued that the United States intentionally shot down the aircraft as part of an effort to assist Saddam Hussein in Iraq's war with Iran. In April 1988, the United States had engaged in a naval battle with Iran. U.S. ships severely damaged two large Iranian vessels and six armed speedboats in what was called Operation Praying Mantis. The Iranians concluded that the shooting down of Iran Air flight 655 constituted a warning of all-out war.

But numerous independent investigations have never shown the shooting was intentional. If the United States was trying to send a message to Iran, it could have done so through additional attacks on military targets, as occurred in Operation Praying Mantis. Intentionally shooting down a civilian airliner made sense neither politically nor from a public relations standpoint. It seems likely that aggressive Navy officers, operating under orders to engage Iranian ships if necessary, erroneously identified Iran Air flight 655 as a hostile aircraft. When the enormity of the mistake became apparent, the Navy covered up the crime.

A 1992 *Newsweek* magazine investigative report explained, "The top Pentagon brass understood from the beginning that if the whole truth about the *Vincennes* came out, it would mean months of humiliating headlines. So the U.S. Navy did what all navies do after terrible blunders at sea: it told lies and handed out medals."[27]

The United States did eventually pay $61.8 *million* in compensation to victims' families but never admitted fault. By comparison, Libya had to pay $2.7 *billion* for its role in the 1988 explosion of the Pan American flight downed over Lockerbie, Scotland. And in perhaps the greatest insult, the crew of the *Vincennes* all got combat ribbons. Lieutenant Commander Scott Lustig, air war coordinator on the *Vincennes*, received the Commendation Medal for "heroic achievement."

The Iran Air flight 655 tragedy is permanently seared in the collective Iranian memory. Two hundred ninety people, including sixty-six children, lost their lives for no reason. What if Iran accidentally shot down a United Airlines passenger plane? The U.S. government might use that as an excuse to wage war. But somehow it's different when innocent Iranians die.

Does Iran Support Terrorism?

Over the years the United States has accused Iran of being the most active state sponsor of terrorism in the world. But that description conflates real incidents of terrorism with armed actions most of the world considers fighting for national liberation.

Iranian Revolutionary Guards helped found the Lebanese group Hizbollah, for example. Iran helps arm Hizbollah, which has killed innocent Israeli civilians. The predecessor group to Hizbollah was also responsible for driving a truck bomb into the U.S. Marine base in Lebanon in 1983, killing 241 service personnel. But that was an armed action intended to drive foreign troops out of their country. If Hizbollah had an air force, it would have dropped bombs on the barracks.

These days Hizbollah is both an armed militia and a political party with considerable power, part of the ruling coalition in the Lebanese parliament. The United States calls Hizbollah "terrorist" as a means to attack a political group that has effectively stymied U.S. plans in Lebanon.

Similarly, Iran gives political and financial backing to the Palestinian group Hamas. Hamas has taken credit for numerous suicide bombings inside Israel that have killed and wounded hundreds of innocent civilians. Hamas also won a plurality of the popular vote in the January 2006 Palestinian Authority election and 56 percent of the parliamentary seats. It provides government services to over one million Palestinians living in Gaza. Hamas is both a political and a military movement. Simply denouncing Hamas as terrorists, while blaming Iran for supporting them, doesn't help resolve the underlying question of Palestinian nationhood.*

I strongly oppose the political ideology of both Hizbollah and Hamas, which are based on ultra-conservative interpretations of Islam. There is no excuse for terror tactics that kill innocent civilians. But for years, the United States has funded and supported precisely such terror tactics by groups and governments that it supports.†
The people of Lebanon and Palestine can determine what to do about Hizbollah and Hamas in their own time and in their own way.

---

* In 2011, Hamas supported the popular Syrian uprising against Bashar al Assad, Iran's ally. Iran cut off financial aid to Hamas and threw its support to Islamic Jihad, a small extremist Palestinian group. By 2018 Hamas and Iran had reconciled but relations have not returned to the pre-2011 level.

† In Nicaragua in the 1980s, the United States trained and financially supported Contra groups, which systematically murdered teachers, medical personnel, and other civilians in an effort to destroy Sandinista reforms in the countryside. The United States has used similar tactics in Chile, Iran, Lebanon, South Vietnam, and numerous other countries.

The United States has also accused Iran of organizing terrorist attacks such as the 1994 bombing of a Jewish community center in Argentina. Evidence of who was behind that bombing remains murky. Authorities in Argentina say Iran is responsible, but Iran denies it. Similarly, the United States accuses Iran of organizing the attack on the Khobar Towers housing complex in Saudi Arabia. The 1996 truck bomb attack killed 19 American military personnel and wounded 372 Americans and Saudis. Iran denies responsibility, and some sources blamed Al Qaeda for the attack.[28] Iranian intelligence agents *were* responsible, however, for the assassinations of Iranian and Kurdish opposition leaders living in Europe, based on police investigations in those countries.[29] In the 1990s, Iranian intelligence services were also responsible for carrying out terrorist assassinations of writers and opposition figures inside Iran.

Gary Sick, a senior research scholar at Columbia University's School of International and Public Affairs, noted that Iran has not been sponsoring terrorist groups outside the Middle East in recent years. He wrote, "Today, Iran's promotion of violence seems to be increasingly focused on support for radical anti-Israeli groups. ... This shift calls for a different and more creative set of responses on the part of the United States."[30]

Some Recent History

In general, U.S.–Iranian relations have remained mutually hostile in recent years. The September 11, 2001, terrorist attacks on the United States briefly changed that. The Iranian government cooperated with the United States in its efforts to overthrow the Taliban in Afghanistan. This may come as a surprise to those who think Islamic extremists are all in cahoots, but Iran solidly opposed Taliban rule. The Taliban murdered nine Iranian diplomats in 1998, almost leading the two countries to war.[31] Iran had supported the Northern Alliance fighting the Taliban.

So when the United States was planning to invade Afghanistan, Iran was happy to help. Iran assisted in forging a coalition of Afghan opposition forces at the Bonn conference that established an interim Afghan government. U.S. officials praised Iran's "constructive role" in the meetings.[32] In January 2002, Iran pledged $560 million for Afghan reconstruction aid, the largest amount offered from a third world country.[33] Iranian officials have told me that they expected the United States to extend the contacts over Afghanistan into a wider dialogue about U.S.–Iranian relations.

Instead, in his State of the Union address in January 2002, President Bush denounced Iran as part of an "axis of evil." The Bush Administration closed off any possibility of reaching a political settlement with Iran and began its campaign for regime change. The Bush Administration regularly reminded Iran that "all options remain on the table," including possible military attacks. Such warnings continued under presidents Obama and Trump.

Washington has remained hostile to Iran, in part, because of the human rights record of the Iranian government. So it's worth exploring who really rules Iran.

Notes

1. Quoted in Stephen Kinzer, *All the Shah's Men*, p. 40 (New York: John Wiley & Sons, 2003).

2. Radio documentary *The Struggle for Iran*, produced by Reese Erlich for KQED Radio News and distributed nationally on NPR stations, 2001 (www.iran-project.org). The media segment quoted here was reported by Deepa Fernandes.

3. Kinzer, *All the Shah's Men*, p. 67.

4. Kinzer, *All the Shah's Men*, p. 155.

5. Kinzer, *All the Shah's Men*, p. 160.

6. CIA, *Clandestine Service History, Overthrow of Premier Mossadeq of Iran*, p. 37, available online from the *New York Times* (www.nytimes.com/library/world/mideast/041600iran-cia-index.html).

7. CIA, *Clandestine Service History*, p. 59.

8. Kinzer, *All the Shah's Men*, p. 178.

9. Kinzer, *All the Shah's Men*, p. 190.

10. Radio documentary *The Struggle for Iran*.

11. Mark Gasiorowski, "Just Like That: How the Mossadegh Government Was Overthrown," *The Iranian*, Apr. 19, 2000 (www.gwu.edu/~nsarchiv/NSAEBB/NSAEBB28/index.html).

12. "Statements on Iranian Oil Accord," AP wire story, Aug. 6, 1954.

13. Institute for Policy Studies, "Background Information on the Crisis in Iran," Washington DC, 1979.

14. Hoover Institution, *Great Expectations: Democracy in Iran*, Apr. 28, 2003 (www.hoover.org/publications/uk/3001451.html).

15. Human rights activist and historian Emad Baghi estimated 88 were killed on Black Friday. Cited in Cyrus Kadivar, "A Question of Numbers," Rouzegar-Now, Aug. 8, 2003 (www.emadbaghi.com/en/archives/000592.php).

16. Massoumeh Ebtekar, interview with author, Nov. 1, 2000, Tehran. Ebtekar wrote a book about her experiences, entitled *Takeover in Tehran* (Vancouver: Talon Books, 2000).

17. Barry Rosen, interview with author, Sept. 6, 2000, New York. Rosen's description also appears in the radio documentary *The Struggle for Iran*.

18. Ebtekar interview.

19. Abbas Abdi, interview with author, Nov. 1, 2000, Tehran.

20. Robert Parry, "The Original October Surprise," *Consortium*, Oct. 25, 2006 (www.consortiumnews.com/2006/102506.html). Parry quotes from former Iranian president Banisadr, who goes into great detail about Iran's negotiations with Republican leaders prior to the November 1980 election.

21. "Text of agreement between Iran and the U.S. To resolve the hostage situation," *New York Times*, Jan. 20, 1981 (www.nytimes.com/1981/01/20/world/text-of-agreement-between-iran-and-the-us-to-resolve-the-hostage-situation.html).

22. Bob Woodward, *Veil*, p. 412 (New York: Simon and Shuster, 1987).

23. "July 3, 1988, Defense Department Briefing on Current Developments in the Persian Gulf." Early U.S. media reports simply echoed the claims by the Defense Department that an "Iranian air-craft" had attacked the *Vincennes*, not mentioning that it was a civilian airliner. By 1:30 p.m. EDT, William J. Crowe, Jr., Chairman, Joint Chiefs of Staff, admitted in a press conference that it was a civilian plane but asserted that the *Vincennes* fired in self-defense.

24. Jeff Cohen and Norman Solomon "30-Year Anniversary: Tonkin Gulf Lie Launched Vietnam War," *Fair*, July 27, 1994 (https://fair.org/media-beat-column/30-year-anniversary-tonkin-gulf-lie-launched-vietnam-war/).

25. Ronald Reagan, Statement on the Destruction of an Iranian Jetliner by the United States Navy Over the Persian Gulf, July 3, 1988.

26. Ted Koppel, *Nightline*, July 1, 1992. *Newsweek* and ABC's *Nightline* did a joint investigative report exposing the Navy's misinformation.

27. John Barry and Roger Charles, "Sea of Lies," *Newsweek*, July 13, 1992.

28. Gareth Porter, "Who Bombed Khobar Towers? Anatomy of a Crooked Terrorism Investigation," *Truthout*, Sep. 1, 2015 (www.truth-out.org/news/item/32589-who-bombed-khobar-towers-anatomy-of-a-crooked-terrorism-investigation).

29. Iranian intelligence agents murdered Kurdish opposition leaders in Vienna in 1989 and Berlin in 1992, and former prime minister Shapour Bakhtiar in Paris in 1991.

30. Gary Sick, "Iran: Confronting Terrorism," *Washington Quarterly*, Autumn 2003.

31. Wilfried Buchta, *Who Rules Iran?* p. 147 (Washington DC: Washington Institute for Near East Policy and the Konrad Adenauer Stiftung, 2000).

32. Agence France Press, Dec. 6, 2001, cited in *Washington Quarterly*.

33. Sick, *Washington Quarterly*.

SIX

Who Rules Iran?

Two impeccably dressed men approached us at a trendy north Tehran espresso bar in 2005. They wanted to know if Sean Penn would like to interview Akbar Hashemi Rafsanjani, then the leading candidate for president. Rafsanjani was known in Iran as "Akbar Shah" (the great king) and is reputedly one of the wealthiest men in the country. He wasn't giving many interviews to the foreign media at the time, so we accepted, figuring nothing would likely happen. But, to our surprise, the interview did eventually take place. We were about to begin a strange and convoluted journey that revealed a lot about how the power structure works in Iran today.

In his five-part series for the *San Francisco Chronicle*, Sean referred to the pin-striped guys at the cafe as "the Siths," the evil characters in the *Star Wars* saga.[1] At the time, we just called them "the Chanels" because one of the guys handed me a business card indicating he ran a boutique selling Chanel perfumes.

Mr. Chanel assured us that he was very close friends with top Rafsanjani advisors. He could get us the interview, really. And by the way, would Sean like to come to dinner at his house? As strange as this may seem to non-Iranians, we must have received thirty unsolicited dinner invitations during Sean's few days in Tehran. Iranians are incredibly hospitable, and people were quite serious about the offer. (I'm not sure what would have happened if we had actually accepted any of the offers, often made by complete strangers on the street. Husband to wife: "Hi, Honey, I'm home, and I brought Sean Penn. Can you throw a few kebabs on the fire?")

We declined Chanel's invitation to dinner. That night Chanel called and said we should meet him at 10:30 p.m. Right—we go meet some stranger, in some strange location, in a strange city in the middle of the night. We politely declined again.

But over the next few days, we found out that the Chanels were real. The first Chanel had a friend, who had a friend, who was related to a guy who really was a top Rafsanjani advisor. That's how a lot of business and political deals get made in Iran. Economic wealth overlaps with family, political, and religious connections. In the shah's time, people said Iran was run by 1,000 families. That's still true, but the families have changed. For example, Iran's former nuclear negotiator Ali Larijani's father was the well-known Ayatollah Mirza Hashem Amoli.[2] Reformist leader Mohammad Reza Khatami, brother of the former president, is married to the granddaughter of Ayatollah Khomeini.[3] And former president Khatami is the son of a grand ayatollah.

The next afternoon we met at a north Tehran rendezvous point and a multi-car convoy chugged up a winding road. We were on a private, military-patrolled street heading to the former home of Ayatollah Khomeini in the Jamaran neighborhood, less than a mile from the shah's old Niavaran Palace.

Khomeini had been an ascetic from the old school, eschewing ostentatious wealth. A guide taking us around the compound stressed that back in 1979 Khomeini had stopped his supporters from an elaborate remodeling of the building. The Ayatollah, we were told, preferred simple rugs, a few chairs, and tables. But that asceticism didn't transfer to Khomeini's allies and successors.

On the way up the private road, we passed by Rafsanjani's enormous compound, protected by a large metal fence. Not bad digs for a man who began life as the son of small-scale pistachio farmers. Technically, the government owns the houses, not the individuals. But the opulence belies the myth of humble religious people living the ascetic life.

Corruption is rampant among top political and business leaders. Iran ranks 30 on Transparency International's 2017 Corruption Perceptions Index, with 1 being the most corrupt and 100 being the most honest.[4] It ranked 130th among 180 countries in the world, equalling such countries as Myanmar and Ukraine. Under the shah's rule, a small group of corrupt officials became fabulously wealthy. Under clerical rule, the corruption remains—it's just covered by turbans.

Iran's Political System

Iran's political system is unique in the world. Iran is neither a secular state nor a theocracy, neither a totalitarian dictatorship nor a representative democracy. Conservative religious, military, and business leaders have institutional control over major government decisions, but they are constrained by elections and sometimes raucous political debate.

Iran has a number of formal government institutions. The president is elected every four years, as are city councils and a national parliament. There's a parallel system of Islamic clerics headed by the Supreme Leader, often called just "The Leader." Ayatollah Khomeini was the first, and Ayatollah Khamenei took over after his death. The Leader has ultimate political power, able to overrule any of the elected officials.

The Leader is selected by the Assembly of Experts, a body of popularly elected clerics. But candidates for that assembly—as well as those for president, parliament, and other elective institutions—must be approved by the Guardian Council, which is appointed by the Leader. Got that? Let me make an analogy to the U.S. political system. Imagine that a popular uprising brings a Christian fundamentalist to power. He declares himself the Supreme Christian Leader, and his religious supporters write a new constitution in which the United States becomes a "Christian Republic." Then the Supreme Christian Leader holds a referendum on the new constitution, and it passes overwhelmingly.

The Supreme Christian Leader appoints Pat Robertson and other Christian elders to the Supreme Court. All members of the Senate, who are popularly elected, are evangelical Christian ministers; even Catholic priests can't get elected. The Congress is still elected in competitive elections. The Congress even sets aside a certain number of seats for Jews, Muslims, and other non-Christians. But the Senate decides who meets "Christian qualifications" to run for any political office and can even disqualify sitting members of Congress from seeking reelection. The Supreme Christian Leader can intervene at any time in any of the political institutions, and his word comes from God.

That's Iran, only they're not Christian.

So Iran certainly isn't democratic, but Iran can be far more responsive to the popular will than governments in such American-allied countries as Saudi Arabia or Kuwait, which are dictatorial monarchies, and where women as well as ethnic/religious minorities have few rights. The Iranian government holds elections in which competing conservative factions and the loyal opposition camps debate issues and vie for support. But when the popular will challenges the power of the ruling elite, the religious and repressive institutions hold sway.[5] So it's critical to understand both the economic and political power of Iran's rulers.

Iran's economy has been called Islamic socialism because so many key industries are nationalized, but clerical capitalism would be a more accurate description. Iran has a free enterprise system with government and quasi-governmental institutions monopolizing large sectors of the economy. Large private businesses exist, and some of their owners wield considerable political power. The economy does little to benefit ordinary Iranians, but it has created a fabulously wealthy new ruling class.

Let's take a look at some of the competing interest groups.

The Bazaar Merchants

After descending into the labyrinth of Tehran's covered bazaar, a visitor passes hundreds of small stands and shops selling every-thing from housewares to handwoven Persian carpets. Thousands of merchants buy, sell, and export products here six days a week. The store owners welcome you with a cup of tea and explain how they can make you a very special deal. They dress casually in slacks and white shirts with open collars. But some of these bazaar merchants (bazaaris) are quite wealthy and constitute a key economic sector in Iran's power structure.

Dating back before the 1979 revolution, some of the bazaaris had long-time ties to the local clergy and were marginalized by the shah. Many of the wealthy bazaaris felt threatened by such modern inno-vations as chain stores. The bazaaris see themselves as upholders of Islamic traditions. Wealthy bazaaris provided the financial backbone for Ayatollah Khomeini in exile, supported his revolution, and became some of his strongest political supporters when he came to power.

Some of the bazaaris went on to become leaders of the Revolutionary Guard and the revolutionary foundations (bonyads). Many of them continue to support conservative candidates for parliament and other elected bodies, although some supported the reformists. Conservative bazaaris control the important chambers of commerce, and the ruling clergy bestow valuable favors on them.

One bazaari living in Dubai wanted to export 15,000 pairs of shoes to Iran. But paying customs duties made the transaction too costly, and smuggling them into Iran on small boats was too risky. So he bribed a Revolutionary Guard intelligence official to facilitate the deal. The shoes arrived in Tehran three days later, shipped by air.

The Bonyads—Revolutionary Foundations

The Islamic Republic set up a vast network of bonyads, non-profit charities, as a way to help the poor, war veterans, and others. The government funded them by turning over property confiscated from the shah and his wealthy supporters, who fled the country after 1979. The bonyads can import luxury goods without paying taxes. Their leaders soon became a major economic force outside the control of the parliament, president, central bank, or anyone else except the Supreme Leader, who appoints them.

Mohammed Forouzandeh, a former defense minister, headed the Foundation of the Oppressed and Disabled, the country's largest bonyad, made up of some four hundred firms. The government gave the foundation factories and other assets confiscated from the shah's supporters. It employs 400,000 workers and has assets of as much as $12 billion.[6] The bonyads run all kinds of businesses and account for an estimated 10 to 20 percent of Iran's gross domestic product.[7]

Because the bonyads operate outside normal government control and don't show their financial books to outsiders, corruption runs rampant. Morteza Rafiqdoost, brother of the former head of the Foundation of the Oppressed and Disabled and himself part of the bonyad, received a life sentence in the mid-1990s for stealing $400 million.[8]

The bonyads are a source of financing for conservative political movements. One bonyad, the Panzdah-e-Khordad, put up the $2.8 million bounty to kill British writer Salman Rushdie after Ayatollah Khomeini issued his infamous fatwa accusing the author of blasphemy.[9]

The Government Bureaucrats

About 70 percent of the economy is state owned. Oil, autos, and petrochemicals and much of banking, shipping, transportation, communication, and import/export are under government control. So the Islamic Republic employs hundreds of thousands of people in state industries, including hundreds of top managers who have a vested interest in maintaining clerical capitalism. They are expected to throw their support behind the current ruling faction in government, and they can lose their jobs when another faction takes power.

Major Tehran hotels are owned by bonyads. For example, the former Intercontinental Hotel, now called the Laleh, is owned by one powerful bonyad. You can still see the Intercon logo on some of the dishes and old furniture. In 2005 I became acquainted with the manager, Mr. Alizadeh. He seemed like a nice enough guy, if a bit long-winded. We stayed in touch by e-mail. After the election of President Ahmadinejad, he stopped returning my e-mails. I later found out he was removed from his position soon after Ahmadinejad's inauguration. His departure was part of a more widespread purge of company managers and the diplomatic corps.

Alliances Form and Break Apart

There's a reason foreigners have a hard time figuring out what's going on in Iran. The ruling elite doesn't break down into easily defined categories, nor do political groupings reflect strong ideological trends. The various power centers come together on some issues, only to break apart at a later time. Both Democratic and Republican leaders in the United States have been befuddled by the Iranian system.

In the 1980s, for example, the Reagan Administration said it was trying to promote Iranian moderates over the hardliners. Reagan officials held secret talks with supporters of President Rafsanjani, whom they thought of as a moderate and realist. During the Iran-Contra scandal, Reagan's boys—among them Lieutenant Colonel Oliver North and Donald Rumsfeld—secretly allowed Iran to obtain missiles, spare parts for American jet fighters, and other sensitive military equipment for its war against Iraq.

The Rafsanjani forces gladly accepted this military aid and helped obtain the release of some U.S. hostages then held in Lebanon. But Rafsanjani was carrying out the policies of Ayatollah Khomeini and other top clerical leaders, not some secret moderate policy that would lead to improved relations with the United States. After the exposure of Iran-Contra, the United States shifted to full support for Iraq in the deadly Iran–Iraq War and dropped all mention of supporting "moderate" Iranian leaders.

U.S. leaders were similarly befuddled by the surprise election of President Khatami in 1997. Promising greater cultural and political freedoms, Khatami prevailed over a badly divided conservative camp. The Clinton Administration was never sure whether to praise or attack Khatami, and eventually did both.

Khatami was elected because Iranians were tired of economic stagnation, official corruption, and harsh cultural and political restrictions. The reformist camp—composed of some former revolutionary student leaders, liberal-minded clergy, professionals, and private-sector businesspeople—tapped a deep vein of discontent among Iranians. In 1997 Khatami won 70 percent of the vote, garnering support across class lines—picking up votes from workers, the poor, and middle-income people.

Khatami ran on a platform of promoting civil society and strengthening democracy, and he wanted Iran to rejoin the international community. At the time, he had the support of some clergy and conservative politicians, including Rafsanjani and Gholam Hussein Karbaschi, the powerful mayor of Tehran.

If Iran had been a third world dictatorship, the conservative forces who had been in power could have engineered a military coup or other illegal seizure of power. But Iran is no typical third world autocracy. Instead, some bazaaris, conservative clergy, conservatives in the Islamic Revolutionary Guard Corps (IRGC), and others bided their time. They knew that the president had limited power, and they exploited that to the max.

For example, in the late 1990s, President Khatami wanted to improve relations with the United States. Clinton's Secretary of State Madeleine Albright gave a speech in which, for the first time, the

United States expressed mild self-criticism about the 1953 CIA coup against the democratic government of Prime Minister Mohammad Mossadegh. The March 17, 2000, speech made a tepid reference in one paragraph that it had been a mistake for the United States to back the coup, but then it went on to list the many U.S. grievances against Iran.[10] Nevertheless, the Clinton Administration hoped the speech would pave the way for a dialogue with Iranian leaders.

After the speech, President Khatami met with Supreme Leader Khamenei to request that they explore possible improved relations with the United States, according to Rutgers professor Amirahmadi, who later interviewed Khatami. Remember, the Supreme Leader controls foreign policy. Khamenei refused to pursue further openings. If Iran opened talks with the Americans, the leaders would lose support among the army, sectors of IRGC, and conservative clerics, even though they make up a minority of the population. The potential opening with the United States went nowhere.*

That one example was repeated on other fields. Khatami allowed much greater press freedom, and the conservative judiciary shut down over a hundred newspapers. Khatami was the first official in Iran to acknowledge that the ministry of intelligence was involved in the serial killing of writers.[11] His government arrested the deputy intelligence minister, who later allegedly committed suicide in jail. Khatami was blocked from pursuing a deeper purge of the intelligence services.

Khatami was willing to allow greater freedom of speech for students, but the intelligence services and Basijis functioned as a law unto themselves. The Basijis gained fame as shock troops in the Iran–Iraq War. They morphed into an organized paramilitary force,

---

* The fact that the Clinton Administration wanted to begin a dialogue was no guarantee that the United States would have ultimately agreed to normalize relations with Iran. Powerful conservative forces within the U.S. ruling elite, particularly the pro-Israel lobby, oppose any rapprochement with Iran. Under Clinton, the United States imposed additional unilateral economic sanctions on Iran.

enforcing religious edicts such as banning alcohol and public interaction between unrelated people of the opposite sex. In an infamous incident on July 8, 1999, intelligence services allied with the Basijis violently assaulted students in their dorm at the University of Tehran, killing at least one and wounding dozens.[12]

Khatami, wherever his personal sympathies lay, failed to respond to these numerous conservative attacks. His failure to deliver on his promises of reform led directly to the defeat of his camp in the 2005 elections.

The Conservative Backlash in the 2005 Elections

Late one night, we were caught in a Tehran traffic jam of honking horns and screaming drivers. Having been born in Los Angeles, I assumed this was just the Persian version of road rage. But in fact, we had stumbled upon a campaign event supporting Rafsanjani for president. Young people, faces painted with the colors of the Iranian flag, were passing out flyers to motorists, who in turn were honking and expressing their support or displeasure. Campaign posters hung everywhere.

On another day, as we left Friday prayers held at the University of Tehran, supporters of conservative candidates were passing out leaflets and explaining to the pious why their candidate was best for the Islamic Republic.

The June 2005 elections displayed how a country can have competitive elections without being democratic. Over 1,000 people declared their candidacies for president. The Guardian Council ruled that the vast majority, including all the women, were not sufficiently Islamic. The Guardian Council is a twelve-person, appointed body that can veto any legislation passed by parliament. It expanded its role to include vetting the qualifications of all candidates for national office.

The Guardian Council also initially disqualified a major reformist candidate, Dr. Mostafa Moeen, a former minister in the Khatami government. Supreme Leader Khamenei realized that disqualification of the leader of a significant political trend would be disastrous. He intervened with the Guardian Council, and they relented. Moeen was allowed to run.

It was a fascinating election. Three candidates represented different trends among the conservatives: Mahmoud Ahmadinejad, then the mayor of Tehran; Ali Larijani, the former head of Iranian state TV and later lead negotiator on Iran's nuclear-negotiating team; and Mohammad Bagher Ghalibaf, a Revolutionary Guard hero of the Iran–Iraq War and former Tehran police chief. Two major candidates were identified with the reformist trend: Moeen and Mehdi Karroubi, the speaker of parliament from 2000 to 2004. Conservative bazaaris and clergy and the Supreme Leader tended to support Ghalibaf. Rafsanjani assumed he would win, given his tremendous personal financial resources and support from some clergy, private businessmen, and sectors of the state bureaucracy.

Ahmadinejad ran an unusual conservative campaign. He rarely mentioned religion, instead making populist promises to increase subsidies for poor and working-class Iranians. He appealed to conservative cultural values by denouncing the evils of drugs and prostitution. In thinly veiled attacks on Rafsanjani, he denounced wealth and corruption. Ahmadinejad had backing from the IRGC, bazaaris, and the Basijis, but the mainstream clerical establishment was wary of his populism. No pollster, analyst, or politician I interviewed gave Ahmadinejad much of a chance.

So most observers were caught off guard when Rafsanjani polled 6.1 million votes and Ahmadinejad got 5.7 million, forcing a runoff election two weeks later.[13] Karroubi, a quirky reformist candidate who came in third, publicly asserted that the vote had been manipulated so Ahmadinejad would come in second. Unable to get the intervention of the Supreme Leader to reverse the fraud, Karroubi said he would have to take his complaint to God.

The reformist camp feared an Ahmadinejad victory, which they saw as a takeover by extreme conservatives affiliated with the IRGC.

They tended to vote for Rafsanjani in the second round. The ultra-conservative camp, which had a long and testy relationship with Rafsanjani, united behind Ahmadinejad. Ahmadinejad won by 62 percent.

How Much Power Did Ahmadinejad Really Have?

Up close Ahmadinejad doesn't look very threatening. He's short (5'4") with a closely shaved beard speckled with gray. He often wears plain slacks and a zipper jacket or wrinkled sports coat. Although he has a PhD in transportation engineering, he doesn't come off as an intellectual. He rose from an obscure professor to a Revolutionary Guard leader; the Tehran City Council later appointed him mayor. He's quick to learn and a good debater. Most of all, said Professor Amirahmadi, the president has charismatic appeal to poor Iranians. "He speaks like them. He dresses like them. He sounds like he's one of them. He's a populist person."[14]

That populism allowed Ahmadinejad to attract support from rural voters, rank-and-file religious conservatives, and working-class and urban poor. His most famous slogan during the 2005 election was "Bring the oil money to the people's table." Partly because of this populism, and partly because Ahmadinejad is not a cleric, the powerful, traditional religious leaders remained suspicious.

For example, early in his term, Ahmadinejad declared that women could attend soccer matches. Previously, governments had ruled it was un-Islamic for men and women to attend sporting events together. Ahmadinejad proposed to allow women into strictly segregated seating as a concession to Iranian soccer mania that reached a crescendo in the months before the 2006 World Cup.[15] Within a short time, ranking religious leaders objected, and Supreme Leader Khamenei asked Ahmadinejad to reverse his decree. The president did so.

Even more significantly, Ahmadinejad had trouble getting key cabinet ministers approved by both conservatives and reformists in the parliament. It took over four months for the Majlis to approve the education, social welfare, and cooperatives ministers. Ahmadinejad had promised during the campaign to clean up corruption in the National Iranian Oil Company, but the parliament rejected his first three nominees for oil minister and finally agreed to the fourth a full six months after the process began.[16]

The traditional clergy doesn't like Ahmadinejad, explained Professor Amirahmadi. "They don't know what to do with him. Khamenei decided to make up with him [because] their base overlaps. They are trying to find a way to get rid of him or make him like them. They are frightened about Revolutionary Guards taking over through him."[17]

In December 2006, Ahmadinejad faced setbacks in the off-year elections for the Assembly of Experts and local city councils. His candidates lost significant ground, as both reformists and traditional conservatives gained. While much of the U.S. media continues to report on Ahmadinejad as if he had the power of a U.S. president, in fact, he—like Khatami—confronted the limits of presidential power in Iran. Iran's Supreme Leader, not the president, controls the military, police, judiciary, and other key institutions.

The Deep State

I've described the various interest groups competing for power in Iran, but by far the most powerful are the Supreme Leader, IRGC, judiciary, and intelligence services—what's known as the Deep State. They exercise the repressive apparatus that keep the ruling elite in power. Let's take a look at the IRGC. After the 1979 revolution, the clerical leaders didn't trust the loyalty of the regular armed forces. So they formed the Islamic Revolutionary Guard Corps as a more reliable military organization. Its soldiers serve a variety of positions, including as a Praetorian guard to safeguard leaders and as border and security police. In recent years the IRGC sent trainers and combat troops to war in Syria and Iraq.

The IRGC has taken over more than 100 economic enterprises to become financially self-sufficient and to avoid financial accountability through the regular government budgeting process.[18] The IRGC controls ports and airports. It controls a web of companies such as Khatam al-Anbia, the 35,000-worker construction company. It holds government contracts in defense industries. An IRGC subsidiary got part of the oil contract to develop the South Pars gas field and a $1.3 billion contract for a natural gas pipeline. The Basiji own interests in major mining, energy, pharmaceutical, and construction companies.[19] Some IRGC and Basiji leaders have become extremely wealthy.[20]

Professor Amirahmadi told me that the Revolutionary Guard uses political influence to bolster its economic power and corrupt practices, including the importation of smuggled goods such as liquor. "A lot of ministers and governors are from the Revolutionary Guard," he said. "They are using the money to buy loyalty and create power bases."[21]

The Revolutionary Guard shows no hesitancy in using that power. In 2005, the IRGC was discovered to be running an illegal airport near Karaj City, close to Tehran. They were able to import and export goods without any oversight. That same year, President Khatami attended a ceremony to open the new Imam Khomeini International Airport in Tehran. After the formalities, the Revolutionary Guard stormed the airport and shut it down. It later reopened, but under Revolutionary Guard management.[22] In early 2018 Supreme Leader Khamenei indicated the IRGC might be getting too powerful. He ordered IRGC generals to sell off those companies "not related to their mission." Western press reports indicated that some IRGC generals had been arrested in an effort by President Rouhani to assert power.

"Mr. Rouhani has told the supreme leader that the economy has reached a deadlock because of high levels of corruption and the guards' massive control over the economy," said one regime insider, who is a relative of the Supreme Leader, according to the *Financial Times*.[23] Other press reports indicated that IRGC generals were pushing back and refusing to sell some holdings. It remains to be seen what companies will be considered "related to their mission."

While fights within the ruling elite will continue, one commentator with first-hand knowledge of the deep state offered his comment. Mehdi Karroubi, the 2009 presidential candidate now under house arrest, wrote in a letter, "The political behavior of some of IRGC commanders has brought about political instability and created a despotism that has deprived the nation of its political rights and has put an end to the idea of the regime being a republic."

Political Prisoners and Hostages

The IRGC's Intelligence Branch plays a key role in Iran's repressive apparatus. It operates as a law unto itself, intimidating and arresting anyone considered disloyal. Its agents and their allies in IRGC affiliated media, such as *Fars News Agency* and *Javan Newspaper*, frequently accuse journalists, human rights activists, and even government officials of being spies.

Take the case of *Newsweek* journalist Maziar Bahari. On June 21, 2009, four Revolutionary Guards came to his mother's house at 8 a.m. The Canadian–Iranian citizen had been covering the Green Movement demonstrations for *Newsweek* and Britain's Channel 4 news. The deep state wanted to make an example of him. IRGC agents took him to Evin, the infamous prison used to house political prisoners.

"On the first day when they arrested me, they told me that they knew I was working for four different intelligence agencies: the CIA, Mossad, MI6, and Newsweek," said Bahari. "When I asked them what was their evidence, they said, 'We don't have to give you any evidence. We're going to give it to the courts.'"

Bahari told me that his interrogators demanded that he confess to their preconceived list of offenses. First, they wanted him to confess to being a spy. Then they wanted him to admit collusion with five prominent reformists. "I wasn't asked about my work," he told me. "By arresting me and showing my confession, they wanted to teach a lesson to a large number of people."[24]

Bahari was held in solitary confinement and subjected to psychological and physical torture. An integrator would punch, kick, and beat him with a belt. He was forced to videotape a "confession," which later aired on Press TV, the Iranian government's international TV network. "I just confessed that the Western media are bad and stooges of capitalist companies. I didn't name any names. I also mentioned that journalists are obvious targets and spy agencies would choose doctors or scientists to act as spies rather than journalists."

The TV confession didn't satisfy the interrogators. Bahari was immediately subjected to more torture because he didn't mention any names and didn't confess to spying.

Family members and Iranians who knew him understood the confession was coerced. In 2000 I worked with Bahari on a public radio documentary, "The Iran Project," and I knew he was no spy. But the intelligence branch forced Bahari to go on camera dressed nicely and seemingly relaxed. He spoke calmly responding to the interviewer's questions. For some Iranians it was effective propaganda.

An international campaign developed demanding Bahari's freedom. Newsweek and other media demanded his release. In October, after 118 days in prison, Bahari was released on $300,000 bail and flew to London. He had been asked to spy on regime opponents living abroad.

"The first thing I did when I arrived in London was to send them an e-mail," he said. He told them "I have never spied for anyone. and I'm not going to start spying for you." Bahari lives in London these days. In 2014 he founded *IranWire*, a Farsi and English wire service focusing on Iran. His best-selling book on his prison experiences was made into the film *Rosewater*, directed by former Daily Show host Jon Stewart.

Bahari's experience was far from unique. Iranian deep state agents have arrested dozens of journalists, NGO workers, and academics on phony spying charges. *Washington Post* journalist Jason Rezaian and the three American hikers (Sarah Shourd, Shane Bauer, and Alex Fattal) were among the best known in the United States. There are dozens of lesser-known cases. Deep state agencies bring phony spying charges against those arrested and then hold them hostage either for money ("bail") or political concessions from their home country. One of the more blatant examples is Nazanin Zaghari-Ratcliffe, a dual British–Iranian citizen, who was arrested in 2016. She was a charity worker who had been visiting family, but she became a target of opportunity in a dispute between Iran and the UK over interest payments on a 450-million-pound debt the British owed to Iran for not delivering tanks in 1979.[25]

Her case was moved from the judiciary to the Foreign Ministry when the judge told her, "The British have accepted to pay the historic debt, but there is still a dispute over calculating the interest rate. It is the Ministry of Foreign Affairs that is finalizing with the UK the calculation of the interest the debt." She won't be released until the British settled the dispute.

I asked a highly placed source in the administration of President Rouhani about this consistent pattern of arrests. The IRGC sees enemies everywhere, he told me. "Their conception of being a spy is different from the normal definition," he explained. "Basically anyone questioning their power is by definition aligning with the U.S., Israel, and other enemies. Therefore he is a spy."

The deep state is so powerful that even high-level officials live in fear. "I could be arrested tomorrow, and there's nothing my family could do," he said.

The Rafsanjani Interview

So whatever happened with our strange 2005 journey to interview Rafsanjani? On a small scale, we experienced the wheeling-dealing and underhanded tactics that pass for politics in Iran's ruling elite.

We agreed with Rafsanjani's handlers that Norman Solomon, Sean Penn, and I would have a half-hour sit-down interview with Rafsanjani. We even negotiated the number of questions we would be allowed to ask.

We were ushered into Kakh Marmar (Marble Palace), a former palace of the shah that now houses the Expediency Council, headed by Rafsanjani.* Security was tight, and it took us nearly an hour waiting in the line to be searched. We were stalled about another hour as Rafsanjani attended a meeting with supporters, mostly government bureaucrats and influential businesspeople.

Then we got a real surprise. Instead of a half-hour sit-down interview, Rafsanjani and a passel of handlers met us in a hallway. We were allowed a few questions and got some stock answers. The campaign photographers took lots of photos of Rafsanjani standing next to Sean Penn. Those photos appeared on the front pages of several newspapers the next day, and the TV stations ran video as well. Rafsanjani's handlers figured that a photo op with Sean Penn would help attract the youth vote. So, apparently, they never intended to allow a real interview with time for follow-up questions. It was a minor disappointment but, unfortunately, all too typical of how Iran's ruling elite operates.

Rafsanjani lost the 2005 election and sought to run again in 2013, but the Guardian Council ruled him ineligible. At a press conference with a member of the Guardian Council, I asked how Rafsanjani, a former president and current leader of the Council of Experts, could suddenly be found to be "un-Islamic." The representative said Rafsanjani was too old to run. Rafsanjani was seventy-nine at the time, only two years older than Ayatollah Khomeini when he was still in office. Rafsanjani passed away in 2017. Many Iranians don't

---

* The Expediency Council mediates disputes between parliament and the Guardian Council. Rafsanjani used his position as head of the Expediency Council to keep himself in the public eye.

trust their rulers. Successive U.S. administrations have hoped to use that sentiment, find a replacement, and install pro-U.S. elite in their place. And that's what we'll explore in the next chapter.[26]

Notes

1. Sean Penn, "Sean Penn in Iran," Day 2, *San Francisco Chronicle*, Aug. 23, 2005. The entire five-part series is available online at www.sfgate.com/cgi-bin/article.cgi?f=/c/a/2005/08/22/DDGJUEAF041.DTL.

2. Gareth Smyth, "Larijani's Pragmatist Reputation Faces Severe Challenge," *Financial Times*, Jan. 10, 2006.

3. Gareth Smyth, "Fundamentalists, Pragmatists, and the Rights of the Nation: Iranian Politics and Nuclear Confrontation," *Century Foundation Report* (www.tcf.org/list.asp?type=PB&pubid=597).

4. Transparency International, 2017 Corruption Perceptions Index (https://www.transparency.org/country/IRN).

5. Darius Bazargan, "Iran: Politics, the Military and Gulf Security," *Middle East Review of International Affairs Journal*, Sept. 1997.

6. Statement of Kenneth Katzman, specialist in Middle Eastern Affairs, Congressional Reserach Service, before Joint Economic Hearing on Iran, July 26, 2006.

7. Paul Klebnikov, "Millionaire Mullahs," *Forbes Magazine*, July 7, 2003.

8. Robert D. Kaplan, "A Bazaari's World," *The Atlantic Monthly*, Mar. 1996.

9. In February 1989 Ayatollah Khomeini issued a fatwa (religious directive) accusing British novelist Salman Rushdie of blasphemy for insulting the prophet Mohammad, and Khomeini called for his assassination. Supreme Leader Ayatollah Khamenei reaffirmed the fatwa in 2005 although, apparently, there have been no efforts to carry it out in recent years.

10. For a full transcript of Albright's speech, see www.gasandoil.com/goc/speeches/albright-17-03-00.htm.

11. Human Rights Watch, "Pour-Mohammadi and the 1998 Serial Murders of Dissident Intellectuals," (http://hrw.org/backgrounder/mena/iran 1205/3.htm).

12. Sources vary on the number of students killed. Ali Akbar Mahdi says five were murdered in "The Student Movement in the Islamic Republic of Iran," *Journal of Iranian Research and Analysis*, Nov. 1999.

13. CNN, "Rafsanjani to Face Tehran Mayor," June 18, 2005 (http://CNN.com).

14. Hooshang Amirahmadi, interview with author, Oct. 7, 2006, Berkeley CA.

15. Nazila Fathi, "Iran Lifts Ban Barring Women from Attending Sporting Events, *New York Times*, May 1, 2006.

16. Abbas Milani, "Iran's New President," *Hoover Digest*, No. 4, 2005. See also Robert Lowe and Claire Spencer, editors, *Iran, Its Neighbours and the Regional Crises*, p. 13 (London: Royal Institute of International Affairs, 2006).

17. Amirahmadi, interview with author.

18. Mohsen Sazegara, "What Was Once a Revolutionary Guard Is Now Just a Mafia," *Jewish Daily Forward*, Mar. 16, 2007.

19. Smyth, "Larijani's Pragmatist Reputation Faces Severe Challenge."

20. Ted Koppel, "An Offer Tehran Can't Refuse," *New York Times*, op-ed, Oct. 2, 2006.

21. Amirahmadi, interview with author.

22. Vali Nasr and Ali Gheissari, "Foxes in Iran's Henhouse," *New York Times*, op-ed, Dec. 13, 2004.

23. Najmeh Bozorgmehr, "Iran Cracks Down on Revolutionary Guards Business Network," *Financial Times*, Sept. 13, 2017 (www.ft.com/content/43de1388-9857-11e7-a652-cde3f882dd7b).

24. Maziaar Bahari, phone interview with auhor, Mar. 21, 2018.

25. Adam Lusher, "Nazanin Zaghari-Ratcliffe Remains in Jail 'because Iran and UK Want to Haggle over Arms Deal Interest Rates,' Husband Claims," *The Independent* (London), Feb. 22, 2018 (www.independent.co.uk/news/uk/home-news/nazanin-zaghari-ratcliffe-iran-arms-deal-tanks-boris-johnson-450m-release-delay-haggling-interest-a8223551.html).

SEVEN

Iran's Protest Movements—Part I

The winter snows hit Tehran in late November and only got worse as winter wore on.

The already clogged traffic crawled at an even slower pace. Taxi drivers cursed other drivers, as if somehow they had never seen sleet and snow before.

The evening air was dropping toward freezing as I walked down the flight of stairs to Shirin Ebadi's office in a middle-class neighborhood. She is perhaps the best-known Iranian human rights activist, having won the Nobel Peace Prize in 2003. The prize is sometimes awarded in hopes the winners will help bring peace and justice to their homeland in the near future. But in the case of Iran, justice remains some years away.

Ebadi sat in a simple, four-room office filled with books, files, and old photos. One shows Ebadi as a beautiful young woman wearing a head scarf. She is perhaps twenty years older now, but still wears her scarf back on her hair as she did in the photo. Ebadi was tired after a long day of work, but she remained upbeat.

In mid-2006, Interior Ministry officials tried to shut down her Center for the Defense of Human Rights. But international pressure, including a support letter from nine Nobel Peace Prize winners, forced them to back off.[1] Ebadi told me ministry officials later called the attempted closing "a misunderstanding." But Iran's ubiquitous security services continued to tap her phone and watch her office. She received numerous, anonymous death threats.

Ebadi explained that by the end of 2006, the popular resistance to the government was more muted than in years past. In part, Iranians were disillusioned with the failure of the reformists such as President Khatami to deliver on their promises. And in part, the security forces under President Ahmadinejad had cracked down even harder than in previous years.[2]

Ebadi was traveling abroad during the 2009 Green Movement protests and decided not to return home, fearing she would be jailed. She lives in exile in the UK.

Ebadi and other human rights activists were at the forefront of promoting democratic reforms. And, significantly, they all opposed U.S. meddling. In fact, they say, the United States makes matters worse. When Congress and the president allocate money to "promote democracy" in Iran, that gives the repressive forces an additional excuse to crack down on the opposition, claiming they are tools of the United States.[3]

Akbar Ganji, a leading dissident journalist, told me, "The U.S. money is no good."[4] During my first two visits to Iran, Ganji was held in Evin prison for having published investigative articles showing the intelligence services participated in the murder of four activists and writers in 1998, something later acknowledged by President Khatami. He went on numerous hunger strikes. I had hoped to interview him in prison, but that proved impossible. Activists inside Iran and internationally had turned his imprisonment into a cause celebre and organized a large movement for his release. In 2006 he was freed after serving his six-year sentence. International pressure made sure he wasn't arrested again, and Ganji left Iran.

In person Ganji was much shorter than I imagined. Standing perhaps 5'3", with a receding hairline and thin beard, he looked like a college professor. In exile, various political groups courted Ganji. U.S. officials even offered him a visit to the George W. Bush White House, but Ganji refused. "The U.S. attempt to support so-called democracy is counterproductive," he told me.[5]

The Opposition Says the Nukes Issue Is Phony

Iranian political activists criticize U.S. attempts to use the nuclear issue. U.S. officials scare Americans and Europeans with nightmares of a nuclear-armed Iran. But focusing on the nuclear issue has the opposite effect inside Iran. Iranians see their government under attack from a foreign power. "Americans shouldn't start a military attack," said Ebadi. "And they shouldn't interfere with the internal affairs of the country."[6]

During ten visits to Iran, from 2000 to 2017, I spoke with many dozens of ordinary Iranians. Most supported the Iranian government position on nuclear power. That's partly because people receive a heavy dose of government propaganda, and it's partly a nationalist rejection of foreign interference.

Ali Mohammadi owns a small grocery store in a working-class neighborhood of south Tehran. "Iran's nuclear power isn't for mass destruction," he told me. "The American government doesn't want any country to have access to technology or become developed. America just wants everything for itself."[7]

Ganji told me that most Iranians resent the hypocrisy of the U.S. position on nuclear weapons. "If Israel, the United States, Russia, Pakistan, and China have the right to a nuclear bomb, Iran must have that same right," he told me. "If Iran doesn't have the right to a nuclear bomb, then no one has that right." But Ganji said, given the reality of international relations, he opposed all nuclear programs in Iran. "Because there are all manner of dangers facing Iran, I am against this program."

Ebadi said activists in Iran don't separate the issue of nuclear power/nuclear weapons from the issue of democracy. "The government of

Iran claims it does not want to make nuclear bombs," she said. "But the international community doesn't believe Iran. What's the solution? Iran isn't a democratic country. And all the decisions are made behind closed doors. The international community can't trust such a government. If the government wants the international community to believe in what it says, it should try to bring real democracy into the country. The political solution to the nuclear energy issue is democracy in Iran."

Ebadi and Ganji are only the most recent in a long line of dissident voices in post-revolutionary Iran who don't align themselves with foreign powers. These opposition movements have ebbed and flowed over the years, but never stopped.

A Short History of Opposition Movements

In 1979 the people of Iran overthrew the hated shah in a genuinely popular uprising. Conservative religious forces led by Ayatollah Khomeini, nationalists, leftist Muslims, and secular Marxists all joined together in hopes of building a new, democratic Iran. In January 1980, in a very competitive election, Iranians elected Abolhassan Banisadr as president with 76 percent of the vote. He was a popular, leftist Muslim who opposed many of the religious conservatives' policies of repression.

The student seizure of the U.S. Embassy in Tehran in November 1979 and then Saddam Hussein's invasion of Iran in September 1980 added to the country's turmoil. The conservative Islamic forces took advantage of the war to intensify attacks on other supporters of the revolution, killing and jailing thousands of nationalists, Marxists, and leftist Muslims. The Majlis impeached Banisadr on phony charges, and he was forced to flee the country in 1981. Repression continued against opposition groups throughout the 1980s, including murders of Marxists and brutal repression of Kurdish rebels fighting in the northwest of the country.

In 1988, in the final days of the Iran–Iraq War, the People's Mujahideen of Iran (Mujahideen-e-Khalq, or MEK) launched an attack on Iran from Iraq in an ill-fated attempt to seize power. The Iranian forces easily beat them back and then launched horrific retaliation inside Iran. Intelligence and judiciary officials murdered as many as 3,800 political prisoners held in jails around the country. Prisoners were asked a series of questions to test their loyalty, including whether they would walk across minefields. If they answered no, they were executed.[8]

Government crackdowns of the 1980s effectively eliminated much of the organized opposition that had hoped to bring democratic reforms to Iran. But a new generation of activists came of age in Iran and participated in a number of important mass movements.

The Students Rebel

Iran's student movement has played an important role at critical junctures in recent Iranian history. In the period leading up to the 1979 revolution, Muslim and leftist students held significant demonstrations against the shah. The student seizure of the U.S. Embassy served as a catalyst for Khomeini's consolidation of power. After Khomeini's death in 1989, the national Muslim student association became more critical of the government, which foreshadowed the rise of the reformist trend in the 1990s.

In a country of 82 million, 39 percent of Iranians are below the age of twenty-five.[9] Iran has a sophisticated system of higher education, but many young graduates can't find work. Youth unemployment hit 24 percent in 2017.[10] Conservative clerical forces feared the growth of a genuine democratic trend among Muslim students. Using the judiciary and intelligence services, they cracked down hard on student protests.

I walked into a nondescript building near the University of Tehran campus. The furniture was threadbare. The whole office needed a fresh coat of paint. But the file cabinets looked familiar. They were U.S. government issue, taken from the U.S. Embassy during the 1979 takeover. We were visiting the Office for Strengthening Unity (OSU), Iran's main student organization in 2000. The OSU had acquired the file cabinets when it was a staunch supporter of the Islamic government. But since 1989, it had become part of the Islamic opposition.

Journalists Keith Porter, Maziar Bahari, and I had just arrived to interview a top leader of Iran's student movement, Ali Afshari. We were preparing an hour-long radio documentary, *The Struggle for Iran*, hosted by Walter Cronkite.[11] Afshari wanted the Islamic state to continue but favored elimination of the ruling elite's privileges. "We need a wider distribution of wealth and more social justice," he told us. He stressed that Iranians should be able to have different interpretations of Islam. "We believe that religion can function in the framework of democracy."[12]

He, like other student leaders, strongly criticized U.S. policy toward Iran. "For over fifty years America has worked to weaken democracy in Iran. The United States must remove forces from the Persian Gulf and remove the sanctions against Iran. America must acknowledge our right to sovereignty."

About a month after our interview, Afshari was arrested for speaking at a large student meeting and accused of "spreading propaganda" against the Islamic Republic. Afshari was tortured into giving a false confession, was sentenced to three years in prison, and later went into exile in the United States.[13]

When Ahmadinejad became president in 2005, the repression worsened. The new president barred students from inviting prominent reformists to speak on campus, banned certain student publications, and purged liberal faculty at major universities. Some students fought back. In an action that gained international publicity in December 2006, students heckled Ahmadinejad, who was speaking at Amirkabir University. They held his photo upside down and forced him to cut short his speech. Students expressed anger at the lack of civil liberties, but also at the high cost of education and the lack of jobs after graduation. And for the first time during his administration, they shouted "Death to the dictator."[14]

The Iranian student movement was far from dead as seen in the massive youth rebellion in 2009. (See next chapter.)

The Battle for Women's Rights

Westerners often confuse the status of women in Iran with their status in reactionary Arab countries. They see photos of Iranian women clad in the black chador and assume the worst. (The chador is a semi-circular piece of cloth draped over the head and shoulders.) The Iranian government, in its defense, notes that Iranian women are far freer than in U.S.-supported Arabic countries. In Saudi Arabia, for example, women can't vote and attend gender-segregated classes in school. By comparison, Iranian women work and receive higher education. Women make up over 60 percent of university students, and they hold high-level jobs in universities, medical fields, and government.

But in the view of many Iranian women, that's not enough. Take the issue of the chador. Women have worn the chador for centuries as part of their religious and cultural tradition. Many women, particularly those in rural areas, would choose to wear it even if no government dress code existed.

But after Ayatollah Khomeini consolidated his power in the 1980s, the government forced women to wear very conservative dress. Those who were caught on the street without proper attire could be arrested and whipped. Yet younger women in particular continued to rebel against these restrictions, allowing bits of hair to peek out from the hijab and taking other risks. Women spearheaded a similar informal rebellion against rules prohibiting unrelated men and women from being together in public.

President Khatami, elected in 1997, responded to pressure from the women's movement and considerably relaxed cultural restrictions.

President Rouhani adopted similar measures after his election in 2013. Today in major Iranian cities, some young women wear jeans with manteaus* and head scarves pushed far back on their hair. Women are still not free to dress as they please, but popular opposition forced significant changes.

The battle for women's rights continues because Iran's interpretation of Islam institutionalizes a great deal of discrimination and oppression. One afternoon I visited the apartment of Pouran Farrokhzad—a writer, women's rights activist, and sister of Iran's most celebrated woman poet, the late Forough Farrokhzad. In the 1960s and 1970s, poet and filmmaker Forough Farrokhzad wrote openly about femininity, sex, and other controversial issues that make her a heroine to the women's rights movement today.[15] Her sister continues the struggle. "Women are still considered half a man in this country," Pouran Farrokhzad told me emphatically.[16]

In the case of an auto accident or other civil matters, for example, Iranians may be required to make a payment to the injured party in what's known as "blood money." Farrokhzad described a case of a family seeking compensation for the life of their relative who died in an accident. "A pregnant woman carrying a male child died recently. The boy baby inside her womb carried twice the blood money as her. You can see how painful these rules and laws are."

Under Iran's interpretation of Sharia law, "crimes against chastity" (adultery, sex before marriage) are illegal. Adultery can be punished with death. A British television documentary exposed the hanging of a sixteen-year-old Iranian girl for "crimes against chastity," although she had been raped by a married man three times her age.[17] In cases of rape or other sex-related offenses, men are likely to go free or receive lighter sentences.

Farrokhzad said, "We live in a very bizarre era. Our lives are like a river. The religion puts a dam to block this river. If this dam is

---

* The manteau is a thigh-length coat similar to a raincoat.

removed, we continue our way and show our true face to the world."
Farrokhzad passed away in 2016 in Tehran.

The women's movement had launched a strong campaign against
the government's policy of execution by stoning. The Iranian judiciary continued to approve death by stoning for those convicted of
adultery and other crimes.

Women's organizations attempted to hold two peaceful demonstrations in 2006, demanding equal rights for women. As women showed
up in a major Tehran square, "police attacked women and beat them,"
Ebadi told me. "One woman ended up with a broken arm. About seventy people were arrested. Some were in jail for one month. One man
spent four months in jail."

In late 2006, non-governmental organizations (NGOs) in Tehran
initiated a campaign to gather one million signatures in support of
women's rights. The petition demanded full equality for Iranian
women. Organizers gathered signatures door-to-door and on the
Internet.[18] Such campaigns indicate the Iranian government has been
unable to crush dissent. "The culture of the Iranian people doesn't
allow the government to drag the country backward," said Ebadi.
"Maybe the government wants it, but the culture doesn't allow it."

Wildcat Strikes and Independent Unions

While the student and women's movements tend to get more publicity in the West, anger also simmers below the surface among working-class Iranians. High inflation and unemployment are persistent
problems. The Islamic government created pro-government trade
unions, but they frequently fail to represent workers' interests. So
workers have launched numerous demonstrations and wildcat strikes,
in some cases led by independent Marxists.

In December 2005 Tehran bus drivers demanded higher wages,
improved working conditions, and an independent union. They refused
to collect passengers' tickets, as a pressure tactic on the city-owned

bus company. When their leader, Mansour Ossanlou, and others were arrested, workers held a wildcat strike. That was only the most widely publicized of numerous spontaneous worker actions around the country.

The bus drivers' strike "was an important incident," Ganji told me. "The workers have legitimate concerns. They were demanding minimum pay and that they should be paid back wages that the government had refused to pay. Their demand was primarily of a trade union type. But because there is such extensive repression in Iran, every trade union demand ultimately becomes political."

Shirin Ebadi confirmed that "the protests are about economic issues. But the economic problems of people in this country are rooted in the political problems. Iran is a rich country. If the people are poor, it's because of the wrong policies of the government and corruption."

Ossanlou was arrested and released several times, ultimately serving a five-year prison sentence. He was released in 2013.

NGOs Try to Create Civil Society

I was surprised when I got off an elevator at an upper floor of a downtown Tehran office building. I had to step around a group of Arab–Iranian women sitting on the floor. The women had come to the office of the Institute to Defend Prisoner's Rights because their male relatives had been convicted of carrying out terrorist bombings in Ahvaz, a southern city with many Arab–Iranians. Their visit to this NGO was a last-ditch effort to gain international attention and stop the men's executions.

Institute director Emad Baghi weaved in and out of the fifty people camped out in his office, offering advice and sometimes stopping to answer cell phone calls from major politicians. He was trying desperately to get the executions postponed. Baghi and his committee carried out the sometimes lonely fight for civil liberties and against the death penalty in a country that executed some ninety-four people in 2005.[19]

People such as Baghi and Shirin Ebadi dedicate their lives to running non-governmental organizations, a type of non-profit group. They focus on human rights and civil society issues without directly participating in elections or similar political activities. The government regularly cracks down on NGOs but must often back off because the UN, human rights, and other international groups protest against the repression. The progressive NGOs helped to create space for a wider opposition movement.

The United States claimed to support the NGOs and other opposition movements in Iran, while clandestinely promoting terrorist attacks. I don't use the term loosely. Terrorism is the intentional killing or injuring of civilians for political or religious ends. Recent actions inside Iran certainly fit that definition. Sometimes the perpetrators are unknown; other times they fit the classic pattern of U.S. black operations.

In June 2005 a bomb exploded in a main square in Tehran, injuring several passersby. Then in 2005 and 2006, at least twenty people died and ninety were injured in bombings in the southern province of Khuzistan, where Iran's Arab minority is concentrated. The Iranian government convicted twenty-three ethnic Arab men and sentenced nineteen of them to death for planting the bombs, claiming they had assistance from British intelligence.

Baghi of the Institute to Defend Prisoner's Rights took up the men's cases as a protest against capital punishment. Baghi admitted to me, however, that ten of the men did plant the bombs and filmed the explosions for propaganda purposes; eight others purchased bomb-making supplies but didn't use them. Baghi thinks the men were influenced by Arabic satellite TV channels advocating separatism for Khuzistan.[20]

In February 2007, bombs destroyed a bus carrying Revolutionary Guards in the southwest province of Balochistan. A total of eleven people were killed, and over thirty soldiers and civilians were wounded.[21] The anti-government Baluchi group Jondollah Organization of Iran officially claimed credit for the attacks.

ABC News aired a report in April 2007 revealing U.S. support for these terrorist attacks. The United States funds Iranian exiles, who in turn provide money to Jondollah leader Abdel Malik Regi. ABC reported, "Regi claims to have personally executed some of the Iranians. 'He used to fight with the Taliban. He's part drug smuggler, part Taliban, part Sunni activist,' said Alexis Debat, a senior fellow on counterterrorism at the Nixon Center."[22]

Seymour Hersh, writing in *The New Yorker*, confirmed that the United States sponsors similar terrorist attacks in other parts of Iran, as well. "The Pentagon has established covert relationships with Kurdish, Azeri, and Baluchi tribesmen, and has encouraged their efforts to undermine the regime's authority in northern and south-eastern Iran."[23]

These terrorist actions resemble past U.S.-sponsored activities. During the 1980s, the United States trained and financed Sunni extremists to attack Soviet troops and civilians in Afghanistan. The Reagan Administration adopted the same tactics in support of the Contras in Nicaragua. But successive administrations can't seem to learn the lessons of history.

Every opponent of the Iranian government that I spoke to criticized the disastrous impact of U.S. policies. When the United States periodically threatens military attacks, funds dissidents, and sponsors terrorism, the administration helps fuel anti-American nationalism, said Ganji. When the United States allocates tens of millions of dollars to overthrow the Iranian government, it makes "our work much more difficult and the work of the democratic forces much more cumbersome in Iran," Ganji told me.

Ebadi explained that Iranian activists also opposed unilateral U.S. economic sanctions that began as far back as Jimmy Carter's presidency. The sanctions prohibit most trade, investment, and many cultural exchanges. "Economic sanctions hurt people more than the government," said Ebadi. "Americans shouldn't start a military attack. And they shouldn't interfere with the internal affairs of the country."

Iranians rally round their government when faced with an external threat, just as Americans did after September 11, according to former Iranian foreign minister Ebrahim Yazdi. He heads the social democratic Iran Freedom Movement. I met Yazdi at his home in north Tehran. Then in his seventies, Yazdi was the éminence grise of the Iranian opposition. He had a private collection of birds that chirped loudly in the background as we sat down to drink strong, black tea and munch pistachios.

Yazdi told me, "The United States doesn't understand Iran." By threatening possible military action and funding terrorist groups, the Bush Administration tosses a lifesaver to the Iranian government, he said.[24]

Iranians understand that Bush's talk of "democratizing Iran" is code for overthrowing a sovereign government and installing a U.S.-friendly regime, Yazdi said. Iranians went through that experience once with the 1953 CIA coup. "Democracy cannot be imported or exported," said Yazdi. "American soldiers don't carry democracy in their backpacks. It has to come from within."

Leading Iranian activists argue that the United States could play a positive role if it changed policies. The United States should stop focusing on Iran's alleged nuclear program, according to Ebadi. "The Americans should pay more attention to the human rights issues in Iran," she told me. Lest human rights violations also end up as an excuse for future military action, opposition leaders call for joint international activities.

Yazdi said the United States should cooperate with other countries to hold hearings before the UN's Human Rights Commission and other international bodies. He saw such actions as a tactic to organize international support to strengthen internal opposition, while avoiding unilateral U.S. action. "The U.S. government as an individual member of the UN can back pressure on the Iranian government to observe their human rights obligations as part of a multilateral effort," he said.

Yazdi was arrested several times during the 2009 Green Movement protests. He passed away in 2017.

U.S. policy toward Iran since the 1979 revolution has failed. The United States must radically shift its policies, according to Ganji. "The United States is a superpower using its military power to force its will on the people. Everyone knows I oppose the Iranian regime. But it is us, the Iranians, who must change it."

As I left Yazdi's home, I bundled up against the cold night air. I walked a few blocks through the quiet neighborhood with satellite dishes sprouting on many buildings. Iran's opposition movements are similar to those dishes. No matter how much the government tries to eliminate them, they sprout right back. As we will see in the next chapter, the opposition to the Iranian government exploded in 2009 and then again in 2018.

Notes

1. Omid Memarian, "Nobel Peace Winner Threatened with Arrest," *Inter Press Service*, Aug. 28, 2006.

2. Shirin Ebadi, interview with author, Nov. 15, 2006, Tehran.

3. Karl Vick and David Finkel, "U.S. Push for Democracy Could Backfire Inside Iran," *Washington Post*, Mar. 14, 2006.

4. Akbar Ganji, interview with author, Aug. 3, 2006, Ross CA.

5. Akbar Ganji, interview with author, July 30, 2006, Berkeley CA.

6. Ebadi, interview with author.

7. Ali Mohammadi, interview with author, Nov. 13, 2006, Tehran.

8. Human Rights Watch, "Pour-Mohammadi and the 1988 Prison Massacres," Dec. 2005 (www.hrw.org/backgrounder/mena/iran1205/2.htm).

9. Iran Demographics Profile 2018 (www.indexmundi.com/iran/demographics_profile.html).

10. Ivana Kottasová, "The Economic Forces Driving Protests in Iran," CNN, Jan. 2, 2018 (http://money.cnn.com/2018/01/01/news/economy/iran-economy-protests/index.html).

11. *The Struggle for Iran*, produced by Reese Erlich, can be heard online at www.iranproject.org/.

12. Ali Afshari, interview with author, Oct. 26, 2000.

13. Afshari now does analysis for Voice of America. Amnesty International detailed his forced confession, "Iran: Student Leader Forced to 'Confess' on Television," (www.web.amnesty.org/web/wwa.nsf/print/irn-011002-wwa-eng).

14. Nazila Fathi, "Iran President Facing Revival of Students' Ire," *New York Times,* Dec. 21, 2006.

15. Forugh Farrokhzad's Open Forum Web Site (www.forughfarrokhzad.com/selectedworks/main.asp).

16. Pouran Farrokhzad, interview with author, Nov. 15, 2006, Tehran.

17. "Execution of a Teenage Girl," BBC, July 27, 2006 (http://news.bbc.co.uk/2/hi/programmes/5217424.stm).

18. The One Million Signatures Demanding Changes to Discriminatory Laws Web site is www.we-change.org. It publishes in several languages.

19. Amnesty International, "Facts and Figures on the Death Penalty," (http://web.amnesty.org/pages/deathpenalty-facts-eng).

20. Emad Baghi, interview with author, Nov. 18, 2006, Tehran.

21. Nazila Fathi, "Iran Says Sunnis, Using Pakistan as Base, Planned Fatal Bombing," *New York Times,* Feb. 29, 2007.

22. Brian Ross and Christopher Isham, "The Secret War Against Iran," *ABC Evening News,* Apr. 3, 2007. See also, *Source Watch,* "Jundollah," (www.sourcewatch.org/index.php/Jundullah).

23. Seymour Hersh, "The Next Act," *The New Yorker,* Nov. 11, 2006.

24. Ebrahim Yazdi, interview with author, Nov. 16, 2006, Tehran.

EIGHT

Iran's Protest Movements—Part II

Thirty-one-year-old Ariya Khosravi is a skilled electrician living in Tehran, yet he has no permanent home. Sometimes he stays with relatives. Sometimes he sleeps in refurbished shipping containers at construction sites. Khosravi is an imposing figure, standing over 6' tall with a shock of black hair. He wears a leather jacket against the winter chill. And he's not afraid to speak his mind.

Khosravi and many of his friends were encouraged by the 2015 nuclear deal in which western countries agreed to lift harsh economic sanctions in return for Iran not building nuclear weapons. They also had high hopes that with sanctions lifted, President Hassan Rouhani, a centrist reelected in 2017, would improve the economy. "We've been expecting change," he told me. "But we've seen very little change for working class people."[1]

When Rouhani issued a proposed budget for the 2018 fiscal year, it was an eye opener. The budget slashed food and other subsidies for the poor and increased gasoline prices by almost 50 percent. These neo-liberal austerity measures resembled those promoted by the International Monetary Fund at a time when overall unemployment was 12 percent and youth unemployment was a staggering

29 percent.[2] Inflation crept up to 10 percent in the last quarter of 2017.[3] Even the price of eggs shot up.

Workers were even more upset when the budget showed religious institutions outside presidential control would receive about $1.2 billion. The religious foundations, originally set up as charities, became owners of major companies (see Chapter 6). Similarly, the Revolutionary Guards, which also own numerous industries, did not face budget cuts.[4]

Then on December 28, 2017, conservative opponents of Rouhani in Mashad, Iran's second largest city, held a rally criticizing the austerity measures. But these conservatives, who traditionally attracted some working-class support, were caught by surprise when young workers around the country responded with marches and rallies demanding economic change. Over the next week, tens of thousands demonstrated in eighty cities. These were the largest anti-government protests since the Green Movement uprising of 2009.

Khosravi heard from friends about the protests, which took place mostly in smaller cities and towns. But he initially thought they would fizzle out, just like previous one-day demonstrations protesting late wages and failed banks. "But this was serious," he said, "both in the demands and the numbers participating."

The spontaneous protests, with no previously known leaders, raised all kinds of demands. Some chanted "Death to the Dictator," referring to the Supreme Leader Ali Khamenei. A few called for the return of the Shah, the son of Iran's dictator, who ruled until 1979. Others criticized Iran's giving billions of dollars to regional allies such as Syria, Lebanese Hizbollah, and Palestinian Hamas.[5] "Not Gaza, Not Lebanon—My Life for Iran" was another popular chant.

"First you have to feed your own people and then go around helping others," explained Khosravi. "The government is always helping other nations and, as a result, we have poverty at home."

Tehran authorities quickly denounced the protests as provocations instigated by the United States and Israel. The government organized tens of thousands of counter-demonstrators in the big cities. The government also forcefully dispersed the protestors, arresting nearly 5,000.[6] Twenty-five people died.[7] Because of the repression, some protestors hedged their bets. "I know people who demonstrated one day against the government," said Khosravi. "When the government held its demonstrations the next day, they went there as well. They don't want this government, but at the same time they are so afraid. The government is too strong. They are afraid they might lose whatever they have."

The mass worker demonstrations stopped after about a week, but isolated protests continued. Vida Moyahed removed her head scarf and put it on a stick. She climbed onto a utility box in central Tehran and waved it like a flag. She was later arrested and became known as "the daughter of the revolution." Dozens of other women were inspired to do the same, often posting their defiant actions on social media.[8] Many Iranian women voluntarily wear the hijab as a sign of devotion to Islam. But many others, particularly the younger and more affluent, deeply resent the government forcing them to wear a head covering. So protests periodically erupt against the mandatory hijab.

Not surprisingly, President Donald Trump tried to jump on the protest bandwagon. He tweeted, "Iran is failing at every level despite the terrible (nuclear) deal made with them by the Obama Administration. The great Iranian people have been repressed for many years. They are hungry for food & for freedom. Along with human rights, the wealth of Iran is being looted. TIME FOR CHANGE!"[9] But a few rhetorical flourishes on Twitter didn't undo a year of anti-Iranian policies, according to ordinary Iranians. Trump banned all Iranians from travel to the United States, even for family visits. He recognized Jerusalem as the capital of Israel, which most Iranians see as an affront to the Palestinians. "Iranians don't like Trump," said electrician Khosravi. "People don't believe that he's supporting the people of Iran."

Big Economic Problems

Previous large opposition movements focused on political issues, and supporters came mostly from middle-income people, students, and intellectuals. The 2018 demonstrations were significantly different because they attracted young workers who protested the country's serious economic problems. These workers were often perceived to be supporters of former President Ahmadinejad and other principalists. (Conservatives are known as principalists because they claim to uphold the principles of Iran's revolution.)

When Ahmadinejad was elected president in 2005, he made populist promises to bring the country's oil wealth to the dinner table of ordinary Iranians. He lowered college tuitions and provided cash subsidies to every Iranian. Such programs lowered the poverty rate from 13 to 8 percent.[10] But inflation quickly ate away at the value of the subsidies. By the time he left office in 2013, Ahmadinejad had overseen skyrocketing inflation that hit 40 percent and an unprecedented reign of corruption.

President Rouhani was elected in 2013 and again in 2017 with promises of economic change. He had some initial successes. Rouhani brought inflation down to as low as 9 percent and implemented a successful national health care plan that helped poor people. Oil production significantly increased between 2015–16 because sanctions were lifted. The economy recovered from -2 percent GDP in 2015 to a +6.6 percent in 2017.[11] But much of the GDP growth failed to trickle down to ordinary people, particularly those living in smaller cities and towns.

Iran's average household budget fell by 15 percent from 2007–17.[12] The household budget, a good method of determining economic prosperity, includes all goods and services consumed by a household. The drop began in 2007, when the United States pressured the UN Security Council to impose strict sanctions against Iran. But it continued even after major sanctions were lifted in 2016. Continued unilateral U.S. sanctions and pressure on European companies not to invest in Iran had negative consequences, but that didn't account for all the problems.

Iran can best be described as a clerical capitalist country. Some 70 percent of the economy is controlled by the government, IRGC, and religious institutions (see Chapter 6). That 70 percent is operated to benefit Iran's ruling elite, not the Iranian people. Iran is subject to the same boom/bust cycle as any other capitalist economy.

When Rouhani came to power, he had to bring down inflation and get the economy growing again. His government privatized some government companies, increased the power of the private sector and scaled back on populist subsidies. Even Ayatollah Khamenei told the IRGC to sell some of its holdings. In January 2018 Brigadier General Amir Hatami said the IRGC will "withdraw from irrelevant economic activities."[13]

But Rouhani's privatization policies led to bank failures, bankrupt pension plans, layoffs, and growing unemployment. For example, the Persian Gulf International Transport Company was privatized in 2016, laid off workers, and failed to pay the wages of others, according to the Iran Labor News Agency. Workers protested in front of a government agency in October 2017. "The payment of our wages and insurance premiums has been in shambles," a worker told the wire agency.[14]

By 2018, over a dozen banks went bankrupt. Rouhani admitted that the Central Bank refunded some $2.5 billion to depositors in bankrupt banks and had told the Central Bank not to provide permits to new private banks.[15] While the principalists ruined Iran's economy with inflation and corruption, the reformists adopted neo-liberal austerity measures. That shouldn't be surprising because many of Rouhani's top economic advisors studied in the United States, said Foad Izadi, a professor at Tehran University. "There are more American PhDs in Rouhani's cabinet than in either Obama's or Trump's," he told me.[16]

Did Iranians Support the Protests?

Many Iranians supported the economic demands raised by the protestors. An opinion poll conducted January 16–24, 2018, by the University of Maryland and IranPoll indicated 69 percent of Iranians said the economy was bad and 58 percent said it was getting worse. Seventy- five percent indicated living conditions have not improved with the passage of the nuclear accord. A staggering 96 percent said the government should do more to fight financial and bureaucratic corruption.[17]

While the economic demands enjoyed widespread support, the protestors' political demands and tactics were far more controversial. The mass protests only lasted one week and no acknowledged leaders emerged. So we don't know which political views prevailed, but based on the demands and interviews done with individual demonstrators, we can discern different trends. Some protesters attacked and burned police stations and other public buildings; others did not. Some wanted change within the Islamic constitution while others wanted to see the elimination of the system altogether.

The poll indicated Iranians as a whole opposed overthrowing the government. Seventy-seven percent of respondents "somewhat" or "strongly" opposed fundamental change in Iran.

The violent tactics and chants supporting the Shah alienated reformists in the big cities. They refused to join the protests, both fearing government repression and because they didn't trust the small-town protesters. As such, the demonstrations had no visible links to 2009 Green Movement leaders. The 2018 protests were very different from those of 2009, and it's worth taking a look to see why.

2009 Green Movement Begins

I spent a week covering the 2009 presidential elections. According to the official count, Mahmoud Ahmadinejad, a PhD in transportation engineering posing as a man of the people, had won. Reformist Mir Hossein Mousavi had lost, despite holding huge rallies around the country in the final days of the campaign. According to official figures, Ahmadinejad won 62 percent of the vote in a field of four candidates.

The election took place on Friday, and I had planned lunch on Saturday with a journalist friend I hadn't seen in years. We never did have lunch. I wrote about the massive demonstrations that erupted around the elections; Maziar Bahari ended up a political prisoner in Evin Prison (see Chapter 6).

But first let's go back a few weeks.

In the days leading up to the June 14 vote, I witnessed tens of thousands of mostly young people pouring into the streets to support Mousavi. There were no speakers or official campaign organizers, just joyful, spontaneous events. Sometimes women removed their hijabs. People chanted support for the reform candidate but also criticized the government. Anti-government demonstrations are illegal in Iran. But election time provides an opportunity for people to gather. Sometimes the police busted up the rallies; sometimes they didn't.

Mousavi's efforts seemed to really take off in the last few days of the campaign. As strange as it seems to outsiders, Iranians often don't decide whom they will vote for until the last days, or even last hours, prior to marking their ballots. So the last minute surge of rallies across the country was very significant.

Tens of millions of Iranians went to bed on Friday, June 12, convinced that either Mousavi had won the election outright or that there would be a runoff between him and Ahmadinejad. When they woke up Saturday morning, the election results hit like a bombshell. They had some early indications of fraud. The government had disabled the text messaging system throughout the country, the main way that election observers used to communicate ballot counts in local areas to a central location.

And then the vote count came less than twenty-four hours after the polls closed. Rouhani's supporters, along with those of another reformist candidate Mehdi Karroubi, said the early vote count indicated fraud. They were convinced the elections had been fixed. "It was a coup d'état," one friend told me, echoing the suspicions of many.

Over the next few days, millions of Iranians poured into the streets in cities around the country. Their efforts became known as the Green Movement, named after Mousavi's campaign color. Reformists organized silent marches through word of mouth and phone calls. Initially these gatherings included women in chadors, workers, and clerics—not just the middle- and upper-income voters who form the reformist base.

Workers resented the 24 percent annual inflation that robbed them of real wage increases. Independent trade unionists had been fighting for decent wages and for the right to organize. Young people of all backgrounds hated the religious police who arrested unmarried couples walking together or women who allowed too much hair to show from under their hijab.

While the largest numbers came from the relatively more affluent, spontaneous marches also took place in the poorer neighborhoods, supposedly the strongholds of Ahmadinejad. Iranians initially protested the rigged elections, chanting "Where is my vote?" But that sentiment quickly evolved as the protests grew in size and breadth. In the week after the election, some 3 million Iranians vented thirty years of pent-up anger at a repressive system.

Not surprisingly, Iran's ruling elite denounced the demonstrations as creations of the United States, Israel, and other foreign powers. They organized counter-demonstrations. The ruling elite minimized the turnouts for the opposition and exaggerated the size of their own rallies. But in later years, important officials had to admit the popularity of the protests. Mohammad Bagher Ghalibaf, former Tehran mayor and conservative presidential candidate, said 3 million people had demonstrated in Tehran. Revolutionary Guard General Hossein Nejat admitted in a 2014 interview that, "a major part of demonstrators were Tehran's ordinary people."[18]

While government officials at the time said the demonstrations would stop after a few weeks, they continued for months. The Green Movement took advantage of the government's tradition of holding large marches on various anniversaries. For example on September 18, 2009, the government planned to mobilize for Al Quds Day to support the Palestinian cause. Instead of pro-government militants, however, hundreds of thousands of Green Movement activists showed up to chant anti-government slogans and wave green banners. The government was helpless and police couldn't intervene.

The Green Movement demonstrations continued for nine months. Much of the early participation by workers peeled away, however, and the movement consisted largely of students, intellectuals, and other middle-income Iranians. The movement demonstrations ended in the face of relentless government repression.

Government Repression

Faced with massive protests that threatened the legitimacy of the Islamic state, the government cracked down hard. The IRGC and police attacked demonstrators. The Basiji, a paramilitary forced controlled by the IRGC, put two people on a motorcycle. While one rode into the crowd, the other swung chains at peaceful demonstrators. The government even positioned snipers on rooftops.

On June 20 Neda Agha Soltan, a twenty-six-year-old woman standing away from the demonstration, was shot and killed by sniper fire. A cell phone video captured her blood-splattered face. She became the symbol for the Green Movement. Official figures show thirty killed and 4,000 arrested. But activists said over seventy-five died.[19] Political activists were systematically abused in prison, according to human rights groups.[20] There were numerous credible accounts of guards raping both men and women.[21]

Presidential candidates Karroubi and Mousavi remained free until 2011 when they spoke out in favor of the Arab Spring. Authorities feared the anti-government protests might spread to Iran. They detained the two leaders, along with political activist Zahra Rahnavard, who is married to Mousavi. As of this writing, they have not been put on trial and remain under house arrest. A wide range of intellectuals worldwide have called for their release.[22]

Just as with the 2018 protests, some demonstrators asked for reform while others demanded revolution. Reform candidate Mousavi issued a five-point program calling for press freedom, freedom to demonstrate, transparent elections, freedom of political prisoners, and freedom to form independent political parties. He later advocated separation of mosque and state, while saying religion would continue to play an important part in Iran's political future.[23]

Other activists considered Mousavi's program too modest because he never directly criticized the Supreme Leader or the Islamic Constitution. They wanted a restructuring of Iran's political institutions. The Mossadegh government of the early 1950s included freedom to organize political parties, trade unions, and civic associations. Media was not censored, and religious groups were free to organize. But such a system would require replacing the Islamic Constitution and a revolutionary change in Iran.

Both reformist and revolutionary trends existed within the Green Movement. Lacking the ability to hold an objective opinion poll amidst the chaotic demonstrations and counter demonstration, let alone a free and fair referendum, it's impossible to know which trend predominated. But the ruling elite acted as if it's very survival was at stake. And Iranian leaders did have some popular support.

Appeal of Right Wing

I refer to Iran's ruling elite as "right wing," although it rankles American conservatives. Iran's principalists have a lot in common with their U.S. counterparts: they both rely on patriotism and nationalism to say in power; they believe that religion should play an important role in government and in people's private lives; they demean women; and they believe young people are far too preoccupied with sex. They are both willing to use state coercion to promote traditional social values.

In 2009 and then again in 2018, Ayatollah Khamenei, the judiciary, IRGC, and security services pulled out all the stops to confront the opposition and conserve the status quo. They mobilized tens of thousands of supporters, particularly in the big cities such as Tehran and Mashad. They used carrots and sticks. Government offices gave workers the day off, provided buses, and gave free food. Government workers not participating in the mobilizations could lose their jobs. Companies with big government contracts were required to send their workers. But the principalists also had genuine popular support.

To better understand that appeal, even years after 2009, I took a taxi with Avasta Yazdi, the gym personal trainer we met in Chapter 3. We drove to his apartment in a working-class neighborhood of South Tehran where he lived with his mother. Yazdi said many of his friends supported Ahmadinejad, who lived in a modest apartment with his family and wore a working class, zipper jacket. Ahmadinejad was street smart and jousted with opponents in terms ordinary Iranians could understand. "The south of Tehran, yes, they favored Ahmadinejad, but not all of them of course," Yazdi told me. "They thought he was more religious."[24]

Islam plays an important role in Iranian politics. While Ahmadinejad was not a cleric, having served as mayor of Tehran, he was known as a pious man. Young people are attracted to principlist politics through Islam, according to ultra-conservative Member of Parliament Ruhollah Hosseinian, who I interviewed in 2015. "Before the revolution if you went to the University of Tehran praying mosque, you would see only a handful praying," he told me. "But if you go to the Tehran university these days, the prayers are held two times because it gets so full."[25]

Professor Javad Etaat, an associate professor of political science at Beheshti University, concedes that some youth support the conservatives for religious reasons. But he said religious practice doesn't always equate with right-wing politics. "The current popularity of religion doesn't mean support for the government," he told me.

"Religion runs deep in Iran because of the culture. It's young people's personal belief, and it's not related to politics. It's because of
Shia beliefs."[26]

Nevertheless, it shouldn't be surprising that some poor and working-class Iranians support right-wing populists, said Professor Izadi.
They have the same appeal as Donald Trump. "Both of them speak
their mind," he told me. "They don't worry about being politically
correct. Both of them are populists. Both cater to people's fears. That's
how Ahmadinejad became president. There are more poor people
than rich people in Iran."

Leftist Confusion

People around the world expressed support for the Green Movement.
Most leftists saw the protests as a popular, progressive effort that
would benefit the people of Iran and continue to oppose U.S. imperialism. Surprisingly, however, a small number of leftists opposed
the Green Movement. They argued that the CIA created, or at least
manipulated the demonstrators. They denounced the movement and
supported Ahmadinejad. I wrote an essay criticizing this leftist confusion, and it got wide circulation.[27] Now we have the advantage of
historical distance. Who was right?

A key question was how the left should view Ahmadinejad.
Alexander Cockburn, then a columnist for *The Nation* magazine,
strongly criticized Mousavi and his ally, former President Hashemi
Rafsanjani. "Compared with this vicious duo," Cockburn wrote,
"Ahmadinejad is relatively wholesome."[28]

Retired Professor James Petras called Ahmadinejad a "nationalist-
populist." He wrote: "The great majority of voters for the incum-
bent [Ahmadinejad] probably felt that national security interests,
the integrity of the country and the social welfare system, with all
of its faults and excesses, could be better defended and improved
with Ahmadinejad than with upper-class technocrats supported by
Western-oriented privileged youth."[29]

As we've seen previously in this chapter, in reality, Ahmadinejad oversaw 40 percent inflation and massive corruption. He ramped up the country's anti-imperialist posturing and promoted himself as the leader of the Islamic world. But his anti-Jewish statements undercut that effort. He claimed the German massacre of Jews needed more study. Ahmadinejad told a national TV audience, "If the Holocaust was a real event, why don't they allow research on it to clear up facts?"[30] That reminds me of the creationists who say there needs to be more study because evolution is only a theory. In practice, Ahmadinejad undercut Iran's' credibility abroad and made him Israel's favorite punching bag. Today, Ahmadinejad is so discredited in Iran that even the Supreme Leader Khamenei, a former supporter, refused to allow Ahmadinejad to run for president in 2017.

Was the Green Movement created by, or at a minimum, manipulated by the United States? Eric Margolis, a columnist for Quebecor Media Company in Canada and a contributor to *The Huffington Post*, wrote: "While the majority of protests we see in Tehran are genuine and spontaneous, Western intelligence agencies and media are playing a key role in sustaining the uprising and providing communications, including the newest electronic method, via Twitter."

Margolis and others on the left got suckered by the mainstream media reports that the mass uprising was a "Twitter Revolution." In reality very few Iranians at that time had access to Twitter. As I pointed out in a Reuters commentary, they mostly relied on text messaging, hardly the latest in Western technology.[31]

Margolis' argument had appeal, however, because the CIA has a long history of overthrowing governments by creating or manipulating mass movements. In 1973 the CIA funded mass demonstrations in Chile against the democratically elected government of President Salvador Allende. U.S. intelligence agencies then worked with the Chilean military to impose a brutal dictatorship. In Panama, U.S.-inspired demonstrations served as a prelude to the 1989 U.S. invasion and overthrow of Manuel Noriega. And, of course, the CIA and British overthrew Iran's Prime Minister Mohammad

Mossadegh in 1953. The CIA organized mass demonstrations, bribed politicians, kidnapped, murdered, and bombed its way into power (see Chapter 5). But these past examples didn't prove the CIA controlled the 2009 events.

The demonstrations arose quickly and spontaneously. They were beyond the control of the reformist leaders, let alone the CIA. The Green Movement expressed popular anger against the country's leaders. As noted earlier, some demonstrated for reform and others for revolution. But neither trend wanted Iran to rejoin a U.S. sphere of influence. The leftist critics of the Green Movement, ironically, joined hands with Ahmadinejad and the reactionary clerics who blamed all unrest on outside agitators.

In 2009 the public had no direct access to U.S. intelligence agency documents concerning the Green Movement. Journalists had to make an analysis based on observations. But now we have both the Wikileaks data dump of 2010 and Edward Snowden's revelations of 2013. What do they tell us about the Green Movement?

U.S. diplomatic cables revealed by Wikileaks show that the United States was caught unprepared. The U.S. Embassy in Iran had been closed since 1979, cutting off an important source of U.S. intelligence. So diplomats scrambled to get information from journalists and embassies in surrounding countries. Even after this intelligence gathering, the State Department wasn't able to provide any insights not already obvious to journalists.

"What started as a movement to annul the election now gives shelter both to those seeking the full set of rights guaranteed them by Islamic Iran's constitution and those seeking a new system altogether," a January 12. 2010, State Department cable reads.[32]

The British made some efforts to influence the protestors. Agents set up a phony URL aimed at attracting and monitoring Green Movement cyber activists. Documents released by Edward Snowden revealed the existence of the Joint Threat Research Intelligence Group (JTRIG). It set up a URL "shortener," which purported to speed up internet access for Iranians. But when Iranians logged on, it tracked their internet usage with the aim of influencing the opposition movement and developing human intelligence. The British deactivated the site in 2010 when the Green Movement ended only to open it again after the Arab Spring began a year later.

But the JTRIG didn't have much impact, according to the Snowden documents. Contrary to the movie image of the sophisticated MI6 intelligence agency, this project was so underfunded that it had no Farsi or Arabic speakers. The site only operated in English. And it was only operational Monday–Friday during normal London office hours. [33] Hmm, do you think any Iranians figured out what was going on?

Nothing revealed in the millions of U.S. government documents made public so far indicates that foreign powers instigated or successfully manipulated the Green Movement.

I'm convinced the people of Iran will bring about fundamental change, but they will do so in their own way and in their own time, and not under U.S. direction.

Notes

1. Ariya Khosravi, interview with author, Dec. 15, 2017, Tehran. Portions of this chapter originally appeared in *The Progressive*, Apr.–May 2018.

2. Trading Economics, The Iran Unemployment Rate 2001–18 (https://tradingeconomics.com/iran/unemployment-rate).

3. Trading Economics, The Iran Inflation Rate 2001–28 (https://trading-economics.com/iran/inflation-cpi).

4. Muhammad Sahimi, "Iran's People Do Not Need U.S. Crocodile Tears," *Truth Dig*, Jan. 9, 2018 (https://www.truthdig.com/articles/iranian-people-not-need-u-s-crocodile-tears/).

5. Gareth Smyth, "Claims About Iran's "Billions" in Military Spending Abroad Not Backed By Evidence," *Muftah*, Jan. 19, 2018 (https://muftah.org/iran-spending-sanctions-fdd/#.WmHNKKhl9PY).

6. Associated Press, "Iranian lawmaker say 5,000 arrested during January protests," Feb. 2, 2018 (http://abcnews.go.com/amp/International/wireStory/iranian-lawmaker-5000-arrested-january-protests-52800024).

7. Thomas Erdbrink, "Compulsory Veils? Half of Iranians Say 'No' to Pillar of Revolution, *New York Times*, Feb. 4, 2018 (www.nytimes.com/2018/02/04/world/middleeast/iran-hijab-veils.html).

8. Eliza Mackintosh, "Iranian Police Arrest 29 for Involvement in Hijab Protests," CNN, Feb. 3, 2018 (www.cnn.com/2018/02/02/middleeast/iran-arrests-29-women-after-hijab-protest-intl/index.html).

9. President Donald Trump, Twitter, Jan. 1, 2018 (https://twitter.com/realdonaldtrump/status/947810806430826496?lang=en).

10. The World Bank in Islamic Republic of Iran Annual Report 2017 (www.worldbank.org/en/country/iran/overview).

11. Nader Habibi, "The Iranian Economy Two Years after the Nuclear Agreement," Middle East Brief, Feb. 2018 (www.brandeis.edu/crown/publications/meb/meb115.html).

12. Behrang Tajdin, "How Sanctions Have Hit Ordinary Iranians," *BBC Persian service*, Jan. 4, 2018 (www.bbc.com/news/world-middle-east-42541170).

13. *Financial Tribune*, "IRGC Told to Lay Off Economic Activities," Jan. 23, 2018 (https://financialtribune.com/articles/economy-domestic-economy/80544/irgc-told-to-lay-off-economic-activities).

14. Radio Farda, "More Labor Protests Show Pains Of Privatization In Iran," Oct. 24, 2018 (https://en.radiofarda.com/a/iran-worker-strikes-spread/28812308.html).

15. Erin Cunningham, "Anti-Government Protests now Look Like an Opportunity for Iran's President," *Washington Post*, Feb. 24, 2018 (www.washingtonpost.com/world/anti-government-protests-now-look-like-an-opportunity-for-irans-president/2018/02/22/17f33326-0b4c-11e8-998c-96deb18cca19_story.html?utm_term=.9d20af3f5d54).

16. Email interview with author, Feb. 27, 2018.

17. It's not easy conducting opinion polls in Iran. But IranPoll has a good track record by using anonymous phone surveys. It has accurately predicted presidential election results (http://iranprimer.usip.org/blog/2018/feb/02/poll-iranians-economy-politics-after-protests).

18. Reza Haghighatnejad, "The Guards Need 'the Sedition' to Survive," *Iran Wire*, Sept. 16, 2017 (https://iranwire.com/en/features/4821).

19. Joshua Schneyer, "Rights Groups Seek U.N. Probe of Iran Rape Charges," Reuters, Sept. 21, 2009 (www.reuters.com/article/us-iran-rape/rights-groups-seek-u-n-probe-of-iran-rape-charges-idUSTRE58K5IL20090921).

20. Human Rights Watch, *Country Report: Iran 2010* (www.hrw.org/world-report/2010/country-chapters/iran).

21. PBS Newshour, "Iranian Women Prisoners Detail Torture: 'Death Was Like a Desire," June 10, 2011 (www.pbs.org/newshour/show/iranian-women-prisoners-detail-torture-death-was-like-a-desire).

22. Saeed Kamali Dehghan, "Academics Urge Rouhani to Speak Out over House Arrests of Iranian Critics," *The Guardian,* June 14, 2016 (www.the-guardian.com/world/iran-blog/2016/jun/14/academics-urge-rouhani-house-arrests-iranian-critics-mir-hossein-mousavi).

23. Abbas Milani, "Iran Primer: The Green Movement," PBS, Oct. 27, 2010 (www.pbs.org/wgbh/pages/frontline/tehranbureau/2010/10/iran-primer-the-green-movement.html).

24. Interview with author, Feb. 25, 2016, Tehran.

25. Interview with author, Aug. 2, 2015, Tehran.

26. Interview with author, Aug. 2, 2015, Tehran.

27. Reese Erlich, "Iran and Leftist Confusion," *Common Dreams,* June 29, 2009 (www.commondreams.org/view/2009/06/28-10).

28. Alexander Cockburn, "Twittergasms," *The Nation,* July 13, 2009.

29. Jams Petras, "Iranian Elections: The 'Stolen Elections Hoax," Petras home page, June 18, 2009 (http://petras.lahaine.org/?p=1781&print=1).

30. Nasser Karimi, "Iran's Ahmadinejad Questions Holocaust," Associated Press, published in the *San Diego Tribune,* Sept. 18, 2009 (www.sandiegouniontribune.com/sdut-ml-iran-ahmadinejad-091809-2009sep18-story.html).

31. Reese Erlich, "It's not a Twitter revolution in Iran," Reuters, June 26, 2009 (http://blogs.reuters.com/great-debate/2009/06/26/its-not-a-twitter-revolution-in-iran/).

32. State Department cable released by Wikileaks, "Iran's Green Party Opposition: Its Birth and Evolution," Jan. 12, 2010 (https://wikileaks.org/plusd/cables/10RPODUBAI13_a.html).

33. Mustafa Al-Bassam, "British Spies Used a URL Shortener to Honeypot Arab Spring Dissidents," Vice News, July 29, 2016 (https://motherboard.vice.com/en_us/article/78kw7z/gchq-url-shortener-twitter-honeypot-arab-spring).

NINE

The Shah, Monarchists, and TV Pretenders

For most people in the world, the shah of Iran died in exile in 1980—dethroned and disgraced. But for some Iranian exiles, the shah lives—in suburban Washington DC, to be exact. Reza Pahlavi, son of the late shah, was crowned king shortly after his father died. Although he has not set foot in Iran since the 1979 revolution, his supporters still call him "your majesty."

"His majesty is quite busy with interviews and meetings," his assistant told me on the phone when I was attempting to arrange an interview. Once Pahlavi had agreed to meet me, however, apparently his schedule loosened up. "He's free several days next week," she confided in a follow-up call.

One cold morning the assistant picked me up in front of my downtown Washington DC hotel. For security reasons she wouldn't reveal the location of the interview in advance. We drove to the home of Colonel Ovissi in tony McLean, Virginia. The colonel, as everyone called him, originally accompanied Reza Pahlavi to the United States in 1978. His living room was filled with the kinds of carpets, paintings, candlesticks, and silver cup holders that I recognized from my travels to Tehran. Pahlavi's supporters like to remember their days of glory.

Pahlavi had his own American security man, who had researched me on the Internet before arrival. "You look like your photos," he said casually. Thank God I had current pictures of myself on the web. The security man carefully searched my briefcase but spared me the indignity of removing my shoes.

At precisely the appointed time, Reza Pahlavi entered the room. He cut a dashing figure, nattily attired in a charcoal pin-striped suit and lavender tie. Born in 1960, his hair is starting to gray but he looks physically fit. He assured me that he wants nothing more than to get rid of the oppressive regime in Iran and allow the people freedom. He talked of democracy, separation of religion and state, and civil liberties. Yet he can't escape the fact that his father and grandfather ran regimes that were far from ideal models of governance. This issue of monarchy versus republican form of government sharply divides the Iranian exile community.

Pahlavi tries to confront the conundrum by saying times are different now. Iranians themselves should choose what system they want. "It's the content of the future system, not its form, that is important," he told me.[1] In other interviews, he used similar dodges, declining to say what he personally advocates. An hour into our interview, and after considerable pushing, he finally admitted that he wants a constitutional monarchy to replace the current government.

> I happen to believe that system is still a valid option for Iran, and we'll do better to have institutionalized democracy in my country than a republican system. That's my personal opinion. ... If I didn't believe that, my entire course of action would have been different for twenty-seven years. The reason I don't discuss it is because I don't think it's a healthy debate to argue about the form.

The monarch should represent the nation and not get involved in day-to-day policy making, he told me. But the shah should, under extreme circumstances, be able to dissolve parliament. Pahlavi clearly wants to return to the throne of his father and grandfather.

Thousands of exiled businesspeople, professionals, and others support him as a future king. The United States has kept him in the wings for a possible return to power. He travels the world seeking support.

The United States is always *trying* to find a new ruler for Iran, according to Paul Pillar, CIA national intelligence officer for the Near East and South Asia from 2000 to 2005. U.S. officials pursue "anything that looks like a potential shortcut to political change that would allow us to parachute someone into power," he told me.[2] That vision "continues to have attraction, even if there's no one figure out there."

"The imperial regime under his father and grandfather was not a popular movement or ever had a large amount of popular support," Pillar said. "The same issues that gave rise to the revolution in the late 70s are ones that would strongly counteract any move by the young shah to gin up a movement in Iran today."

Of course, that's not how Pahlavi sees it.

His supporters claim Pahlavi has significant support inside Iran as the inheritor of three thousand years of imperial history. In fact, his grandfather, Shah Reza Pahlavi, was a military officer who seized power and got himself crowned king in 1925. His original name was Reza Khan, and he simply appropriated the name Pahlavi. At times Reza Shah stood up to Britain and took steps to modernize the country. But Britain and the Soviet Union forced him to abdicate in 1941, fearing that his official neutrality in World War II was a cover for pro-German sympathies. His son, Mohammad Reza Pahlavi, was crowned shah that same year.

By the early 1950s, a popular, democratic movement led by Prime Minister Mohammad Mossadegh diminished the power of the new shah. After the CIA and British government engineered a reactionary coup against Mossadegh and restored the shah to full power, he became notorious for his brutal, authoritarian rule. So Reza Pahlavi did not inherit a 3,000-year dynasty but a sixty-four-year family dictatorship.

Reza Pahlavi, of course, strongly disagreed with that characterization of his family. But he said setting the historical record straight could take days. Besides, that's all in the past, he told me. "I'm my own man. This is my vision. It's not based on what my predecessors have or have not done."

But the past is very relevant because Pahlavi echoes key political views of his forebears. During the 1950s, his father used anti-communism to justify repression. The supposed threat of a Soviet takeover of Iran was the excuse.

Immediately after World War II, the Soviet Union, as well as Britain, had troops stationed in Iran. The USSR supported the Tudeh (communist) Party and briefly backed the establishment of independent Kurdish and Azerbaijani states led by leftists. The Soviet Union withdrew its troops from Iran, however, and by the early 1950s posed no threat of invasion. The shah continued to use the excuse of a Soviet takeover to crush opposition, much like other U.S.-backed anti-communist regimes throughout the region. Even today, Pahlavi blames the USSR for not allowing Iran to modernize and become a bastion of civil liberties.

"At the time, there was a Cold War," he said. "That was a major issue undermining our ability as a country to fulfill the goals we had in terms of liberalization. Most of the problems that occurred in terms of restricting political freedoms were directly related to elements that were pretty much doing the bidding of the Kremlin, in the form of the Tudeh Party and some other leftist groups."

In fact, the Tudeh and other leftist parties backed the nationalist forces seeking democratic reform. The shah used anti-communism as the excuse for brutal repression to keep himself in power, along with U.S. and British oil interests.

Pahlavi offered this decidedly un-civil-libertarian explanation for his father's repression and how innocents were caught in a repressive net: "It's almost like tuna fishing and a lot of innocent dolphins get caught in the middle. And that is something that frustrates, or puts a dent into, the liberalization program." Pahlavi clearly sees himself as the fisherman, not the dolphin.

The Terrorist Threat Replaces Anti-Communism

These days, Reza Pahlavi uses the terrorist threat as his father once used the communist threat. He asserted, in a wonderfully mangled metaphor, that Iran is the major source of terrorism in the world. "You have been dispatching your fire trucks all over the world, trying to put out fires lit by these terrorists. But have you once gone after the guy with matches in his hand? Who is the chief arsonist in all this? The head of the octopus is Tehran."

Well, actually, Iran is not the mollusk with matches. Iran backs armed groups in Lebanon, Iraq, Palestine, and Yemen. Those groups have carried out armed attacks on armed enemies, but also on civilians. Iran also strongly opposes Sunni groups such as Al Qaeda and the Taliban in Afghanistan. Pahlavi and successive U.S. governments intentionally mislead the public about terrorism by lumping together disparate groups that have little in common politically.* In our interview, I pushed Pahlavi about how he could say Iran supports violent, Sunni groups.

"We say the wolf is the brother of the jackal. ... I'm not saying what is represented by bin Laden is from the Islamic Republic [of Iran], but at the end of the day, when you look at the regime in Iran, it has been a source of backing and support."

In fact, there is no credible information that Iran is backed bin Laden or Al Qaeda. The Bush Administration used similar misinformation to scare the American public into supporting the 2003 U.S. invasion of Iraq. Saddam Hussein was an evil dictator, but he wasn't supporting Al Qaeda.

Pahlavi's biggest problem is that he has little political support inside Iran. During the 2018 protests in Iran's smaller cities and towns, some demonstrators chanted pro-Shah slogans. But the shah's

---

*   The United States claims Americans are threatened by everyone from real terrorist groups (Al Qaeda, Islamic State) to groups that have used terrorist tactics but are considered legitimate political parties in their homeland (Hizbollah in Lebanon, Houthis in Yemen). The United States also calls Marxist guerrillas and armed nationalists terrorists.

supporters can't point to any significant organizations or movements inside Iran that champion their cause. Iranians have a strong memory of the Pahlavi dynasty, and no sweet words from the aspiring shah will alleviate their fears.

As former CIA officer Pillar told me, Pahlavi can't lead a movement of any political significance. "I suspect he and his supporters, ... with each passing month and year, are getting progressively more out of touch with the realities back in their homeland."

Before the 2003 invasion of Iraq, the Pentagon and neoconservatives promoted Ahmad Chalabi as the future ruler of Iraq. Chalabi even met with international oil companies to discuss allocation of Iraq's future production. But after the invasion, Chalabi proved to be far more unpopular than his backers ever imagined. In 2005 Chalabi couldn't even get elected to parliament. Unwilling to learn the lessons of Iraq, however, U.S. officials continue the search for a pro-American Iranian leader.

Mohsen Sazegara

Mohsen Sazegara has the kind of pedigree treasured in Washington. He was an aide to Ayatollah Khomeini and helped found the Revolutionary Guard in the early years of the revolution. He broke with the government in 1989, becoming an outspoken critic of the government and an editor of reformist newspapers. Imprisoned for his political views, Sazegara suffered eye problems and was eventually allowed to leave Iran for medical treatment.

US Seeks Alternative Leaders

In 2004 Sazegara became known for helping organize a petition drive to hold a referendum for a new Iranian constitution. Patrick Clawson, a hardliner who is director of research at the Washington Institute for Near East Policy, brought Sazegara to Washington.[3] Sazegara has held various academic posts in the United States in recent years and resided at Harvard University in 2007. In 2009 he gained notoriety for producing daily video commentaries viewed widely in Iran during the Green Movement demonstrations.

Sazegara's history, liberal views, intimate knowledge of the Revolutionary Guard, and insights into splits within Iran's ruling elite make him appealing to sectors of the U.S. ruling circles. Sazegara isn't getting with the program, however. He doesn't agree with Bush Administration hardliners, who continually threaten military action against Iran. Sazegara favors negotiations, and he warns U.S. authorities not to anoint anyone as a single leader of the opposition movement.[4]

So the search continues.

In 2006, neoconservative and former Pentagon advisor Richard Perle offered support to a recently exiled political prisoner named Amir Abbas Fakhravar. Perle claimed that Fakhravar was a well-known student leader who escaped from the infamous Evin prison and then secretly fled from Iran to the West. Fakhravar ended up testifying on Capitol Hill and was invited to attend a meeting of Iranian exile leaders at the White House.

Unlike Sazegara or former political prisoner Akbar Ganji, Fakhravar seems to echo the neoconservative views on Iran. In a secret meeting at the U.S. Embassy in Dubai, as released in a Wikileaks document, an embassy official wrote that Fakhravar said he "will not publicly advocate a limited military strike against Iran, Fakhravar thinks such a strike on Iranian nuclear infrastructure would lead to a popular uprising."[5] So Fakhravar's star dimmed as his connections to neoconservatives became more apparent, and the exile community questioned his bona fides as a student leader. Several former student activists said they had never heard of him when he was supposedly leading the student movement in Iran.

U.S. Conservatives Support a Cult

Some conservatives have thrown support behind an even stranger ally: the People's Mujahideen of Iran (Mujahideen-e-Khalq, or MEK).

The MEK began in the 1970s as an organization combining leftist and Islamic ideologies to fight the shah. The MEK bombed U.S. and Iranian targets during the 1970s, killing U.S. citizens. The State Department listed the MEK as a terrorist organization.

The MEK developed a significant base of support in Iran immediately after the revolution, but it suffered extreme repression by the government and eventually moved its headquarters to Iraq, which was at war with Iran. This alliance with the hated Saddam Hussein embittered most Iranians and largely eliminated whatever respect the MEK may have won from its earlier resistance.

After the 2003 U.S. invasion of Iraq, the United States allowed the MEK to keep its small arms and control its own military base, originally established by Saddam's officials. The United States didn't officially allow the MEK to attack Iran and instead developed a work-around. Members needed only declare that they had left the MEK and now support democracy. The United States then used them for armed attacks inside Iran.[6]

Ideologically, the MEK has renounced its leftist history, and it claims to favor free markets and democracy. But critics question that commitment, given the cult of personality built around MEK's leader, Maryam Rajavi. MEK members must hold the leaders in adulation and shun contact with outsiders—even other anti-Iranian government activists. Former MEK members allege that the MEK separates children from their families and trains them as guerrilla fighters.[7] "They are easily categorized as a cult," Massoud Khodabandeh, a former MEK member now living in London, told me.[8]

Nevertheless, prominent American conservatives such as Florida Republican Representative Ileana Ros-Lehtinen have long supported the MEK as a legitimate alternative to the current government. After an intense lobbying campaign, in which high ranking Republican and Democratic officials endorsed the MEK, it was removed from the terrorist list in 2012.[9]

Abraham Sofaer, a top State Department official from 1985 to 1990, and now George Schultz, senior fellow at Stanford's conservative

Hoover Institution, said both Clinton and Bush administrations have tried to overthrow the Iranian government by backing dissident organizations. "The U.S. has supported groups opposed to the Iranian government," he told me. "It hasn't worked for years."[10]

So, divided among themselves and lacking credible choices, U.S. officials continue the search for an Iranian Idol. And what could be a more appropriate locale than a locale near Hollywood?

A Visit to Tehrangeles

In 2017 there were 387,000 people of Iranian origin living in the United States and 226,000 in California. Most of those lived in southern California. Iranian students and former students had settled in Los Angeles during the 1960s and 1970s. But after 1979, the area saw a huge influx of wealthy businesspeople, former military and intelligence officials, professionals, and ordinary Iranians. So many Iranians moved to the Westwood section of LA that it became known as Tehrangeles.

To learn more about that community, I didn't have to go far. I just drove back to the neighborhood where I lived as a child. I grew up in a middle-income section of Los Angeles just south of UCLA. I used to walk up Westwood Boulevard toward Westwood Village, past a stockbroker's office and the Crest movie theater.

Today, some fifty-five years later, Iranian groceries, bakeries, book stores, and music shops take up nearly every storefront. A New England-style warren of small offices used to house the ultra-right-wing John Birch Society. Today those offices hold Asian and Iranian businesses providing immigration advice and passport photo services. Where white kids in Madras shorts used to tread, Iranians speaking Farsi now stride. And, to tell you the truth, it's an improvement. The neighborhood has more character now. What do you prefer: white bread or saffron rice?

The San Fernando Valley area of Los Angeles is best known for shopping malls and valley girl lingo. Now the valley town of Tarzana has another claim to fame. The city is home to a bevy of monarchists intent on reclaiming the glory days of the shah. And they are intent on using their Farsi-language TV stations to promote the future rulers of Iran.

Take a drive north on the 405 freeway from west Los Angeles toward Van Nuys. A few exits later sits Tarzana, originally a working-class suburb that still has lots of low-rise warehouses. It really was named after Tarzan—a tribute to the city's native son and Tarzan author, Edgar Rice Burroughs. In 2006 I drove past the Red Barn Feed and Pet Food store where a nondescript warren of small offices pops up. Inside sit the offices of PARS TV and AFN TV. Just down the road, in Canoga Park, sits a third TV station, Channel One.

These and other Los Angeles TV stations broadcast via satellite to North America, Europe, and Iran. I watched several of the LA stations while in Tehran one evening. They appear to be big-time operations. A commentator sits behind an expansive news desk. His fax machine is in plain view, reminding viewers they can fax their comments any time. An impressive array of graphics appears behind the commentator, perhaps a famous Tehran monument or a rippling Iranian flag.

But viewed from inside the studio, the sets look considerably less impressive. The production values are limited. A commentator with a few notes sits in front of a green screen. At PARS TV, two scrawny TV cameras and a few lights fill the small studio. Everything is run from a control room about the size of a large walk-in closet. At AFN TV the day I visited, a grand total of two employees were present; one came specifically for the interview with me. The owner doubles as the technical crew.

The stations did share one thing in common. The owners of the top three political TV stations all had pictures of the late Shah Mohammad Reza Pahlavi prominently displayed in their offices. When asked if they were monarchists, all declined to state. "Of course I have my own view," Shahram Homayoun, president of Channel One TV, told me. He said the issue remains extremely controversial in the exile community. "If I tell you my views, the person who disagrees won't sit next to me."[11]

Many of the LA broadcasters are out of touch with reality, according to Bijan Khalili, owner of Ketab Books and the Iranian yellow pages phone service. The LA media are so conservative and engage in so much infighting that they have little credibility in Iran. "All the TV stations attack one another," he told me.[12]

Los Angeles boasts some twenty cable and satellite TV stations broadcasting in Farsi, along with numerous newspapers and magazines and countless websites. Amir Shadjareh, owner of PARS TV in Tarzana, claimed his station had 1 million viewers in the United States and Canada, and another 1.4 million inside Iran.[13] Shahram Homayoun, head of Channel One TV, claims a total of 10 million viewers.[14] While the station owners concede that the entertainment stations draw far larger audiences, each claims to have the largest number of viewers for a political station. The estimates of Iranian viewership appear to be widely exaggerated; no independent companies can verify them. The number of viewers in the United States is too small for the Nielsen rating service to even track.

Exaggerating their audience size is just the beginning. The conservative exile media also have the unfortunate habit of overestimating their political support inside Iran. One notorious incident illustrates the cockeyed contortions of both the conservative opposition forces and their supportive media. It was something right out of the Keystone Kops.

On May 27, 2005, the Hakha Movement issued a press release announcing an upcoming press conference at the National Press Club in Washington DC. Hakha is a cult-like organization centered around its leader, Ahura Pirouz Khaleghi Yazdi, with a satellite TV program in Virginia. In the press release, Yazdi said Iranian mullahs must "hand over the government to the people of Iran before or on June 16, 2005, at 10:00 a.m. Tehran time. Otherwise, like a swift-moving hurricane, the People of Iran will stand united and will force the mullahs to give up their power and leave the country."[15] Yazdi was going to personally fly to Tehran to oversee the uprising.

This press release was treated seriously by some of the conservative exile media. On the appointed day, Yazdi and some followers appeared on Hakha TV calling for massive demonstrations to overthrow the regime. Hakha TV got a call reporting that major Iranian leaders were at the Tehran airport preparing to flee. What should they do? The Hakha programmer instructed them to detain the leaders. A later phone call indicated that the leaders had escaped to southern Iran, and he urged that they be detained there. Of course, none of this ever took place, and Yazdi never set foot in Iran. Iranian exiles suspect that Iranian agents had made the phone calls to make Hakha look silly. That appeared to be the case when excerpts of the show were broadcast on Iranian state TV and reprinted in a daily newspaper the next day.

When groups such as Hakha are treated seriously by the exile media, it destroys their credibility inside Iran. Iranians like to watch the exile stations that broadcast music and entertainment. But the political stations' reputation is so bad that, during street interviews, some Iranians asked me if the people on air were really Iranian.

The exile media have also become famous for distorting their news accounts to promote a cause. In May 2006, Amir Taheri, a neoconservative columnist for the *National Post* of Canada, wrote that Iran's Majlis had passed a law requiring Jews to wear a yellow stripe on their clothing. Christians and other minorities would be forced to wear distinctive badges as well.

Wire services and other mainstream media quickly picked up the story as an example of the Iranian government's rampant anti-Semitism. However, reporters, including those from the Jewish press in the United States and Canada, quickly discredited the story by simply looking up the Majlis debate and legislation online. Majlis members, including Jewish members of parliament, flatly denied the story. Iran had passed a law encouraging Iranians to wear traditional Iranian clothing, but there was no mention of special dress or markings for religious minorities.[16] The *National Post* quickly retracted the story and issued an apology a few days later.

Nevertheless, the LA exile media continued to play the story for weeks. When asked about his inaccurate coverage of the issue, Channel One owner Homayoun insisted to me that the story was valid. "That story wasn't untrue," he insisted. Iranian officials "floated it to see how people would respond. The minority leaders in the parliament are paid by the government. So you can't trust what they say."[17] Homayoun never cited any sources to indicate Majlis members were "floating a story," and in-depth investigations of the article found no basis for that claim, which was only made after the original story proved false.[18]

With each phony or exaggerated story, the LA newscasters and commentators think they are helping the popular struggle against the Iranian government. But repeated over time, the distortions discredit the exile media and, by extension, all the exile opposition. Abbas Milani, director of the Iranian Studies Program at Stanford University, told me many Iranians say, "If this is the alternative to the regime, we don't want this change. Is this the best the opposition has to offer?"[19]

Where's the Money?

All the exile broadcast owners I interviewed denied receiving U.S. government funding. But they would all grab some if they could. In the spring of 2006, owners of the major Tehrangeles stations met individually with representatives of the U.S. State Department. Many ended up applying for government money to help their stations.

PARS TV owner Shadjareh told me that he welcomed money for technical support, such as getting his network onto Hotbird, the most popular satellite broadcasting to Iran and the Middle East. The State Department had a total of $85 million to disburse, mostly for media outlets. Kazem Alamdari, a sociologist at California State University, Los Angeles, said the LA stations destroyed their own credibility by constantly trying to undercut each other during the State Department meetings. U.S. officials got tired of "these TV stations attacking each other," said Alamdari.

The State Department has publicly announced that it is spending $50 million to beef up its own media, including the satellite TV version of Voice of America. The United States is also upgrading Radio Farda, the Iranian equivalent of Radio Free Europe.[20]

The U.S. government is not really interested in supporting democracy in Iran. As proof we need look no further than its policies towards religious and ethnic minorities.

Notes

1. Reza Pahlavi, interview with author, Jan. 16, 2007, McLean VA.

2. Paul Pillar, interview with author, Jan. 18, 2007, Washington DC.

3. Connie Bruck, "Exiles," *The New Yorker*, Mar. 6, 2006.

4. Mohsen Sazegara, interview with Council on Foreign Relations, Oct. 20, 2006 (www.sazegara.net/english/archives/2006/10/sazegara_strong.html).

5. Wikileaks, "Iranian Student Activist View Of Iran And US Policy," May 15, 2006 (http://wetheiranian.blogspot.com/2011/09/wikileaks-released-secret-documents.html).

6. Reese Erlich, "The Celibates of Ocalan," *Mother Jones*, Mar.–Apr. 2007.

7. "Mojahedin Members' Families Meet in Baghdad to Free Their Children," *Iran-Interlink News*, July 17, 2003 (www.iran-interlink.org/files/child%20pages/families%2017july.htm).

8. Massoud Khodabandeh, phone interview with author, Jan. 22, 2007, London.

9. Scott Shane, "Iranian Dissidents Convince U.S. to Drop Terror Label," *New York Times*, Sept. 21, 2012 (www.nytimes.com/2012/09/22/world/middleeast/iranian-opposition-group-mek-wins-removal-from-us-terrorist-list.html).

10. Abraham Sofaer, phone interview with author, Nov. 11, 2006, Stanford University, Palo Alto, CA.

11. Shahram Homayoun, interview with author, Oct. 17, 2006, Los Angeles.

12. Bijan Khalili, interview with author, Oct. 16, 2006, Los Angeles.

13. Amir Shadjareh, interview with author, Oct. 16, 2006.

14. Homayoun, interview with author.

15. Hakha press release, May 27, 2005 (www.ahura.info/pressroom/press-release_06022005.html).

16. Larry Cohler-Esses, "Yellow Journalism: Anatomy of a Hoax," *The Jewish Week* (New York), May 25, 2006 (http://thejewishweek.com/news/newscontent.php3?artid=12511).

17. Homayoun, interview with author.

18. Cohler-Esses, *The Jewish Week.*

19. Abbas Milani, interview with author, Oct. 5, 2006, Palo Alto CA.

20. U.S. State Department fact sheet, issued Feb. 15, 2006, Washington DC.

TEN

Iran's Ethnic Minorities: Turmoil on the Borders

I arrived at the rather large office compound thirty minutes early, having miscalculated the Tehran traffic—again. Dr. As'ad Ardalan hadn't arrived yet, so I hung out on the front porch, raising quizzical looks from the entering officials. When they spoke to me in Farsi, I just nodded my head and hoped they were saying "good morning," rather than "we're calling the Revolutionary Guard, American spy."

When Ardalan arrived exactly on time, we went upstairs to his modest office. He's an ethnic Kurd and a researcher with a major government think tank. But he stressed that he was speaking as an individual. Ardalan told me that since the 1979 revolution, Kurds in Iran have been considered "second-class citizens. ... They don't have access to the country's wealth, face discrimination in getting government jobs, and can't learn Kurdish in school. Even when development money is allocated by the central government, the contractors are not Kurdish. So there's a lot of corruption. The money goes back to Tehran, and doesn't stay in the Kurdish region."[1]

Supporters of the Islamic Republic argue that ethnic minorities don't face discrimination. They concede that some minority regions lack economic development, but those problems can be resolved within the country's constitutional system. Ethnic-minority calls for autonomy or federalism will result in separatist movements, the argument goes, and rip apart the territorial integrity of Iran.[2]

So who's right? The answer is crucial to the future of Iran and to U.S. policy. The U.S. government has a history of supporting dissident ethnic minorities, and in some cases, sponsoring terrorist attacks inside Iran. Some conservative Americans are openly advocating the breakup of Iran along ethnic lines. Edward N. Luttwak, a leading conservative military analyst, wrote, "Certainly there is no reason why Iran should be the only multinational state to resist the nationalist separatism that destroyed the Soviet Union."[3] John Bolton, President Trump's National Security Advisor, said in 2008 that the United States should have supported ethnic minorities and youth to stir up revolutionary unrest and regime change in Iran.[4]

Meanwhile the Iranian government cracks down on dissenters, causing even greater resentment among the minority peoples. The future of Iran, in no small part, rests in the hands of the country's minorities.

Most Americans use the terms *Iranian* and *Persian* interchangeably, as do many Iranian exiles. In fact, Iran is a multi-ethnic country with a greater percentage of minorities than exist in the United States. Fars (Persians) make up only 51 percent of Iran's 82 million people. Azerbaijanis (24 percent), Kurds (7 percent), Arab-origin (3 percent), Baluchis (2 percent), and other minorities make up nearly half the population.[5] The ethnic minorities don't call themselves Persian.

The Iranian government also discriminates against religious minorities. Sunnis, who make up about 9 percent of Iran's population, cannot hold government office; the government won't allow the building of even a single Sunni mosque in Tehran.

The clerical government says Bahais, members of a faith founded in Persia in the mid-1800s, are unprotected infidels. Iranian clerics see Bahais as apostates and tools of foreign imperialist powers, particularly Israel and the United States. A Bahai holy site in the city of Babol was destroyed in 2004. Some 300,000 Bahais live in Iran, and they try to win converts to their religion, which angers the Shiite leaders.[6] Anyone converting from Islam to another religion can face the death penalty. Bahais face systematic discrimination in jobs, education, and political rights.

Anger seethes among Iran's ethnic and religious minorities and periodically boils to the surface. In recent years, Kurds and Azerbaijanis held large, spontaneous demonstrations, which were brutally suppressed by authorities. "The regime is worried," Iran expert at Stanford University Abbas Milani told me. "President Ahmadinejad has traveled to all these peripheral areas to throw money at the problem, money that he doesn't have."[7] The United States hopes to exploit the Iranian government's vulnerabilities on this issue by supporting various ethnic groups politically and militarily.

The Kurdish Struggle

In the early 1970s, I remember attending a forum hosted by the Confederation of Iranian Students in Berkeley. The Iranians introduced a Kurdish speaker dressed in baggy pantaloon pants and a traditional head scarf. He spoke about the oppression of the Kurds and their fight against the shah's regime.

That was my introduction to a people many Westerners have never heard about. I still remember his distinctive clothing and eloquent explanation of Kurdish history. Kurds are a distinct ethnic group, neither Arab nor Persian. The majority of the estimated 30 million Kurds living in Turkey, Syria, Iraq, and Iran are Sunni Muslim, but in Iran 50 percent are Shiite.[8] After World War I, Britain and France carved up the old Ottoman Empire. Oil was soon to supplant coal as the world's main energy source, and control of Middle East oil became a major colonial concern. The traditional Kurdish homeland contained a lot of oil.

The Western powers and Turkey intentionally drew maps that divided ethnic Kurds into four different countries. Britain and

France hoped that, divided and conquered, the Kurds would not rebel. But some Kurds have been fighting for an independent homeland ever since. Most other Middle Eastern peoples have formed their own independent nations, with the notable exception of Palestinians. So, they ask, why not the Kurds? Other Kurds identify strongly with their country of origin and oppose separatism. In practical terms, Kurdish support for independence hinges on how they are treated politically and economically in their home countries.

At the end of World War II, both the USSR and Britain had troops stationed in Iran. Britain wanted to reassert its neocolonial control while the USSR supported leftist and communist parties hoping to make a revolution. It soon became clear that the Iranian Tudeh (communist) Party couldn't lead a successful revolution in all of Iran. But Kurds and Azerbaijanis were angry at their treatment by Britain and the shah. Both ethnic groups established independent nations in 1945, led by leftist parties. Iranian troops, with full Western backing, crushed those uprisings and reasserted control from Tehran. Every year, Iranian Kurds still unofficially celebrate that short-lived Republic of Mahabad.

In 1978 the Kurdish movement came alive once again as the shah's regime began to crumble. The Kurdish parties supported the 1979 revolution and at first tried to negotiate greater autonomy with the central government. Ayatollah Khomeini ultimately rejected greater local control, fighting broke out, and he sent troops to crush the Kurds.

The armed peshmurga, which means "those who face death," enjoyed early successes and considerable popular support. But they ultimately lost the war against the central government's superior numbers of soldiers and technology. For a better understanding of that era, check out Iranian director Azizollah Hamidnejad's powerful award-winning film *Tears of Cold*. It portrays a fictional love affair between an Iranian soldier and a Kurdish guerrilla.

Kurds make up about 7 percent of Iran's population and are concentrated in the northwest provinces, although they live in the major cities as well.* Reformist President Khatami tried to improve conditions for Kurds, appointing Kurds to various government posts. He tried to improve the local economy by creating a "free economic zone" in Sanandaj, the capital of Kurdistan province. He implemented long-ignored provisions of the Islamic constitution that allowed local city council elections, but Kurdish resentment against Tehran authorities has continued over the years. During the 2005 presidential elections, first-round voter turnout was only 37 percent in Kurdistan province, which includes other nationalities. In some all-Kurdish areas, voter turnout was less than 16 percent.[9]

In 2005, spontaneous protests broke out against police brutality in the town of Mahabad. Authorities accused a Kurdish man of supporting Kurdish autonomy. He "was shot by police, tied to a car and dragged all the way to a police station, where he was allegedly tortured until he died," according to the BBC.[10] People in Mahabad took to the streets. Kurdish political parties quickly got involved and spread the demonstrations to numerous other Kurdish cities.

During his two electoral campaigns, President Rouhani promised to improve the lives of Iranian Kurds by increasing economic investment and giving representation to Kurds in government offices. But Kurdish critics noted that he had failed to appoint Kurds to the cabinet or even as governors in the Kurdish provinces.[11]

Foreign journalists aren't allowed to visit the minority areas of Iran to do political reporting. So to find out more about the Kurdish movement, I had to journey to northern Iraq, where the major Kurdish parties have their headquarters.

Guerrilla Camps in Northern Iraq

I was scheduled to fly from Tehran's Imam Khomeini airport to Erbil in northern Iraq. The airport, finished in 2004, sparkled with new

---

* Official statistics put the Kurdish population at 7 percent. Opposition Kurdish leaders says it's closer to 10 percent.

entry halls, gift shops, and cafes. The Ahmadinejad administration had a policy of delaying American reporters coming in and out of Iran, a tit-for-tat response to how Iranians were being treated by U.S. customs. I had to wait forty-five minutes to finish the processing— and I was just leaving!

I arrived in Erbil late at night, hired a taxi, and drove straight through to Suleimanyah, the region's second city. Such a nighttime journey, unaccompanied by an armed convoy, was impossible anywhere else in Iraq. So I was impressed that the Kurdish Regional Government (KRG) was relatively safe and secure.

The KRG has an interesting history. In 1991 the United States declared a no-fly zone in northern Iraq, thus effectively taking that Kurdish region out of Saddam Hussein's control. For twelve years, Iraqi Kurds controlled their own territory under U.S. protection. After the 2003 U.S. invasion, the Kurds formally established the KRG, which functioned as a virtually independent country. The KRG allows Iranian Kurdish parties to operate on its soil.

Those parties face a ticklish situation. The KRG maintains good relations with neighboring Iran. Kurdish leaders, including Iraqi President Jalal Talabani, met regularly with Iranian officials and historically received financial and political support from them. Talabani lived in Iran for years while fighting Saddam Hussein and speaks fluent Farsi. At the same time, KRG officials feel sympathy for the plight of Iranian Kurds. So they have worked out a compromise.

KRG leaders allow Iranian Kurdish parties to have compounds for their followers and to train peshmurga militias so long as they don't carry out armed actions inside Iran. They can quietly organize among Iranian Kurds living in the KRG but cannot hold public events. Some parties abide by those rules and others do not.

The oldest and best-known of the Iranian Kurdish parties is the KDPI (Democratic Party of Iranian Kurdistan). I traveled to the KDPI compound outside of Koya, Iraq, about halfway between Suleimanyah and Erbil. We went through a number of KDPI-controlled checkpoints in a maze of six compounds for its leaders and peshmurga. KDPI Secretary General Mustafa Hejri welcomed me into a room with thick carpets on the floor. Hejri wore nicely tailored, Kurdish slacks and jacket with a traditional gray cummerbund wrapped around his waist. He spoke in English, although he seemed tired that day. An assistant immediately brought out glasses of strong, black tea.

Hejri explained that the KDPI is the oldest Kurdish resistance party, having led the independent Republic of Mahabad back in 1945–6. It supported the revolution against the shah in 1979. Hejri and other KDPI leaders were elected to the Majlis but never allowed to serve. When the clerical government failed to respect Kurdish rights, he said, the KDPI led an uprising that didn't completely stop until 1988.

After the end of that unsuccessful rebellion, KDPI faced a lot of repression. Iranian intelligence services assassinated two KDPI leaders in infamous incidents. In 1989 KDPI leader Abdul Rahman Qassemlou was assassinated in Vienna. On September 18, 1992, Iranian Kurdish leader Sadik Sharafkindi and three others were murdered in a Berlin restaurant when they went to meet with Iranian government representatives.

After 1988, according to Hejri, the KDPI shifted tactics to focus on political organizing against the regime. "Strategically we have not opposed armed struggle," he told me. "But for now we believe political activity benefits the party more than armed struggle. Inside Iran we organize people clandestinely. Sometimes we create NGOs. It's very difficult. A lot of our followers and membership are still in jail. Many have been executed."[12]

KDPI began as a leftist party sympathetic to the Soviet Union. Over time, however, it evolved into a democratic socialist party affiliated with the Socialist International. These days it supports democratic federalism within the Iranian state, not independence. The central government would control international affairs, the military, and treasury. All other government functions would devolve to local ethnic-minority provinces. "The Iranian regime states that federalism will lead to separation," said Hejri. "But I believe that if all the nationalities have a federal system where their rights are respected, they will stay in Iran."

Hejri visited Washington numerous times to meet with State Department and other U.S. government officials. "We have had contact with Americans for a long time," he said. Hejri and other KDPI leaders denied accepting U.S. financing, although he said KDPI would accept such aid if offered.

In December 2006, the KPDI announced a split in its ranks. Abdullah Hassan-Zadeh led a dissident group that calls itself KDP-I. While at least some of the issues leading to the split focus on personal and internal power issues, the Zadeh group did criticize Hejri for cooperating too closely with the United States.[13]

Hejri's faction encouraged the United States to take a hard line against Iran. The KDPI opposed the 2015 nuclear accord and called for intensified sanctions against Iran. "If sanctions are lifted," Hejri told me in a phone interview, "Iran will get resources to continue support for terrorists and dictatorships that sponsor terrorists such as [Syria's] Bashar al Assad. They will get more resources to make more turbulence in the Middle East."[14]

Because of its ties with the United States and failure to take up armed struggle, the KDPI found itself losing support to other more militant Kurdish groups. In 2015 it resumed armed struggle with the Iranian government, clashing with IRGC troops along the Iraqi border and killing Iranian soldiers inside Kurdish provinces. Iran retaliated by assassinating KDPI leaders living in northern Iraq.[15]

The Komala Compound

I expected a different political perspective when I visited the Komala compound in Zerguizala village, just a thirty-minute drive from Suleimanyah. In the 1970s, Komala, which means "association" in Kurdish, was the second-largest Kurdish party in Iran and drew inspiration from the ideology of Mao Zedong. At one time, it held sharp differences with KDPI, but at least on major issues, that's hard to find these days.

When I got to their camp, Komala had just finished a major meeting. Its leaders from Iran, Iraq, and western Europe were still gathered at the compound. Komala General Secretary Abdulla Mohtadi welcomed me into a meeting room, speaking flawless English. I was able to spend part of the day with him and later visit Komala's peshmurga training camp.

Like the KDPI, Komala supports federalism, not separatism. It emphasized political organizing and eschewed armed struggle at the time. It trains peshmurga for internal security in Iraq but doesn't rule out future action in Iran.

Mohtadi told me Komala engaged in armed propaganda from 2001 to 2005, in which guerrillas carried out political organizing while armed. But they didn't clash with Iranian authorities. From 2005–17, they stopped the armed propaganda, according to Mohtadi. "The KRG asked us not to do [armed] incursions," he told me. "We could do much more if we didn't respect their legitimate interests."[16] But in 2017 Komala joined the other Kurdish groups and resumed armed struggle along the border area with Iran.[17]

Komala describes itself as a democratic socialist party with aspirations to join the Socialist International. "The Soviet Union and eastern European countries were all failures," said Mohtadi. "We like the Scandinavian model."

Komala also welcomed U.S. financial support while denying it has actually received any. I posed a query to the room full of Komala leaders, many of whom were veterans of the revolutionary movement of the 1970s. "All over the world, supporters of national liberation shout 'Yankee go home.' But here in Kurdistan you yell 'Yankee come here.' Why?" The room broke out in laughter, and then there was an embarrassed pause. Finally, Mohtadi said, "We're pragmatists." The United States "can't make democracy, but it can topple dictators."

Unfortunately, the United States doesn't just topple dictators, allow free elections, and then go home. It's a lot more complicated. And to understand U.S. policy toward Iranian Kurds, I had to travel high into the Qandil mountains along the Iran–Iraq border.

Finding the Party of Free Life (PJAK)

The green and brown scrub brush covering the earth quickly acquire a thick layer of snow in winter. The majestic Qandil mountains straddle the border between Turkey, northern Iraq, and Iran. The peaks suddenly dip into fertile valleys. In happier times the mountains could provide scenic views for tourists. But these days they make the perfect cover for Kurdish guerrillas crossing the border into nearby Iran. AK-47s slung over their shoulders, they dart into Iran for political organizing and clashes with Iranian troops. In May and August 2006, Iranian artillery shelled Kurdish villages in Iraq in retaliation for those guerrilla raids.

KRG authorities at the time said the rugged terrain made it impossible to locate, let alone control, the guerrillas. But after only two cell phone calls, I arranged to interview the top leaders of PJAK (Party for a Free Life in Kurdistan), the third major trend within the Iranian Kurdish movement. My colleague Yerevan Adham and I drove in his car to the small Iraqi town of Ranya and then, after looking around a bit, found a driver with a four-wheel-drive SUV. He and other local drivers knew the exact location of the guerrilla camps.

Hmm. If the local drivers know how to find the guerrillas, why can't the KRG?

In reality, KRG officials look the other way when PJAK launches armed incursions into Iran. That's because the guerrillas are "Kurds helping Kurds," Lieutenant Colonel Dennis Chapman told me.[18] He was a U.S. military officer involved in training Iraqi Kurdish troops. He denied any knowledge of U.S. support for the PJAK guerrillas.

I learned from other sources that the Bush administration was funding and training at least some of the Iranian guerrillas. "The USA funds

PJAK," a Kurdish political activist living in exile told me. "It channels the money through Kurdish groups in [Iraqi] Kurdistan." Seymour Hersh wrote an article in *The New Yorker* indicating that PJAK was supported by both the United States and Israel.[19] The Obama administration dropped the support and put PJAK on the Treasury Department list of terrorist organizations.[20]

The PJAK camps are located in inhospitable terrain. During winter months, the snowy roads are accessible only on foot or by tractor. Luckily the snows hadn't yet blanketed the area, and we drove up easily—if slowly—over winding dirt roads. Suddenly, young women in green pants and the distinctive Kurdish head scarf were walking along the road. They were female guerrillas. PJAK says its troops are almost 50 percent women.

At the camp, a group of guerrillas welcomed us into a threadbare room with a thin carpet on the floor and a kerosene stove blasting heat. Just then I remembered reports that every year some Kurds die from kerosene fumes leaking from faulty heaters. I looked around the room. There were no windows. So in case of excessive fumes, I would have to make a mad dash to the doorway.

We chatted while waiting for the guerrilla leaders to descend from the mountains. I asked one of the women fighters, a Kurd from Turkey, what they did to stave off boredom. "We watch satellite TV," she said, insisting that they cared only for news programs. After a few more questions from me, she confessed with a shy smile, they also watch American movies. "We like Brad Pitt and Mel Gibson." I asked what they thought of Sean Penn. They had never heard of him. In fact, they thought I was asking about Sinn Fein, the northern Irish political party.

About four hours after our scheduled interview time, two top PJAK leaders arrived. The party's top leader, Akif Zagros, had recently died in a flash flood, and the new leader from the political bureau introduced himself by his nom de guerre, Zenar Agri. He stood at perhaps 5'5" and was in his forties with prematurely gray hair. He was the very model of a modern commando general. He carried a cell phone, watched satellite TV, and surfed the Internet. He claimed PJAK was the leading party in the struggle against the Iranian regime.

PJAK grew out of, and remains closely affiliated with, the Turkish PKK (Kurdistan Workers Party). The PKK is led by Abdullah Ocalan, who is jailed in Turkey. The U.S. State Department lists the PKK as a terrorist organization.[21] PKK supporters point out that the group engages in legitimate armed struggle against military and government targets, although sometimes civilians are killed. At the camp, posters of PKK leader Abdullah Ocalan hung on the wall along with the PKK flag. Some Kurds say the PKK and PJAK operate as a cult built up around Ocalan. PJAK forbids guerrillas to have sex, for example, although I wonder how stringently that's enforced.

Agri assured me that Abdullah Ocalan has developed a new global ideology for the liberation of Kurds and all oppressed people in the world. Every other sentence was studded with references or quotes from Ocalan. He informed me, for example, that before the PKK, "the Kurds didn't know about their history and how to struggle." Now, under Ocalan's guidance, Kurds and all people of the world can follow his road to liberation, Agri told me with a straight face.[22]

PJAK has earned a certain amount of respect among Kurds as the first group to engage in armed struggle against Iran in recent years. Even rival political leaders admit that some young people are attracted to PJAK's militancy. PJAK claimed to have killed hundreds of Iranian soldiers, mostly near the Iraq–Iran border.[23] The Bush administration understood that PJAK couldn't spark a Kurdish uprising, let alone overthrow the Iranian government, but it could destabilize the region

The Bush administration played a similar game with the Mujahideen-e-Khalq (MEK), an Iranian guerrilla group once allied with Saddam Hussein and later protected by U.S. troops in a military camp in occupied Iraq. The U.S. government listed the MEK as a terrorist organization in 1997 and delisted it in 2012 after a fierce lobbying campaign spearheaded by conservative U.S. politicians. The Iraqi government, pressured by Iran, wanted the MEK camp closed. In 2016 MEK members remaining in the Iraqi camp were moved to Albania where they continue to operate a camp closed even to Albanian authorities.

Paul Pillar, a former CIA official in charge of Iranian intelligence, called the MEK more of a cult than a legitimate resistance group. "These are not the kind of partners you want to have," he told me. "We should have no truck with them."[24]

The State Department declined my repeated requests for a response to the charges of helping PJAK or the MEK. PJAK leader Agri flatly denied that his party received money or training from the United States or Israel. "But we would welcome American support," he said with a smile.

I really didn't expect a group getting secret U.S. military aid to fess up in an interview. But I was surprised how closely PJAK allied itself with U.S. policy. PJAK called for U.S. attacks on Iran. "We are happy if the United States bombs Iran, because it might change the regime," said Agri. In a region where the United States faces massive setbacks and political isolation, the Bush Administration took whatever allies it could find.

So do the Israelis.

Kurds Receive Israeli Support

Northern Iraq emits an air of international intrigue. One day on the streets of Suleimanyah, I saw a group of four Americans walking down the main street. They sported civilian haircuts and clothes but admitted to being U.S. military. Later I learned they were Special Forces (Green Berets) engaged mainly in intelligence gathering.

"Suli is like some Balkan city years ago," one U.S. officer told me. "You've got spies everywhere. Everyone wants to know what everyone else is doing."

I stayed one night in the seedy Ashti Hotel, once a hangout for Saddam's minions. It was like something out of a Graham

Greene novel. The smoke-filled lobby served as a meeting place for diplomats, businessmen, soldiers, and spies. Men sat around staring at glasses of strong tea. Every now and again, one would pour a bit of tea into his saucer, let it cool, and slurp it down. I met a Kurdish military advisor there, and when the U.S. Army came to escort me for a story on its operations, the Humvees pulled up near the hotel.[25]

Israel participates actively in the intrigue. Mossad agents posing as businessmen set up shop in the KRG soon after the 2003 U.S. invasion. BBC Television discovered Israeli former special forces soldiers training Kurdish security at the new airport near Erbil and also training a special antiterrorism security squad.[26] The Israelis are also helping train PJAK for its armed forays into Iran.[27] But given sentiment among Arabs and Muslims, the Israeli government tries to keep its activities quiet.[28]

Israel historically tried to ally with non-Arabs in the region against Arab countries. In the past, Israel had close ties with the shah of Iran and Emperor Haile Selassie of Ethiopia. In the 1970s and 1980s, Israel worked closely with Turkey, which severely oppresses its Kurdish population. Israeli–Kurdish relations were frosty because the Kurds supported the Palestinians. All that changed in recent years as Israel focused on Iran as the most significant enemy. Israel now champions the Kurds, causing tremendous friction with its one-time ally, Turkey.

Iraqi Kurdish officials wouldn't comment on the record about relations with Israel, but a Kurdish military advisor and I had a fascinating conversation. I asked him if the Israeli government was training Kurds. He smiled and said, "Israel is a wonderful country." Then he admitted that he visited Israel for training. After a few minutes of discussion, he reached under his shirt to pull out a gold chain with a Star of David attached. The advisor is a Muslim Kurd, but he got it in Israel. "I can't wear this publicly," he says, "But I have it around my neck all the time."

At least some Iranian Kurdish parties appear to have the same smile-and-wink policy toward Israel. American KDPI representative

Esfandiari told me, "We recognize Israel's assistance. We have good relations with Israel. The aspiration of Iraqi Kurds is to create a state like Israel."[29]

Israel doesn't hide its political support for the KRG. In 2017 the Iraqi Kurdish government held a controversial referendum calling for independence. Kurds voted for separation from Iraq, which backfired politically and allowed Baghdad to take back territory that had been under Kurdish control. The United States, Turkey, and almost every country in the region opposed the referendum. The one exception was Israel.

Azerbaijanis—the Largest and the Least Known

The Kurdish struggle has received lots of world attention over the years. The same can't be said for other Iranian minorities. Azerbaijanis make up almost a quarter of Iran's population, and even more if you listen to Azerbaijani exiled activists.[30] Yet their situation is little known outside the country.

Azerbaijanis are a Turkish-speaking people, almost all Shiites, ethnically the same as people in the nation of Azerbaijan. The provinces with significant numbers of Azeris are in the northwest of Iran. Nationalists often refer to their region as "South Azerbaijan" with the "North" being the former Soviet republic. In return, the Iranian ruling elite periodically talks about the former Soviet republic of Azerbaijan as actually being part of Iran.[31] Aren't ethnic politics fun?

Azerbaijanis are relatively more integrated into Iranian society than other ethnic groups. As Shiites, they don't face the same religious discrimination as Sunni Kurds, for example. Wealthy Azerbaijani traders dominate a sector of the Tehran bazaar. Supreme Leader Khamenei and Ayatollah Moussavi Tabrizi, the former chief justice of Iran's revolutionary courts, and some other leaders are Azerbaijani. But Azerbaijanis can't study their own language in school.

That and other forms of discrimination date back to before 1979. Nasser, an Azerbaijani activist living in the Washington DC area who asked that I use only his first name, told me that as a schoolboy in 1970, he had to pay a fine for speaking Azerbaijani in school. "We had an old saying," he said. "Azerbaijanis had to speak Turkish, pray in Arabic, and write in Persian."

Nasser pointed out that the mullahs spoke Azerbaijani while the shah's officials did not. Initially, that generated support for the clerical revolution. But Azerbaijanis became disillusioned with the system as the new government failed to recognize their language and cultural rights.

The region exploded in May 2006 when the state-owned newspaper *Iran* published an insulting and racist cartoon likening Azerbaijanis to cockroaches. Tens of thousands of people demonstrated in Tabriz and other cities. The government closed the newspaper and jailed the editor and cartoonist. But demonstrations continued. Several thousand gathered in front of the parliament building in Tehran, but security forces prevented them from demonstrating. Over the two weeks of protests, Azerbaijani activists say dozens were killed and hundreds were injured,[32] but local newspapers reported four killed and seventy injured.[33]

In September 2006 activists called for a boycott on the first day of school to protest the prohibition on students speaking in their own language. Some activists said 40 percent of students in Tabriz participated in the boycott, although it's not possible to verify that number. Dozens of organizers were arrested and imprisoned.

By most accounts, Azerbaijanis want to remain part of Iran with expanded political and cultural rights. A sector of Azerbaijani exiles favors federalism, like their Kurdish counterparts, but another sector favors independence and unification with the country of Azerbaijan. Reza Salahshour, the U.S. representative of the World Azerbaijan Congress, told me that "over 75 percent of the [Azerbaijani] people want independence now."[34]

That assertion runs counter to both my interviews, as well as the opinion of many analysts. Nayereh Tohidi, a fellow at UCLA's

Center for Near Eastern Studies, wrote, "the overwhelming majority of ethnic rights activists in Iran declare themselves to be
against secessionism."[35]

Arabs in Iran

When word got out that I was writing this book, I was besieged with
emails and phone calls from Arab–Iranians. As one of the groups
most under attack in 2006–7, they felt a particular urgency to get
their story told. Many people outside Iran don't even know that
roughly three percent of Iran's population are of Arab origin. They
mostly live in the province of Khuzistan, a center of Iranian oil production located near the Iraqi border in southern Iran. It was one of
the poorest Iranian provinces under the shah and remains so today.

Miloon Kothari, a UN human rights investigator, said Iran's general housing situation is better than that of most developing countries
because it has few homeless and no large slums. But during a 2005
visit to Khuzistan, he said living conditions in the province lag far
behind the rest of Iran. "There are thousands of people living with
open sewers, no sanitation, no regular access to water [or] electricity and no gas connections," he said. In addition, he noted that new
development projects just outside the provincial capital have displaced
"200,000–250,000 people."[36]

In recent years, Khuzistan has seen a reawakening of a movement
for national rights. In April 2005 thousands of people demonstrated
when a 1999 document surfaced, indicating the central government
planned to forcibly relocate Arabs to other parts of Iran and give
Persian names to Arab cities. Scores were killed and some 333 more
arrested in a brutal government crackdown.[37] The government said
the 1999 document was a forgery, but the large-scale demonstrations
indicated the Arab population found such threats credible.

Terrorist bombs went off in Khuzistan in 2005 and 2006, and the
government convicted nearly two dozen Arab-Iranians of committing

the crimes. It sentenced ten to death.[38] The Iranian government claimed some of these Arab–Iranians received terrorist training in southern Iraq, which was controlled by the British.

Most Arab–Iranian groups oppose separatism. Numbering only about two million and located next to volatile Iraq, Khuzistan residents would have a tough time surviving as an independent nation. Karim Abdian, leader of an Arab–Iranian human rights group, told me federalism could work in Khuzistan if the central government genuinely wants it. "If Arabs can get a fair share of the oil revenues and run their own affairs, then people won't want separation." Speaking of ethnic minorities in general, he added, "If the standard of life is better inside Iran, the minorities won't secede."[39]

U.S. Conservatives Seek to Use Minorities, but It Won't Be Easy

American conservatives have championed the cause of ethnic minorities in Iran. In October 2005 the conservative American Enterprise Institute sponsored a conference with Iranian ethnic minorities, seeking to put the issue into play in Congress and at the White House.

In July 2006 the White House called a meeting of Iranian opposition leaders including ethnic exiles. Attendees included Nicholas Burns, an under secretary of state, and Elliot Abrams, of Iran-Contra fame and a national security advisor in Bush's second term.* They didn't take a position on federalism but instead focused on participants' views on Iran's weapons of mass destruction.[40]

Dr. Alireza Nazmi, founder of the South Azerbaijan Diplomatic Commission, attended the White House meeting. "There was a general discussion about minority rights," he told me, "with a lot

---

*   Elliot Abrams was heavily involved in the illegal arms and money deals between Iran and Nicaragua. He pled guilty to two counts of withholding information from Congress about the Reagan Administration's illegal aid to the Nicaraguan Contras.

of yelling and shouting."[41] The exiled leaders couldn't agree among themselves about numerous issues, including federalism and the boundaries of their respective regions.

The Bush administration sought to use Iran's ethnic minorities to destabilize the Iranian government. Officially, the United States wants to maintain Iran as a single nation. But by sponsoring Kurdish military attacks inside Iran and promoting nationalist groups with questionable backgrounds, the Bush Administration played a very dangerous game.

When Obama was elected, the United States stopped funding and arming ethnic minority groups. The Obama camp realized that eight years of Bush administration meddling had not produced anything and had strengthened support for Iran's hardliners. But under the Trump administration, some of the same hawkish officials are back in power. They keep all options on the table, including the use of ethnic minorities, in an effort to overthrow the Iranian government.

During the Cold War, the U.S. government consciously promoted nationalist groups among ethnic minorities in Yugoslavia and the USSR. For years, the Voice of America broadcast the views of separatists and ethnic nationalists as a means to weaken those governments. Officially, the United States wanted to maintain the territorial integrity of those countries, but it helped unleash reactionary nationalist movements with all their ethnic cleansing and war crimes. U.S. leaders don't seem capable of learning from past mistakes.

Stanford's Abbas Milani told me that ethnic minorities certainly have legitimate complaints. "But trying to use that fissure in Iranian society will eventually backfire and consolidate the regime."

Notes

1. As'ad Ardalan, interview with author, Nov. 16, 2006, Tehran.

2. Hamidreza Jalaeipour, a leading reformist and former government official in Kurdistan in the 1980s, wrote an analysis of the unsuccessful Kurdish rebellion against the central government that lasted from 1979 to 1988.

He criticizes the Kurdish movement, and by extension all ethnic minorities. He wrote that had the Kurds rejected autonomy and kept their struggle confined to the "provisions of the Islamic Republic of Iran's constitution, their struggle would have been more peaceful, less costly for Kurds and Kurdistan would have better developed." Hamidreza Jalaeipour, academic paper, *The Rise and Decline of Kurdish Movement in Years 1978–88.*

3. Edward N. Luttwak, "Persian Shrug," *Wall Street Journal,* op-ed page, Feb. 27, 2007.

4. Robert Dreyfuss, "John Bolton Reads 'Em and Weeps," PBS, Dec. 5, 2008 (www.pbs.org/wgbh/pages/frontline/tehranbureau/2008/12/john-bolton-reads-em-and-weeps.html).

5. Iranian ethnic leaders say minorities actually total over half the population, arguing the state census figures undercount their numbers. Such claims can't be verified without a freely conducted census, however, so I've used the CIA research figures. *The World Fact Book,* 2018 (www.cia.gov/library/publications/the-world-factbook/geos/print_ir.html).

6. The estimate of 300,000 Bahais comes from the Bahai International Community based in the United States (http://info.bahai.org/persecution_iran.html).

7. Abbas Milani, interview with author, Oct. 5, 2006, Stanford University, Palo Alto CA.

8. Estimates of the total number of Kurds in the four countries run from 27 to 36 million because of inaccurate census counts. Ralph Peters, "Blood Borders," *Armed Forces Journal,* June 2006.

9. Walter Posch, "Islamist Neo-Cons Take Power in Iran," Ljubljana Institute for Security Studies, *Occasional Paper No. 3,* July 2005.

10. Frances Harrison, "Iran Press Reports Kurdish Riots," *BBC News* Web site, July 7, 2005.

11. Ava Homa, "Iranian President visits Kurdistan Province," *Kurdistan24,* March 25, 2017 (www.kurdistan24.net/en/news/c5a4a7f9-6d90-49a3-9160-b9bcb55dfe71/iranian-president-visits-kurdistan-province).

12. Mustafa Hejri, interview with author, Nov. 24, 2006, Koya, Iraq.

13. Information about the KDP-I is based on follow-up interviews done by Yerevan Adham in December 2006. He helped me arrange interviews and translated during my trip to northern Iraq in 2006.

14. Mustafa Hejri, phone interview with author, June 12, 2015.

15. Fazel Hawramy, "Assassinations mount as Iranian Kurdish militants clash with Tehran,"*Al-Monitor,* March 7, 2018 (www.al-monitor.com/

pulse/originals/2018/03/iran-kdpi-kurdish-opposition-iraq-assassinations-rahmani.html).

16. Abdulla Mohtadi, interview with author, Komala compound, Nov. 25, 2006, Iraq.

17. *EKurd*, "Leftist Kurdish Komala Party Resumes Armed Struggle Against Iran,"April 30, 2017 (http://ekurd.net/kurdish-komala-struggle-iran-2017-04-30).

18. Lt. Col. Dennis Chapman, interview with author, Nov. 21, 2006, Suleimanyah, Iraq.

19. Seymour Hersh, "The Next Act," *The New Yorker*, Nov. 27, 2006.

20. U.S. Department of the Treasury, "Treasury Designates Free Life Party of Kurdistan a Terrorist Organization," Feb. 4, 2009 (www.treasury.gov/press-center/press-releases/Pages/tg14.aspx).

21. The State Department's justification for listing PKK as a foreign terrorist organization can be found at Country Reports on Terrorism, Apr. 28, 2006 (www.state.gov/s/ct/rls/crt/2005/65275.htm).

22. Zenar Agri, interview with author, Nov. 26, 2006, PJAK guerrilla base, Qandil mountains, Iraq.

23. Zenar Agri, interview with author.

24. Paul Pillar, former CIA national intelligence officer for the Near East and South Asia, interview with author, Jan. 18, 2006, Washington DC.

25. Reese Erlich, "Calm amid a Storm," *Dallas Morning News*, Dec. 22, 2006.

26. "Kurdish Soldiers Trained by Israelis," *BBC News* Web site, Sept. 20, 2006.

27. Hersh, *The New Yorker*, Nov. 27, 2006.

28. The Israeli government tried to keep the training secret, but reports surfaced inside Israel. See Conal Urquhart and Michael Howard, *The Guardian* (London), Dec. 2, 2005.

29. Esfandiari, interview with author.

30. Reza Salahshour, representative of the World Azerbaijan Congress, told me Turkish-origin Iranians, including Azerbaijanis, make up 52 percent of the Iranian population, a figure not backed up by other credible sources. Phone interview with author, Oct. 23, 2006, Washington DC.

31. On Oct. 12, 2006, the Supreme Leader's personal envoy, Ayatollah Moshen Mujtahed-Shabestari, responded to those who want to secede from Iran, "If there is to be any union, (Azerbaijan) should join Iran." "Iran Adopts Firm Stance on Minority Rights Issue," Oct. 20, 2006 (http://Eurasianet.org).

32. Amnesty International, "Incommunicado Detention, Abbas Lisani," June 8, 2006 (UA 163/06).

33. Nazila Fathi, "Ethnic Tensions Over Cartoon Set Off Riots in Northwest Iran," *New York Times*, May 29, 2006.

34. Salahshour, interview with author.

35. Nayereh Tohidi, "Iran: Regionalism, Ethnicity and Democracy," June 29, 2006 (www.opendemocracy.net/democracy-irandemocracy/regionalism_3695.jsp).

36. Miloon Kothari, UN Commission on Human Rights Special Rapporteur on Adequate Housing, interview with http://IRINnews.org, May 2, 2006.

37. Accurate figures were hard to determine because foreign reporters weren't on the scene in Ahwaz. I took my figures from Amnesty International, "Iran: Need for Restraint as Anniversary of Unrest in Khuzestan Approaches," Apr. 13, 2006; and also from Islamic Republic News Agency, "Defense Minister Praises Arab Iranians' Role in Sacred Defense," May 3, 2005 (www.webneveshteha.com/en/article.asp?id=-1181330580).

38. I explain this case in greater detail in the Chapter 7 section about NGOs.

39. Karim Abdian, executive director of the Ahwaz Human Rights Organization, interview with author, Jan. 15, 2007, Washington DC.

40. Shahin Abbasov, "Iran: Ethnic Azeri Activist Predicts More Protests," July 31, 2006 (http://Eurasia.net).

41. Alireza Nazmi, phone interview with author, Nov. 2, 2006, Tulare CA.

ELEVEN

What the U.S. Media Didn't Tell You

After a hard day, reporters working abroad often gather like herds of gazelles at an isolated watering hole. Journalists covering a foreign election, for example, might hang out at a hotel bar to informally exchange information. Iran is no exception—except there are no bars.

During one presidential election, I stayed at Tehran's Laleh Hotel along with dozens of other foreign reporters. The coffee shop at the former Intercontinental Hotel substituted for the bar. We got to know one another informally and tended to group together by species: TV reporters, photographers, and print journalists.

It became obvious that American reporters, in particular, had a certain mindset about Iran. As *Newsweek* reporter Babak Dehghan Pisheh said in another context, "A lot of Western journalists, particularly Americans, come to Iran with a set of stereotypes expecting to see a country more like Saudi Arabia where women aren't allowed to drive. So the stories they write are often very black and white."[1]

Most American reporters I met saw Iran as an evil society and a danger to the United States. While some expressed disagreement with U.S. policies, prior to 2015, they believed Iran was developing a nuclear weapon that threatened America. In short, their views tracked the political consensus emanating from Washington.

Rather than proceeding from reality, they filtered their reporting through a Washington lens. When Bush, Obama, or Trump made a statement, even a false one, the major media dutifully reported it with few opposing sources. When those in power lie, accurately reporting their views is not journalism; it's stenography.

Professional reporters from Britain and other European countries attended the same events and interviewed similar sources but came to very different political conclusions. In our book *Target Iraq: What the News Media Didn't Tell You*, Norman Solomon and I described in detail the economic and political reasons why major U.S. media distort reality.[2]

Uncritical mainstream reporting changed somewhat during the Trump era. His lies are just too big and too frequent. But the mainstream media's false portrayal of Iran as a national security threat didn't change much. In this chapter, I offer pointed criticisms of mainstream U.S. news coverage of Iran and then suggest some ways you can figure out what's really going on. I focus on the *New York Times* because it's considered the paper of record, and because it plays a key role in shaping other media coverage.

Aircraft Carriers for Peace

At the end of December 2006, Thom Shanker wrote a frontpage article in the *New York Times*, detailing the decision to send U.S. aircraft carrier groups to the Persian Gulf. Shanker, paraphrasing unnamed American officers, wrote that the deployment "would be useful in enforcing any sanctions that the United Nations might impose." In addition, he wrote, the ships "entered the Persian Gulf ... to practice halting vessels suspected of smuggling nuclear materials in waters across the region."[3]

First of all, the UN Security Council had specifically ruled out military force to impose sanctions against Iran, and there were not any prospects of that changing. So the claim that the U.S. Navy entered the Gulf to help the UN was clearly wrong. Second, neither Shanker nor anyone else offered credible evidence that Iran plans to smuggle nuclear materials by sea. The *Times* relied solely on U.S. and British military officials. Shanker didn't even pretend to offer balance by quoting Iranian officials or anyone else critical of U.S. policy. The article assumed Iran was a threat to the American people and the United States was responding defensively. In reality, the United States sent an armada to the Persian Gulf to pressure Iran and prepare for possible unilateral military action.

That kind of one-sided story most often appears with a Washington dateline, where top leaders cultivate reporters who aspire to become chief stenographer. The Lewis "Scooter" Libby perjury trial in February 2007 laid bare the incestuous relations between top officials and major media figures. Vice President Dick Cheney's Chief of Staff Lewis Libby and presidential advisor Karl Rove called selected journalists, such as Judith Miller of the *New York Times* and Matt Cooper of *Time* magazine, to plant stories discrediting a whistleblower who told the truth about the non-existent nuclear weapons program in Iraq. Deputy Secretary of State Richard Armitage leaked a story to national columnist Robert Novak that the whistleblower's wife, Valerie Plame, was a CIA officer, and she eventually had to leave her job.[4]

While Washington reporters are the worst offenders, reporters in the field can accept the most preposterous stories as well, so long as they come from official American sources. On January 20, 2007, men dressed as U.S. soldiers and carrying U.S. identification cards attacked a meeting of Iraqi and American soldiers in the city of Karbala, Iraq. Five Americans eventually died as a result of the assault, which took the United States completely by surprise and constituted a huge embarrassment. A few days later, Iraqi and American military investigators floated the story that Iranians may have prepared the attack. CNN quoted unnamed "officials" as saying, "This was beyond what we have seen militias or foreign fighters do."[5]

The officials presented no physical evidence or other proof of Iranian involvement, just conspiracy theories. The allegation dovetailed nicely with the U.S. campaign to demonize Iran for killing American soldiers in Iraq. It's possible that senior Iraqi officials were involved, because the attackers knew the exact time and location of the high-level meeting. We now know that the predecessor group to the Islamic State used the tactic of dressing up in Iraqi Army uniforms in order to attack Iraqis, as they did in later years.[6] The Pentagon never provided evidence of Iranian sponsorship of the raid, and the story quietly died out.

The election of Donald Trump as president in 2016 led to changes in mainstream media coverage. His policies were far to the right of consensus politics that had prevailed among high-level Democrats and Republicans. He also had the habit of blatantly lying, as opposed to the nuanced lies of his predecessors. So some mainstream media occasionally broke with the tradition of objective journalism and directly challenged Trump's misinformation.

Trump consistently misrepresented the 2015 nuclear accord, claiming Iran "has committed multiple violations of the agreement." Mainstream media ran stories pointing out that international inspectors have consistently found Iran to be in compliance.[7] Unfortunately, the *Times* reverted back to its traditional coverage when it came to reporting on what Iran was doing in the Middle East and what danger that might pose to the United States. In a front-page article published in 2018 some of the *Times* top Middle East reporters resurrected the specter of an all-powerful Iran threatening war against Israel.[8] The article described how Iranian-backed militias had gained strength in Iraq, Syria, and Lebanon. They wrote, "Iran and its allies are seeking to establish a land corridor from Iran to the Mediterranean, via Iraq, Syria and Lebanon." This land corridor would allow Iran to supply Hizbollah in Lebanon. The article stated, "Some people in Israel have started referring to a potential 'First Northern War,' meaning that Israel will have to fight across both the Lebanese and Syrian frontiers."

The reference to a "land corridor" omits the fact that Iran had been supplying Hizbollah with arms since the mid-1980s when no such land corridor existed. It seems unlikely that trucking missiles through volatile Iraq is going to be any more secure for Iran than its current "air corridor" for arms deliveries. But the idea of massive arms shipments going from Iran to the Mediterranean does sound really scary.

The article assumes Iran is an aggressive power threatening both the United States and Israel. It only quotes sources hostile to Iran, including a number of think tanks and Israeli sources who have long advocated bombing Iran.[9] The *Times* never mentioned the 5,000 U.S. troops stationed permanently in Iraq, nor the over 2,000 in northern Syria. The Pentagon is at war with six Muslim countries: Afghanistan, Yemen, Libya, Somalia, Iraq, and Syria. So Iran has good reason to fear for its safety. With articles like this one, the *Times* provides justification for future U.S. military aggression in the region.

These examples are more than aberrations. A careful reading of major U.S. media shows a particular bias, one so ingrained that reporters don't even see it.

The Assumptions of Empire

To put the U.S. media coverage in perspective, imagine for a moment that we're living in Britain in 1946. Politicians, military leaders, business tycoons, and the media all agree that Britain has a splendid empire. We have just won a world war. We have brought prosperity, culture, and Christianity to natives throughout the world. True, the locals periodically complain or even riot (there *is* that pesky Gandhi fellow). But certainly no one would suggest that we grant them independence. What an absurd idea!

Within fifteen years, anti-imperialist movements forced the collapse of that very splendid empire. But don't look to the mainstream British media to have hinted at that possibility until the empire had already begun to crack. More typically, they provided distorted news about the anti-colonial movements by quoting only official British sources.

For example, the BBC reported that widespread "riots" had broken out on the British Crown Colony of Cyprus in 1956. "Archbishop Makarios, the leader of the 'enosis' campaign to unify Cyprus with Greece, was arrested for 'actively fostering terrorism' and has been deported to the Seychelles. British security forces have searched the archbishop's residence and say they have found one petrol bomb and ten similar bombs."[10] In reality, the people of Cyprus were rebelling against colonial rule. The demonstrations continued and by 1960 Cyprus had won independence. Archbishop Makarios was elected president, proving once again that yesterday's terrorist is today's statesman.

Today, the U.S. empire dwarfs that of its British precursor. America is the only superpower. The United States has the largest military in world history, with some 800 military bases in seventy countries around the world.[11] And like their Fleet Street counterparts of old, today's U.S. media defend the empire. News coverage might agree or disagree about a particular policy, roughly reflecting the differences between high-ranking Republicans and Democrats. Some reporters might question the country's leadership when policies go very poorly, but few question the underlying assumptions of empire.

The Corporate Owners Call the Shots

The content of the media reflects the interests of their corporate owners. These days, five companies own a large section of news and entertainment media in the United States: Time Warner (CNN), Disney (ABC), Murdoch's News Corporation (Fox), and Comcast (NBC), and CBS, one of America's original big three broadcast networks, is owned by the corporate parent of Viacom.[12] Other significant news companies include the *New York Times*, the *Washington Post* (owned by Amazon's Jeff Bezos), and Michael Bloomberg's media conglomerate. Major media corporations will continue to merge and consolidate their power. These companies have vested corporate interests to protect. None want to see critical stories about its own holdings, which in some cases include war industries. And corporate executives certainly don't want to alienate government officials who handle antitrust matters, renew Federal Communications Commission licenses, and offer lucrative government contracts. No one wants to be seen as undercutting national security by publishing embarrassing articles.

Reporters deny that corporate owners have ever called them to dictate how a story should be written. That's undoubtedly true. The corporate owners call the publisher, who calls the senior editors. In subtle and not so subtle ways, owners make clear their media enterprises should avoid certain topics. Will an investigative story damage parent company profits? Editors and reporters who have survived on the job usually internalize those lessons.

In theory, major media don't allow government officials to censor the news. But when the story is sensitive enough, editors check with top government officials prior to publication, using the argument that the editors want to protect national security. On several occasions, top editors at the *New York Times* admitted to delaying publication and changing the content of important investigative stories because government officials objected.

In December 2005 the *New York Times* published an expose of how the National Security Agency wiretapped American phone calls without warrants. It had held up the story since before the November 2004 elections—in effect, allowing the administration to censor the newspaper's content. It only ran the article when *Times* reporter James Risen was going to publish the material in a book. A similar process took place during the editing of a 2006 story about improper U.S. pressure on European banks to track alleged terrorists.[13]

That process of corporate and government pressure certainly applies to mainstream coverage of Iran.

Iran's Activities in Iraq—A Case Study

In December 2006, the Bush Administration launched a propaganda blitz to blame Iran for killing American soldiers in Iraq. In press briefings and speeches, the United States alleged that Iran was supplying mortars, rocket-propelled grenades, and other small arms to certain Iraqi militia groups targeting Americans. The Iranian government was allegedly manufacturing highly sophisticated explosively formed penetrators (EFPs) to blow up armored Humvees.

In the beginning, the major media dutifully and uncritically reported those assertions. CBS *Evening News* anchor Katie Couric said, "The U.S. military says it has proof positive" of Iranian weapons in Iran.[14] *New York Times* reporter Michael R. Gordon, who had co-authored false stories about Saddam's weapons of mass destruction back in 2003, also promoted the Pentagon's views about the new crisis. Writing from Washington, Gordon quoted U.S. military sources alleging that top Iranian leaders, including Supreme Leader Ali Khamenei, were responsible for providing EFPs to Iraqi militias.[15]

In February 2006 the military held a Baghdad briefing for reporters, in which unnamed officials presented a table overflowing with weapons allegedly made in Iran. They claimed similar weapons killed 170 American soldiers over the previous three years. To their credit, some U.S. reporters questioned parts of the presentation. James Glanz in the *New York Times* asked why the briefers insisted on anonymity and how they could prove high Iranian officials were responsible. He also asked in his story if the information was being presented now to justify war with Iran. By the low standards set during the 2003 run up to the Iraq invasion, these questions constituted fiery dissent from administration propaganda.

But most American reporters accepted the underlying premise of the military presentation. Glanz wrote, "Whatever doubts were created about the timing and circumstances of the weapons disclosures, the direct physical evidence presented on Sunday was extraordinary."[16] That became the framework for much of the coverage in other U.S. media: Iran is providing deadly munitions to Iraqi militias, but the administration hasn't proven top leaders had approved. That angle on the story got repeated in countless other media throughout the United States. In the weeks after the original February 11, 2007, press briefing, some articles in the *Times* and other major media became more skeptical about whether the EFPs could have originated only in Iran. But none of them accurately described the phony intelligence as well as the same-day reporting by some of the British and alternative press.

As someone who writes for mainstream dailies and broadcast networks, I know how hard it is to file a story the day of a bombshell U.S. announcement. Every other journalist around you will report the official version of events, perhaps with some caveats. Your editor doesn't want to run something different and risk attack by the administration and its supporters.

But it is possible to scrutinize the conventional wisdom in real time. That's what some of the British media did. Public opinion in Britain overwhelmingly opposes the occupation of Iraq and any military assault on Iran. So the British media have greater political space to write contrary—and truthful—stories. Accurate journalism, in turn, increases public sentiment against war with Iran.

On the same day that the *New York Times* reported the "extraordinary" evidence, London's *Independent* newspaper ran a front-page article that said, in its second paragraph, "The allegations against Iran are similar in tone and credibility to those made four years ago by the U.S. government about Iraq possessing weapons of mass destruction in order to justify the invasion of 2003."[17]

Paul Reynolds, a BBC world affairs correspondent, dug through old articles and official statements to come up with one of the first articles to question the underlying premise of the U.S. military propaganda. He noted that British army officers no longer claimed that Iran makes the EFPs. Reynolds wrote that British officers say that "the technology matched bomb-making found elsewhere in the

Middle East, including Lebanon and Syria."[18] Reynolds wrote that, contrary to U.S. military reports, the manufacture of EFPs does not require sophisticated equipment. He pointed out that "Iraqis themselves would be capable of copying a design and therefore do not need to get bombs from Iran."

Several weeks prior to the Baghdad press briefing, the *Los Angeles Times* ran an excellent article pointing out that U.S. troops in the field had found little evidence of Iranian munitions being used against them.[19] Plenty of alternative media in the United States wrote stories showing that Iran played no significant military role in the deaths of American soldiers.[20] Some politicians in the future will probably claim that they were fooled by the Bush Administration lies about Iran, but those lies were exposed publicly within days of the press briefing. And you didn't need access to classified documents to figure out the Bush plans. You just had to take off the blinders provided by the empire builders.

I contacted *New York Times* reporters criticized in this chapter, but none gave substantive responses to my e-mails. *Times* Public Editor Byron Calame did respond publicly in his column to readers' criticism of Iran coverage.[21] He gave the *Times* a clean bill of health!

Calame even praised Michael Gordon's incredibly one-sided and downright inaccurate story of February 10, 2006, about Iran creating the EFPs. In a piece of legerdemain conducted best by the *Times*, Calame praised Gordon for seeking out dissenting views. The Gordon article, he wrote, "cited interviews with 'civilian and military officials from a broad range of government agencies,' and pointed out that group included 'some whose agencies have previously been sceptical about the significance of Iran's role in Iraq.'"

And so we have the perfect defense of empire. The *Times* remains balanced so long as it seeks out dissenting views within the government. The *Times* has no need to find sources outside the Washington Beltway or those who oppose intervention in Iran altogether.

Calame did raise one criticism of Gordon's work. Since June 2005, the *Times* decided to explain to readers why a given source must remain anonymous.* Public Editor Calame chastised Gordon for not mentioning why his sources requested anonymity, but not for using them in the first place.

In 2017, Gordon moved from the *Times* to the Washington Bureau of the *Wall Street Journal,* where he continued to act as a stenographer for the administration in power. Gordon seems particularly susceptible to getting exclusive leaks from those in power. Quoting unnamed administration officials, he wrote that Trump wanted Sunni Arab countries to send troops to replace the 2,000+ American troops fighting in northern Syria.[22] The proposal was absurd on its face as no Arab country would send troops to the predominantly Kurdish region and risk immediate guerrilla insurgency. But if Trump floats an idea, the mainstream media is right there to give it legitimacy.

Controlling the News

I've filed stories from around the world. By far the worst cities for doing good journalism in the developed world are Washington DC and Los Angeles. They are both home to powerful elites who want to control the news. In Los Angeles, the power mongers of the entertainment industry manipulate the media to create favorable coverage and retaliate against reporters who don't play ball. The top political, business, and military leaders of Washington play the same game, but the stakes are much higher.

Just for starters, most government officials won't talk to reporters on the record. We can quote them but not use their names. That's why papers are filled with so many anonymous sources. By refusing

---

* The results of this policy are sometimes hilarious. In one article, *Times* reporter Nicholas Wood quotes a Western diplomat, "who requested anonymity because he was not permitted to comment on the matter for attribution." In other words, the source remained anonymous because he wanted to remain anonymous. Nicholas Wood, "Serbs to Vote on Document That Is Faulty, Critics Say," *New York Times,* Oct. 23, 2006. In May 2006, the *Times* editors changed the policy, supposedly to allow more flexibility and avoid this kind of tautology. This absurd example came out five months after the new policy began.

to be quoted by name, bureaucrats can avoid responsibility for their statements, and journalists lose credibility with the public.

I tried to interview middle-level State Department officials for this book, but by official policy, they wouldn't speak on the record. So I asked to meet with people who could use their names. No one agreed. I even tried to interview a person at Freedom House, a human rights group, but she wouldn't talk on the record. Giving anonymous quotes has become the norm, not the exception, in Washington. Apparently, media manipulation is contagious.

Reporters quickly learn to play the Washington game. If you write stories favorable to your sources, you get interviews with higher-ups. If you don't interview powerful people, the editors notice, and you're weeded out. Young reporters spend years waiting for plum jobs covering the State Department, Pentagon, or White House. Those beats have lots of prestige and six-figure salaries. Sometimes they are gateways to higher positions in the media; other times they lead directly to jobs in politics or with corporations.

I have seen many young reporters work their way up through the mainstream press. They like the increased pay and prestige that comes with writing for a major daily or big network. But the pressure to conform is intense. You learn quickly not to cause waves. Former National Public Radio correspondent Sara Chayes wrote about her experiences reporting from abroad. "When in doubt, you conform. It is the safest course, and it is the course your editors feel comfortable with. That stuff about scoops was never my experience. ... My editors ... never liked having me out on a limb."[23]

So for those conservatives who believe that liberals have conspired to control the major media and destroy America, take heart! Yes, more reporters register Democrat than Republican, but most shed their personal views on the job like a snake in the desert sun. The long crawl to the top changes their thinking, and their desire to keep the cushy job keeps them aligned with whoever is in power.

Just to make reporters' lives even more complicated, journalism is going through a major crisis as people abandon traditional media in favor of online news. Newspapers are shrinking in size and number. Major magazines have converted to online only. The corporate journalism business model is in crisis. Major media are pouring resources into online news but haven't figured out how to make a profit from it. Online advertising doesn't generate enough revenue and paywalls, in which readers must pay a fee to access news, hasn't worked either. Smaller web news sites are popping up in major cities, but lack of steady revenue makes journalism jobs far from secure.

This economic uncertainty has accelerated a wave of mergers, takeovers, and corporate dismemberments. Companies take on debt and then lay off reporters and editors. They close foreign and domestic bureaus. Reporters at formerly stable media companies suddenly fear losing their jobs. The prospect of imminent unemployment isn't conducive to taking risks.

So it's easier for journalists to keep their heads down and report the same things as everyone else. But occasionally they don't. And that's when the story gets really interesting.

The Journalistic High Jump

Occasionally, courageous reporters come up with important stories that shatter the conventional wisdom. In 2003, Carlotta Gall, a *New York Times* reporter then based in Kabul, Afghanistan, dug out a story of how the U.S. military tortured and murdered two prisoners at Bagram air base in Afghanistan.[24] She even found the prisoners' official death certificates indicating homicide, signed by an American pathologist. The story sat unpublished for weeks. Editors sent her out to do more reporting.

That's what editors do with stories challenging conventional Washington wisdom. An editor can always demand more reporting, raising the journalistic bar to impossible heights. By contrast, stories reflecting the Washington consensus can be published with the bar at knee level.

Doug Frantz, who was the *New York Times* investigative editor, revealed to the *Columbia Journalism Review* some of the internal

Times discussions about Gall's article. Top editor Howell Raines and others, according to Frantz, insisted that the torture story "was improbable; it was hard to get their mind around. ... Compare Judy Miller's WMD stories to Carlotta's story. On a scale of one to ten, Carlotta's story was nailed down to ten."[25] Finally, after sitting for a month, the story ran on page 14, not on page 1 as originally pushed by her editor. It ran just a few weeks prior to the U.S. invasion of Iraq and had little public impact.

Washington Post reporter Dana Priest faced a different kind of problem. Priest has written some excellent articles exposing U.S. prisoner abuse and the "extraordinary rendition" (i.e., kidnapping) of alleged terrorists to other countries for torture. In late 2005, Priest published a front-page article about the CIA's secret prisons.[26] The article hit a nerve in Washington because the war in Iraq was becoming increasingly unpopular, and European media was exposing the CIA activities.

Instead of moving to stop the illegal and immoral CIA kidnappings, official Washington reacted by threatening to prosecute those who leaked information to the *Post*. The Justice Department and House Intelligence Committee launched probes into the leaks—but ignored the U.S. policy of torture and kidnapping.

But such articles are the rare exception. The administration in power usually gets full cooperation in efforts to demonize the enemy du jour.[27] And in the last few years, that process has gotten some new media cheerleaders.

Bring in the Clowns

So far I have intentionally not mentioned media distortions from Fox News and other outlets with obvious right-wing bias. Fox pioneered the intentional blurring of the line between reporting and commentary. It set up programs that looked like news shows but featured right-wing blowhards spouting unsubstantiated opinion. For a time MSNBC and CNN followed suit in an effort to grab ratings and advertisers.

The cable TV networks thrive on sensationalistic stories about rampaging serial killers or astronauts attempting to kidnap their lovers' girlfriends.* But Iran also provides perfect fodder because the United States can be presented as the good guy going after evil mullah extremists. Earlier in this chapter I described the journalistic high-jump bar required to air a particular story. In the case of Fox News, they just throw the bar to the sidelines. *Fox and Friends* co-host Steve Doocy once reported Iran was only sixteen *days* away from building a nuclear bomb, citing an unnamed source at the U.S. Embassy in Moscow. That preposterous story was quickly dropped.[28]

In 2006, CNN hired Glenn Beck, a right-wing radio talk-show zealot and self-described rodeo clown, to host an evening prime-time program. While Beck admits he is not a journalist, he presented video clips of the day's events, interviews guests, and otherwise appeared to be one. He regularly exaggerated the threat that Iran presented to the United States, referring to President Ahmadinejad as "President Tom." Beck said on one program, "In 1938 it took Hitler roughly six months to march across Europe after Chamberlain's big 'peace in our time' moment. How much longer do we have with President Tom? Six months, twelve months?"[29]

Beck once interviewed Keith Ellison, a progressive Muslim elected to the House of Representatives. Beck revealed a deep-seated anti-Muslim bias by somehow equating an African American Muslim with terrorists. Beck said, "I have been nervous about this interview with you because what I feel like saying is, 'Sir, prove to me that you are not working with our enemies.'"[30]

---

* In early February 2007, astronaut Lisa Nowak allegedly tried to kidnap the girlfriend of her astronaut lover. The cable news networks devoted extensive coverage to the rather bizarre story and made it a major news event right up until former *Playboy* model Anna Nicole Smith died a few days later.

Such claptrap would be laughable, except some people take it seriously. President Trump openly praises Fox and has helped create an alternate media universe in which anything contradicting his views is "fake news." In actual numbers, conservative cable TV reaches relatively few people. Fox News reached a nightly viewership of 1.36 million viewers during one week in 2018[31], compared to over 8.8 million for ABC TV news.[32]

The evening news programs at MSNBC have emerged as a liberal alternative to Fox. Rachel Maddow, in particular, has developed an impressive following. MSNBC comes close to rivaling Fox in ratings, with 1.23 million nightly viewers.

But because the right-wingers are favored by sectors of the ruling elite, they have a political impact beyond their limited audience. Fox impacts CNN and other channels to play up conservative views, which get echoed on conservative talk radio and in right-wing blogs. Pretty soon, the most outrageous charges begin to sound legitimate.

Decoding the Media

Okay, the right-wing and mainstream media have the uncomfortable habit of lying. How do I figure out what's going on? Glad you asked.

If you want to find the location of a radio transmitter, you get a fix on its signal from two other directions. The process is called triangulation. You can use a similar method to figure out the truth from the media. Read as much as you can and triangulate from there.

I read three newspapers a day (*San Francisco Chronicle, New York Times*, and *Wall Street Journal*). I watch broadcast TV and listen to public radio. I regularly read alternative newspapers, magazines, and websites. On important stories, I might consult British media (BBC, the *Guardian*, the *Independent*), Al Jazeera English language service, or various newspapers from Europe and Latin America.

I don't expect the average reader to devote that much time to the media, but by understanding mainstream media biases and adding alternative information, you can figure out what's going on. Here are some handy hints.

• *Watch for the dateline.* Washington politicians love to cultivate reporters favorable to their causes. So the administration in power starts its propaganda blitzes with reporters high up in the Washington food chain. Anything datelined Washington should be read with particular scrutiny. Beat reporters at the Pentagon, for example, rely on current and former military officers as sources. (I've yet to meet a beat reporter for the peace movement.) Looking carefully at the sources, you can usually figure out who initiated the story: someone in power (usually), or someone going after those in power (occasionally). The Washington dateline can be helpful when one section of the ruling elite wants to attack another. Sometimes Washington reporters break very interesting stories about disagreements between the Defense and State departments, for example. In the run up to the Iraq war, some intelligence and diplomatic officials leaked stories undercutting the Bush Administration's arguments for invading Iraq. The Trump White House is full of leakers, with officials spilling the beans just prior to their firing. But just because one sector of the ruling elite disagrees with the other doesn't necessarily mean either one is right.

• *Scrutinize the sources.* Always be suspicious of articles that describe events in foreign countries with sources based only in the United States. Some mainstream journalists reporting from abroad have the uncomfortable habit of phoning back to the United States to find so-called experts to explain policy issues. If they can't find an expert inside the country, the story may not reflect the views of local people.

• *Look carefully at the so-called experts.* Are they former government or corporate officials? Major media almost always use experts who reflect the policy debate between top-level Democrats and Republicans or between various branches of government.

If the story doesn't quote sources genuinely critical of the new policy being advocated, for example, find some additional sources on the Internet.

• *Get to know the bylines.* Some reporters report more honestly than others. Some are shills for the ruling elite. I don't agree with everything that they write, but I respect the reporting of *Times* reporters such as Carlotta Gall, and, now retired from the Times, Stephen Kinzer and Chris Hedges. *Washington Post* reporters Dana Priest, Jason Rezaian, and Dafna Linzer have written excellent stories. Seymour Hersh stands in a class of his own for digging out contrary views among intelligence officials.

As a media consumer, you might get angry at a particular article and fire off a letter to the editor. But if you see a particularly good article, you should also send a letter or e-mail of support. Good reporters are like Maytag repairmen; they can get pretty lonely.

• *Read the foreign press and alternative media.* As a college student at the University of California, Berkeley, in the 1960s, I had to wait five days for European newspapers to arrive at Dave's Smoke Shop, and months longer for more esoteric journals. Today such information is available online in real time. But more is not always better. Learn to distinguish between websites that offer unsubstantiated rumors and those with hard facts, between those promoting conspiracy theories and those offering a sharp critique of the empire. Would you believe everything contained in a leaflet handed out on the street? Take the same attitude toward the Internet.

As with all media, keep in mind the biases of the particular webpage. I don't trust the BBC's coverage of Northern Ireland, for example, because it hews too closely to the British government's viewpoint. The BBC and the *Guardian*, on the other hand, often provide good coverage of Iran and the Middle East. I provide an updated list of mainstream and alternative media at my homepage: https://reeseerlich.com/other-news-sources/.

Notes

1. Babak Dehghan Pisheh as quoted by Omid Memarian, "Western Journalists in Iran: Fast Food Stories," website presentation for University of California, Berkeley, Graduate School of Journalism, Apr. 26, 2006.

2. Norman Solomon and Reese Erlich, *Target Iraq: What the News Media Didn't Tell You* (New York: Context Books, 2003).

3. Thom Shanker, "U.S. and Britain to Add Ships to Persian Gulf in Signal to Iran," *New York Times*, Dec. 21, 2006.

4. CNN, "Armitage Admits Leaking Plame's Identity," Sept. 8, 2006 (www.cnn.com/2006/POLITICS/09/08/leak.armitage/).

5. CNN, "Iran Involvement Suspected in Karbala Compound Attack," Jan. 31, 2007 (http://www.cnn.com/2007/WORLD/meast/01/30/iraq.main/index.html).

6. Jack Moore, "ISIS Cell Dressed in Police Uniform Kills 31 in Suicide Bomb Attack on Iraq's Tikrit," *Newsweek*, Apr. 15, 2017 (www.newsweek.com/dressed-policemen-isis-cell-kills-31-suicide-bomb-attack-iraqs-tikrit-579269).

7. Eugene Kiely, "Trump on Iran's 'Multiple Violations,'" *The Wire*, Oct. 13, 2017 (www.factcheck.org/2017/10/trump-irans-multiple-violations/).

8. Ben Hubbard, Isabel Kershner and Anne Barnard, "Iran, Deeply Embedded in Syria, Expands 'Axis of Resistance,'" *New York Times*, Feb. 19, 2018 (www.nytimes.com/2018/02/19/world/middleeast/iran-syria-israel.html).

9. Robert Wright, "How The New York Times Is Making War With Iran More Likely," *Intercept*, Mar. 17, 2018 (https://theintercept.com/2018/03/17/new-york-times-iran-israel-washington-think-tanks/).

10. "Riots Erupt in Cyprus over Archbishop," BBC News website, Mar. 10, 1956 (http://news.bbc.co.uk/onthisday/hi/dates/stories/march/10/newsid_4216000/4216931.stm).

11. David Vine, "Where in the World Is the U.S. Military? *Politico*, July/Aug. 2015 (www.politico.com/magazine/story/2015/06/us-military-bases-around-the-world-119321).

12. Ben Bagdikian in his classic book *The New Media Monopoly* (Boston: Beacon Press), describes the process of media consolidation and the dangers it poses to U.S. democracy (www.benbagdikian.com).

13. Public Editor Byron Calame, "Behind the Eavesdropping Story, a Loud Silence," *New York Times*, Week in Review, Jan. 1, 2006; Calame, "Secrecy, Security, the President and the Press," July 2, 2006; Calame, "Eavesdropping and the Election: An Answer on the Question of Timing," *New York Times*,

Aug. 13, 2006. The public editor at the *Times* functioned like an ombudsperson at other newspapers until the position was abolished in 2017.

14. CBS *Evening News*, Jan. 29, 2007.

15. Michael R. Gordon, "Deadliest Bomb in Iraq Is Made by Iran, U.S. Says," *New York Times*, Feb. 10, 2007.

16. James Glanz, "U.S. Says Arms Link Iranians to Iraqi Shiites," *New York Times*, Feb. 12, 2007.

17. Patrick Cockburn, "Target Tehran: Washington Sets Stage for a New Confrontation," *Independent* (London), Feb. 12, 2007.

18. Paul Reynolds, "US claims against Iran: Why now?" BBC News website, Feb. 12, 2007 (http://news.bbc.co.uk/2/hi/middle_east/6353489.stm).

19. Alexandra Zavis and Greg Miller, "Scant Evidence Found of Iran-Iraq Arms Link," *Los Angeles Times*, Jan. 23, 2007.

20. The Institute for Public Accuracy (IPA) offered media interviews with two experts who directly criticized the military intelligence. IPA press release, Feb. 13, 2007. See also Reese Erlich and Muhammad Sahimi, "Fabricated Evidence: Round Two?" *TruthDig*, Mar. 13, 2007.

21. Byron Calame, "Approaching Iran Intelligence with Intelligent Scepticism," *New York Times*, Week in Review, Feb. 25, 2007.

22. Michael R. Gordon, "U.S. Seeks Arab Force and Funding for Syria, *Wall Street Journal*, Apr. 16, 2018 (www.wsj.com/articles/u-s-seeks-arab-force-and-funding-for-syria-1523927888).

23. Sara Chayes, quoted in the *Bulletin Online*, Global Security News, and Analysis (www.thebulletin.org/article.php?art_ofn=so06chayes).

24. Carlotta Gall, "U.S. Military Investigating Death of Afghan in Custody," *New York Times*, Mar. 4, 2003.

25. Quoted from Eric Umansky's excellent analysis of the failures of major media to expose U.S. use of torture. Eric Umansky, "Failures of Imagination," *Columbia Journalism Review*, Sept.-Oct. 2006.

26. Dana Priest, "CIA Holds Terror Suspects in Secret Prisons," *Washington Post*, Nov. 2, 2005.

27. Do a Google search for "Fidel Castro and Hitler," "Saddam Hussein and Hitler," "Slobodan Milosevic and Hitler," and "Ahmadinejad and Hitler." You'll find an amazing number of media references showing that every few years the United States is threatened by a new Hitler.

28. Steve Doocy, *Fox and Friends*, Apr. 13, 2006. To view the video clip, see www.newshounds.us/2006/04/13/fox_news_spreading_panic_on_iran_nuke_plans.php.

29. Glenn Beck, transcript, Sept. 19, 2006 (http://CNN.com).

30. Glenn Beck, transcript, Nov. 11, 2016 (http://CNN.com). Beck left CNN for Fox News and then in 2011 left TV altogether to do an online radio broadcast.

31. A.J. Katz, "Fox News Marks 11 Weeks at the Top in Total Day," *Adweek*, Mar. 27, 2018 (www.adweek.com/tvnewser/fox-news-marks-11-weeks-at-the-top-in-total-day/360374).

32. Chris Ariens, "8.8 Million Weekly Viewers on ABC, Top Rated," *Adweek*, Mar. 20, 2018 (www.adweek.com/tvnewser/evening-news-ratings-week-of-march-12-3/359767).

TWELVE

Learning the Lessons of Iraq

In the months leading up to the U.S. invasion of Iraq in March 2003, I spoke at dozens of community centers, churches, and campuses across the country. I argued that Saddam Hussein had no weapons of mass destruction and that he posed no immediate threat to the people of the United States. A U.S. occupation of Iraq could lead to splintering the country to the benefit of Iran.[1]

But I still remember a question from a young college student in southern Oregon. "What if Saddam Hussein gives nuclear weapons to terrorists, and they attack the United States?" she asked. "Isn't it worth the risk of war to stop such devastation?" I responded by saying that Saddam didn't have ties with Al Qaeda and that what she described was an administration myth. I don't know what impact my response had on the young woman. I was responding with a rational argument while Bush was appealing to the gut. Many Americans supported the Iraq war in the early years, fearing that if we didn't stop the terrorists in Iraq, we would have to stop them in America.

Obama and Trump engaged in the same kind of propaganda campaign against Iran. But in order to understand it, we must look at the real lessons of the Iraq war.

A small group of neoconservative Republicans had hoped to invade Iraq for years. This was a group of fiercely right-wing intellectuals, some of whom had once considered themselves leftists. They took a hard line against communism and later against Islamic countries. In 1998 the neoconservative group Project for the New American Century wrote a position paper calling for the overthrow of Saddam Hussein. The project included such future luminaries as Vice President Dick Cheney, Secretary of Defense Donald Rumsfeld, and Deputy Secretary of Defense Paul Wolfowitz.

The neoconservatives advocated that nut-brain policy, which had few adherents until the atrocity of September 11, 2001. They tried to blame the 9/11 attacks on Iraq but didn't have any evidence. So they bided their time. In the fall of 2002, the Bush Administration thought it had won in Afghanistan and had strong support from the American people. It cooked up intelligence that Iraq possessed chemical and biological weapons, had restarted its nuclear weapons program, and was supporting Al Qaeda. In fact, the United States invaded Iraq for the same reason it threatened Iran: hegemonic control of the Middle East.[2] Even former National Security Advisor Zbigniew Brzezinski, a Democratic hawk, said many people in the Middle East fear a "new and enduring American imperial hegemony" in the region.[3]

Many politicians criticized the Bush Administration for having no plan for the Iraq occupation. In fact, the administration did have a plan. The people of Iraq just didn't cooperate. The United States would gain quick military victory over Saddam Hussein, and residents would greet U.S. troops as liberators, throwing flowers and candy. The United States would remove the country's top leaders but maintain the army, police, and civilian bureaucracy. A pro-U.S. strongman would emerge as Iraq's leader.

The United States would privatize Iraq's oil industry to pay for the occupation. Once Iraq became stable, the United States could affect regime change in Iran, Syria, and Lebanon and force the Palestinians to accept whatever deal the Israelis offered. The government has declassified documents that show American official plans were truly out of touch with reality. The plan called for the reduction of U.S. troops in Iraq to 5,000 within thirty-two to forty-five months of the war's start.[4]

Of course, the plan was fatally flawed. The Iraqi people welcomed the overthrow of Saddam, but never wanted U.S. domination. The army had largely disintegrated even before the U.S. authorities formally dissolved it. Iranian-backed Shiite political parties gained the most votes in elections. The United States backed Iyad Allawi, who lost the 2005 election and went into self-imposed exile in London. He later returned and became vice president. Ahmad Chalabi, once promoted by the Pentagon as Iran's future leader, never got elected to high office and later developed close ties with Iran. Without an effective central government, opportunistic political leaders used ethnic and religious divisions to build up their own power. In February 2006, right-wing Sunni extremists bombed the holy Shiite shrine in Samara, setting off a full-scale civil war between Sunnis and Shiites. While certainly differences had existed during Saddam's rule, the two communities had lived side by side without violence.

Almost 4,500 American soldiers were killed in Iraq with hundreds of thousands injured. The Iraq and Afghanistan wars will cost an estimated $6 trillion, including ongoing care for veterans. Some 450,000 Iraqi civilians died due to the war.

In 2014 the Sunni extremist group Islamic State (IS) seized important cities in northern and central Iraq, including the second largest city, Mosul. The U.S. began a bombing campaign against IS but wouldn't send significant numbers of ground troops until a more friendly government was created in Baghdad. Prime Minister Nouri al Malaki was ousted and Prime Minister Haider al Abadi came in.

Incredibly, neoconservatives such as Trump's National Security Advisor John Bolton continue to defend the Iraq invasion.[5] Former U.S. ambassador to Saudi Arabia Charles Freeman, Jr., told me, "The neoconservative group think their good ideas were poorly implemented in Iraq."[6]

These days neoconservatives offered the same skewed analysis of Iran. They argued that the Iranian government is unpopular with its own people and only needs a shove from the United States for the people to rise up. Michael Ledeen, a leading neoconservative at the American Enterprise Institute, wrote "Antiregime demonstrations erupt in Iran all the time, and most experts believe the vast majority of Iranians detest Mr. Khamenei and his henchmen. With U.S. support, these millions of Iranians could topple the Islamic Republic and establish a secular government resembling those in the West."[7]

Freeman said the neocon argument is extremely moralistic. "If you're an inherently good power like the United States," he said, "you must use your power to make sure good, justice, and the American way prevail over evil. Somehow there will be an uprising in Iran." He summarized the neocon lesson of the Iraq war: "If at first you don't succeed, do the same thing again somewhere else."

Starting in the fall of 2006, the United States began a concerted campaign to blame Iran for U.S. casualties in Iraq as both a diplomatic pressure tactic and a prelude to possible military strikes against Iran. The clerical government does have strong ties to Iraq. But that was easily predicted before the war.

Iran's Influence in Iraq

Just outside Tehran's old bazaar, dozens of vendors and store owners have set up shop. During the Iran–Iraq war, an estimated 600,000 Shiite Iraqis were expelled or fled to Iran. Merchants established small stores in this neighborhood as a way to survive during years of exile. My interpreter and I wandered into a variety of stores and were welcomed with cups of tea and nut-filled pastries.

We found a hole-in-the-wall shop selling beads. We squeezed inside and heard the owner's tales of abuse and torture at the hands of Saddam Hussein's regime. Many Iraqi exiles welcomed the 2003 U.S. invasion as a means to rid their country of dictatorship. Zuhair Razavi, the bead shop owner, told me Iraqis "kiss the hands of the Americans" in thanks for overthrowing Saddam. He now thinks it's time for Iraq to establish an Islamic state.[8]

That lays bare the contradiction of U.S. policy. Iran had close ties with the two Kurdish and three Shiite political parties that made up the majority of Iraq's ruling coalition since 2003. Shiites are the majority in Iraq, and Iran always planned to play an influential role in whatever government emerged.

Leaders of the political Islamist Dawa Party lived in Iran for years. The Supreme Council for the Islamic Revolution in Iraq (SCIRI), with its armed Badr Brigades militia, was founded in Iran. One day, I decided to interview the SCIRI spokesperson in Iran.

I took a taxi to a prosperous section of Tehran full of commercial buildings. SCIRI occupies a large, four-story office building, which sources told me is paid for by the Iranian government. Before the 2003 fall of Saddam, two hundred people worked here, but most have now returned to Iraq. SCIRI received the second-highest number of seats in the 2005 elections.

"Iran and Iraq have a very, very good relationship," Majid Ghammas, head of SCIRI in Iran, told me. "The Iranian government understood the situation in Iraq better than other countries."[9] SCIRI favors an ultra-conservative interpretation of Islam. "Iraq should be an Islamic state," said Ghammas. "Islam should be the source for our constitution, and no law should be approved that is against Islam." Iranian leaders are quite pragmatic, having supported SCIRI and Dawa. They also supported Muqtada al-Sadr, a fiery Muslim cleric who at times fought Americans and at other times participated in electoral politics. For years, Iran threw support behind the Kurdish leader Jalal Talabani, who was the first president of Iraq.

"We think America has done the best work for us, removing Saddam, our worst enemy," Mehdi Rafsanjani told me. He is the son of former president Ali Akbar Hashemi Rafsanjani and was a campaign manager for his father's 2005 presidential campaign. "Anyone who comes to power in Iraq, it's no problem. These are all our friends."[10]

Asked if it's ironic that when the United States withdraws, Iran could have greater influence than the United States, Hamid-Reza Asefi, deputy foreign minister under President Khatami, told me, "That is true. But that's not our fault. When Americans are working for us, we'll let them do it."[11]

The United States accused Iran of not only giving political and economic support but also providing critical munitions to groups attacking U.S. soldiers in Iraq. Philip Zelikow, counselor of the Department of State from 2005 to 2006, told me that since 2005, "Iran was very actively involved in assisting insurgents and gangs inside Iraq in killing Americans and in killing British soldiers and civilians as well."[12] He wouldn't specify which particular insurgent groups.

Iran certainly isn't supporting Al Qaeda or other fundamentalist Sunnis in Iraq. In fact, the Iraqi branch of Al Qaeda wants Iran destroyed. Abu-Umar al-Husayni al-Qurayshi al-Baghdadi, the leader of Al Qaeda in Iraq, encouraged the United States to drop a nuclear bomb on Iran. "Our battle with the Persians has started," he said in a 2007 audio statement monitored by U.S. intelligence.[13] The emergence of the Islamic State in 2013 heightened tensions even more. The Sunni-based terrorist group considers Iran a mortal enemy. Iranian troops and military advisors fought IS in Iraq and Syria.

Iran benefits from having Shiite Muslim allies in power, not Sunni extremists. Yet in November 2017 CIA director Mike Pompeo tried to link Iran with Al Qaeda by disseminating documents taken from Osama Bin Laden's captured computer.[14] Bin Laden emails indicated Iran had provided sanctuary for some al Qaeda operatives in the aughts but didn't contain any new revelations about Iran forging a military or political alliance with al Qaeda.[15] Former CIA analyst Paul Pillar told me that Trump, like Bush before him, cherry-picked

intelligence to reach a predetermined conclusion. The Trump administration publicizes "a couple of lines in one seized document out of
hundreds of documents that point in other directions," explained
Pillar. "That's not objective intelligence analysis."[16] But it does lay
the groundwork for increased hostility towards Iran, including a possible military attack.

Military Attack?

A sector of the American ruling elite strongly advocates military
strikes against Iran that they hope will topple the government. They
don't envision an invasion and occupation. Rather, aerial bombing
would lead to a popular uprising and regime change. That's the real
goal, not deterring Iran's nuclear threat or stopping Iran's support for
militias in the region.

Thomas McInerney, a retired Air Force lieutenant general and
military analyst for Fox News, wrote, "If we were to carry out an air
campaign, it would probably unleash a new Iranian revolution. ... We
could use the Afghan model of precision airpower supporting covert
and indigenous forces."[17]

Seymour Hersh reported as far back as spring of 2006 that, in
the words of one former defense official, the Bush Administration
was considering a "sustained bombing campaign, ... [which would]
humiliate the religious leadership and lead the public to rise up and
overthrow the government. I was shocked when I heard it, and asked
myself 'what are they smoking?'"[18]

U.S. plans to bomb Iran receded under Obama when negotiations
on the nuclear accord began in earnest. But they increased again with
the election of Trump and his promises to scuttle the agreement. The
appointment of John Bolton as national security advisor in 2018 consolidated hawkish policy in the Trump administration.

Bolton had long advocated war with Iran using the excuse of
stopping its nuclear weapons program. In reality he sought to

install a pro-U.S. regime in Tehran. Bolton said the United States should bomb key nuclear facilities in coordination with the Israeli Air Force.

"The United States could do a thorough job of destruction, but Israel alone can do what's necessary," he wrote in 2005. "Such action should be combined with vigorous American support for Iran's opposition, aimed at regime change in Tehran."[19] Trump continued to build a coalition of Sunni Arab countries and Israel to isolate Iran. Officially, Saudi Arabia, the Gulf countries, Jordan, and other U.S. allies in the region were united in opposition to Iranian "aggression." In reality, the United States encouraged Saudi Arabia to fund and arm right-wing Sunni groups in Lebanon, Yemen, Iraq, and Syria. The Saudis funded the Al Qaeda affiliated group in Syria, as I reported in 2013.[20] And Saudi backed forces in Yemen fought alongside Al Qaeda in Yemen, as documented by the BBC.[21]

This kind of strategic coalition is not new. The United States promoted a similar alliance in the 1980s with Saudi Arabia and Pakistan to fight the Soviet occupation of Afghanistan. Some guerrillas and others who worked with the United States, such as Osama bin Laden, ended up forming Al Qaeda.

Israel's ruling elite also strongly supported an attack on Iran. For decades Israeli Prime Minister Benjamin Netanyahu claimed that Iran posed an immediate and mortal threat to Israel.[22] In 2007 Israeli military authorities leaked information to the British press that they had active contingency plans to bomb Iran's nuclear facilities with atomic weapons.[23]

But Israel won't initiate an attack on Iran without explicit approval from the United States. Logistically, Israeli planes would have to fly over Iraq, which would require U.S. and Iraqi permission. Politically, the United States loses credibility with Sunni Arab countries if it allows Israel to attack. The United States prevented Israel from attacking Iraq during the 1991 Gulf War, although Saddam Hussein was raining rockets onto Israel. Israel's direct involvement would have shattered the U.S. alliance with Arab countries such as Saudi Arabia and Syria, which was then an ally against Saddam Hussein.

Significantly, not a single European ally supports U.S. military action against Iran. Even Britain's former Prime Minister Tony Blair spoke out publicly against U.S. military strikes.[24] During the invasion of Iraq, the United States bribed and cajoled a paltry group of countries into what it called the "Coalition of the Willing." If the United States attacks Iran, it will spearhead the "Coalition of the Nonexistent."

The United States certainly has the military capability of dropping bombs and launching missiles against Iran with few or no American casualties. Initially, the public, Republican and some Democratic Party leaders would rally round the president for acting tough against the Iranian threat. But what would happen after the first few days and weeks?

The Results of a U.S. Attack

To explore that question, Colonel Sam Gardiner (U.S. Air Force, retired) conducted a mock war games exercise for the *Atlantic Monthly* magazine.[25] The war games revealed a number of critical military and political problems. Some of the Iranian nuclear sites are hardened to protect them against aerial bombardment. So massive and repeated strikes may be necessary. Many Iranian civilians could be killed. If the bombings release radioactive materials, they may drift over civilian areas and even into neighboring countries. The Iranian public will likely rally around its leadership in the face of a horrific external attack.

Iran will respond militarily, although not necessarily with a conventional attack on U.S. ships or bases. "There's no doubt in my mind that this would be an act of war," former CIA intelligence officer Paul Pillar told me. "There would be Iranian retaliation."[26]

Iran could close the Strait of Hormuz, through which 25 percent of the world's oil supplies pass. Even the threat of such a closing would send oil prices skyrocketing. Iran could encourage Hizbollah to launch missiles into Israel. Any U.S. attack against Iran would outrage Muslims, igniting large demonstrations in Europe, the Middle East, and Asia. Iran could mobilize that anger and encourage allies in Iraq and Syria to attack U.S. troops. Finally, in a truly nightmarish scenario, Iran could encourage terrorist attacks inside the United States and in allied countries.

The Trump administration is dusting off the old George Bush plans for a military strike on Iran. But as the war games showed, Iran is not Iraq under Saddam Hussein. Iranian leaders have long prepared for asymmetrical war, trying to avoid direct confrontation with the superior U.S. military. The death of U.S. soldiers would undermine the war politically and fatally undermine the Trump administration as well.[27]

Luckily for the world, no everyone in power favors the military option.

Not just Republicans versus Democrats

One afternoon I drove down to the Hoover Institution at Stanford University. The Hoover Tower looms over the idyllic campus, a conservative fortress in an otherwise liberal village. The immediate problem, however, was parking. There wasn't any. After wandering around various parking lots and idling in front of people not inclined to leave their precious parking spaces, I found a metered spot. I trudged over to meet Abbas Milani at an office building for Hoover fellows.

A gaggle of Army officers had gathered in the lobby. They were consulting with some of the Hoover fellows, just another day in an institution stuffed with former cabinet members and assorted conservatives. Abbas Milani, an academic and former leftist, doesn't fit the typical Hoover mold. But he's become known as one of the country's top Iran experts.

In April 2006, President Bush met with Milani at the Hoover Institution. "I was very pleasantly surprised at how involved he was with the Iran issue," Milani told me. Far from his image as an inarticulate doofus, Bush asked intelligent questions about the different political tendencies within Iran's ruling class. "He knew the factions. He knew their names. This notion of him as someone who knows nothing about the world was simply not my experience."[28]

Milani explained that based on his conversations with officials, two camps existed within the Bush Administration. One advocates military strikes against Iran as soon as possible. Vice President Cheney headed this group. "They think the regime is incorrigible and the only way is to take them out," said Milani.

Another camp within the administration, which included Secretary of State Condoleezza Rice, favored other forms of pressure. "They don't think Iran is an easy target. They want to see if they can work with the European Union, and with Russia and China, to bring economic pressure to get the Islamic regime off the nuclear track."

Milani and other experts say neither camp is prepared to live with a clerical government in power in Iran; they differ mainly on the tactics to remove it. "Both sides ultimately think that this regime is up to no good," said Milani. "The only long-term way the United States can coexist with them is if there is regime change." Milani's analysis of the Bush administration applies to Trump and Congressional Democrats today.

When Clinton and Obama were in power, they didn't plan to attack Iran militarily, but they stepped up economic pressure by championing new sanctions. Hilary Clinton, as a U.S. senator and later as secretary of state, took a hawkish line on Iran. "We cannot, we should not, we must not permit Iran to build or acquire nuclear weapons. In dealing with this threat, ... no option can be taken off the table."[29]

Representative Nancy Pelosi, a liberal Democrat from San Francisco who has been both speaker of the house and minority leader, takes a hawkish line on Middle East issues affecting Israel. She told a meeting of the American Israel Public Affairs Committee, "The greatest threat to Israel's right to exist, with the prospect of devastating violence, now comes from Iran."[30]

A few Democratic politicians, such as House member Barbara Lee and former representative Dennis Kucinich, take a principled stand against intervention. Writing in *The Nation* magazine, Kucinich called for negotiations with Iran. "The Administration is escalating tensions with Iran, laying the groundwork for an attack and attempting to make a case to bypass Congressional authorization."[31] But such principled stands are rare within the upper reaches of the Democratic Party.

A few Republican congressmen hold anti-interventionist views. They had opposed Bill Clinton's 1999 military attacks against ex-Yugoslavia. The Republican Party has a small isolationist wing that opposes some U.S. military interventions. Conservative columnist and one-time presidential candidate Pat Buchanan strongly condemned mainstream conservatives for supporting an attack on Iran.[32] But Buchanan and other isolationists have little impact on Trump and mainstream Republican officials.

Conservative corporate interests, right-wing think tanks, and the pro-Israel lobby pressure both parties to take a hard line against Iran. Peace groups, a sector of Iranian-Americans, and progressive think tanks urge alternative strategies.

Is There Another Way?

Mainstream policy makers argue that the United States can't live with a clerical government in Tehran. They think the Iranian government will never give up its nuclear ambitions, seek peace with the United States, stop supporting terrorism, or agree to a Palestinian–Israeli settlement. Well, in fact, Iranian authorities once offered to do just that.

In the spring of 2003, Iran contacted Swiss Ambassador Tim Guldimann, who represented the United States diplomatically in Tehran, and proposed comprehensive negotiations that could resolve many of the outstanding U.S.–Iranian issues. The United States had just invaded Iraq, and Iran was worried. In a proposal approved by Supreme Leader Khamenei, Iran agreed to provide intelligence information from Al Qaeda suspects being detained in Iran, agreed to stringent international inspections of nuclear sites, offered to stop military support for Hizbollah and Hamas, and agreed to support a two-state solution to the Israeli–Palestine issue.[33]

The written proposal from Ambassador Guldimann was both faxed and hand delivered to the U.S. State Department. It was promptly ignored by the Bush Administration. The neoconservative faction argued that the United States shouldn't have any dealings with supporters of terrorism. Condoleezza Rice and other Bush officials later denied ever receiving the offer, but receipt of the proposal was confirmed by Flynt Leverett, an analyst with the National Security Council, and by Lawrence Wilkerson, Colin Powell's chief of staff.[34]

We can't know if the Iranians would have negotiated in good faith in 2003. But the Bush Administration didn't even try. It has a history of similar blunders. Starting from its opening months in power, at a time when North Korea did not have nuclear weapons, the Bush Administration unilaterally undercut a 1994 U.S.–Korean agreement that had been negotiated under Bill Clinton. In February 2007, Bush officials went back and negotiated essentially the same agreement—except by then, North Korea had the Bomb.[35]

Successive Democratic and Republican administrations have made a mess of U.S.–Iranian relations since 1979. The United States has tried economic embargoes, UN resolutions, propaganda broadcasts, covert terrorist attacks, detainment of Iranian diplomats living in Iraq, and strident military threats. None have resulted in significant changes inside Iran.

A number of leading experts suggest an alternative. The people of Iran must be left alone to change the government as they see fit. Meanwhile, the United States must implement the nuclear accord and negotiate with Iran to lower tensions throughout the Middle East.

Former CIA official Pillar told me, "I believe it is a big mistake not to engage the Iranians. ... Among the parallel interests are overall stability in their neck of the woods. We worked together in Afghanistan after the overthrow of the Taliban."[36]

Sane voices in Washington can help lower tensions with Iran. But I personally don't trust mainstream politicians, lobbyists, and think tank gurus to resolve anything soon. Nor do I trust the clerics in Tehran to stop their belligerence. A pro-peace, pro-democracy movement exists within Iran. I think people in the United States need to build one as well.

The anti-war Iraq movement has already begun educating people about Iran. We need more educational events, people-to-people exchanges, demonstrations, and anti-intervention votes by city governments, all of which can build grassroots pressure to change U.S. policy.[37] If the governments of the United States and Iran won't make peace, the people of our two countries must.

Notes

1. Norman Solomon and Reese Erlich, *Target Iraq: What the News Media Didn't Tell You*, p. 37 (New York: Context Books, 2003).

2. Norman Solomon and Reese Erlich, *Target Iraq*, pp. 113–15.

3. Zbigniew Brzezinski, testimony before the Senate Foreign Relations Committee, Feb. 1, 2007.

4. Michael Gordon, "Prewar Slide Show Cast Iraq in Rosy Hues," *New York Times*, Feb. 15, 2007. See www.nsarchive.org for the original documents.

5. David M. Drucker, "John Bolton: No Regrets about Toppling Saddam," *Washington Examiner*, May 14, 2015 (www.washingtonexaminer.com/john-bolton-no-regrets-about-toppling-saddam/article/2564463).

6. Charles W. Freeman, Jr., interview with author, Jan. 19, 2007, Washington DC.

7. Michael Ledeen, "To Break the Moscow-Tehran Alliance, Target Iran's Regime," *Wall Street Journal* commentary, Feb. 13, 2017 (www.wsj.com/articles/to-break-the-moscow-tehran-alliance-target-iran s-regime-1487030972? mg=id-wsj).

8. My interview with Zuhair Razavi and others in this section first appeared in my article "Iran's Waiting Game," *St. Petersburg Times*, July 3, 2005.

9. Majid Ghammas, interview with author, June 16, 2005, Tehran.

10. Mehdi Rafsanjani, interview with author, June 11, 2005, Tehran.

11. Hamid-Reza Asefi, interview with author, June 12, 2005, Tehran.

12. Philip Zelikow, phone interview with author, Feb. 6, 2007, Charlottesville VA.

13. "Islamic State of Iraq Amir Announces Plans to Counter US Security Plan," Open Source Center—Jihadist websites, Feb. 3, 2007.

14. CIA, "CIA Releases Nearly 470,000 Additional Files Recovered in May 2011 Raid on Usama Bin Ladin's Compound, Nov. 1, 2017 (www.cia.gov/news-information/press-releases-statements/2017-press-releases-statements/cia-releases-additional-files-recovered-in-ubl-compound-raid.html).

15. www.theatlantic.com/international/archive/2017/11/iran-mike-pompeo-bin-laden-documents-cia/545093/.

16. Paul Pillar, interview with author, Washington DC, Jan. 8, 2018.

17. Thomas G. McInerney, "Iran Escalates," *Wall Street Journal,* op-ed page, Mar. 31, 2007.

18. Seymour Hersh, "The Iran Plans," *The New Yorker,* Apr. 17, 2006.

19. John R. Bolton, "To Stop Iran's Bomb, Bomb Iran," *New York Times,* op-ed, Mar. 26, 2015 (www.nytimes.com/2015/03/26/opinion/to-stop-irans-bomb-bomb-iran.html?utm_source=NIAC+Grassroots+Email+List&utm_campaign=14b098eeaf-EMAIL_CAMPAIGN_2018_03_30&utm_medium=email&utm_term=0_27c1480181-14b098eeaf-255556877).

20. Reese Erlich, "Saudi Youth Fighting Against Assad Regime in Syria," *Ground Truth,* Mar. 13, 2013 (http://thegroundtruthproject.org/saudi-youth-fighting-against-assad-regime-in-syria/).

21. BBC, "Yemen Conflict: Al-Qaeda Seen at Coalition Battle for Taiz," BBC, Feb. 22, 2016 (www.bbc.com/news/world-middle-east-35630194).

22. Peter Hirschberg, "Netanyahu: It's 1938 and Iran Is Germany; Ahmadinejad Is Preparing Another Holocaust," *Haaretz* (Tel Aviv), Dec. 19, 2006.

23. "Focus: Mission Iran," *The Sunday Times* (London), Jan. 7, 2007.

24. Tom Baldwin and Philip Webster, "Fears Grow Over Iran," *The Times* (London), Feb. 23, 2007.

25. James Fallows, "Will Iran Be Next?" *The Atlantic Monthly*, Dec. 2004. Col. Gardiner updated his information in *The End of the "Summer of Diplomacy": Assessing U.S. Military Options on Iran* (Washington DC: Century Foundation Report, 2006).

26. Paul Pillar, interview with author, Jan. 8, 2007.

27. Trita Parsi, "War With Iran Won't Be Iraq All Over Again. It'll Be Much Worse," *Huffington Post*, Mar. 30, 2018 (www.huffingtonpost.com/entry/opinion-parsi-war-with-iran_us_5abd46fde4b055e50acc2e82).

28. Abbas Milani, interview with author, Oct. 5, 2006, Palo Alto CA. Milani is the director of Iranian Studies at Stanford University and codirector of the Iran Democracy Project at the Hoover Institution.

29. Associated Press, "Hillary Clinton Calls Iran a Threat to U.S., Israel," Feb. 2, 2007.

30. Nancy Pelosi, Speech to the American Israel Public Affairs Committee, May 23, 2005.

31. Dennis Kucinich, "Collision Course with Iran," *The Nation*, Feb. 27, 2007.

32. Patrick J. Buchanan, "Of Imperial Presidents and Congressional Cowards," syndicated column, *San Francisco Chronicle*, May 1, 2006.

33. Gareth Porter first broke the story in "Burnt Offering," *The American Prospect*, June 6, 2006. The story was confirmed by Glenn Kessler, "U.S. Missed Chance with Iran, Ex-Officials Claim," *Washington Post*, June 18, 2006.

34. Gareth Porter, "First Rejected, Now Denied," *The American Prospect*, Feb. 9, 2007. See also Kessler, *Washington Post*.

35. Charles Scanlon, "The End of a Long Confrontation?", *BBC News* webpage, Feb. 13, 2007.

36. Pillar, interview with author.

37. Some groups working against intervention in Iran and related issues include Campaign Against Sanctions and Military Intervention in Iran (http://www.campaigniran.org/casmii), Just Foreign Policy (www.justforeignpolicy.org), Global Exchange (www.globalexchange.org), United For Peace and Justice (www.unitedforpeaceandjustice.org), the National Iranian American Council (www.niacouncil.org/), and Jewish Voice for Peace (www.jewishvoiceforpeace.org).

Index

Note: Page numbers followed by an 'n' refer to notes.

women: dress code for 9; PJAK (Party
    for a Free Life in Kurdistan) and
    165; rights of 8, 114–16
Woodrow Wilson Center 36
Woolsey, James 15
workers' interests 116–17
World Cup 99

xenophobia 67–8, 191–2

Yazdi, Ahura Pirouz Khaleghi
    150–1
Yazdi, Avasta 31, 46, 133
Yazdi, Ebrahim 120–1
Yazdoneh, Farzad 41

Zaghari-Ratcliffe, Nazanin 104
Zagros, Akif 165
Zelikow, Philip 203